ACADEMICAL DRESS
of
British and Irish Universities

a. Warwick masters' gown.

b. Bath masters' gown.

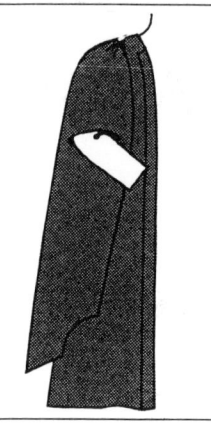

c. Lancaster masters' gown.

d. Leicester doctors' undress gown.

e. St Andrews doctors' undress gown.

f. Oxford convocation habit.

g. Oxford gimp gown.

h. Cambridge Litt.D. undress gown.

i. Cambridge M.D. undress gown.

ACADEMICAL DRESS
of
British and Irish Universities

George W. Shaw

M.A., M.Sc., D.Phil., D.Sc., F.I.Biol.

University of Wales, Wadham College,
Oxford & Girton College, Cambridge

Phillimore

1995

Published by
PHILLIMORE & CO. LTD.,
Shopwyke Manor Barn, Chichester, West Sussex

© George W. Shaw, 1995

ISBN 0 85033 974 X

Printed and bound in Great Britain by
BOOKCRAFT LTD.
Midsomer Norton, Avon

Contents

List of Illustrations ix
Acknowledgements xii

Introduction 1
Abbreviations of Degrees 9
Illustrations 15
Specifications 33
    Aberdeen, University of 44
    Abertay, University of, Dundee 47
    Anglia Polytechnic University 49
    Aston University 51
    Bath University 53
    Queens University, Belfast 55
    Birmingham University 58
    Bolton Institute of Higher Education 61
    Bournemouth University 63
    Bradford University 65
    Brighton University 67
    Bristol University 69
    Brookes University, Oxford 71
    Brunel University, West London 73
    Buckingham University 75
    Caledonian University, Glasgow 77
    Central England, University of, Birmingham 79
    Central Lancashire, University of, Preston 81
    City University, London 83
    Cambridge, University of 35
    Council for National Academic Awards 85
    Coventry University 87
    Cranfield University, Bedfordshire 89
    De Montfort University, Leicester 90
    Derby, University of 92
    Dundee, University of 94
    Durham, University of 96
    East Anglia, University of, Norwich 99
    East London, University of 101
    Edinburgh, University of 103
    Essex, University of, Colchester 106

Exeter, University of	108
Glamorgan, University of, Pontyprydd	110
Glasgow, University of	112
Greenwich, University of, London	115
Guildhall University, London	117
Hallam University, Sheffield	119
Heriot-Watt University, Edinburgh	121
Hertfordshire, University of, Hatfield	123
Huddersfield, University of	125
Hull, University of	127
Humberside, University of, Hull	129
John Moores University, Liverpool	131
Keele, University of	133
Kent, University of, Canterbury	135
Kingston University	137
Lancaster University	139
Leeds University	141
Leeds Metropolitan University	144
Leicester University	146
Liverpool University	148
London University	150
Loughborough University	153
Luton University	243
Manchester University	155
Manchester Institute of Science and Technology, University	157
Manchester Metropolitan University	158
Oxford, University of	41
Queen Margaret College, Edinburgh	160
Middlesex University	162
Napier University, Edinburgh	164
Nene College, Northampton	166
Newcastle University	167
Northumbria University, Newcastle	170
North London University	172
Nottingham University	174
Open University	176
Paisley University	177
Plymouth University	179
Portsmouth University	181
Reading University	185
Robert Gordon University, Aberdeen	187
Salford University	188
Sheffield University	190
South Bank University, London	192
Southampton University	194
St Andrews University	196
Stafford University	198
Stirling University	200

CONTENTS

Strathclyde University 202
Sunderland University 204
Surrey University, Guildford 206
Sussex University, Falmer 208
Teesside University, Middlesbrough 210
Thames Valley University, London 212
Trent University, Nottingham 214
Ulster University, Coleraine 216
Wales, University of 218
Warwick University, Coventry 221
West of England University, Bristol 223
Westminster University, London 225
Wolverhampton University 227
York University 229

Irish Universities

Trinity College, Dublin 231
National University of Ireland 233
Dublin City University 237
Dublin Institute of Technology 238
Limerick, University of 239
St Patrick's College, Maynooth 241

List of Illustrations

Frontispiece: Various gowns

1. Parts of bachelors' gown 17
2. Parts of masters' gown 17
3. Basic bachelors' gown 17
4. Basic masters' gown 17
5. Standard yoke 18
6. Flap collar yoke 18
7. Oxford commoners' gown 18
8. Oxford scholars' gown 18
9. Trinity College, Dublin, undergraduates' gown 18
10. London undergraduates' gown 18
11. Scottish universities' undergraduates' gown 18
12. Christ's College gown 19
13. Clare College gown 19
14. Corpus Christi College gown 19
15. Downing College gown 19
16. Emmanuel College gown 19
17. Fitzwilliam College gown 19
18. Churchill, King's, Peterhouse, Queens', Robinson College gown 19
19. Clare Hall, Hughes Hall, Lucy Cavendish College and Wolfson College gown 19
20. Girton College, Homerton College, Newnham College, New Hall gown 19
21. Gonville and Caius College gown 20
22. Jesus College gown 20
23. Magdalene College gown 20
24. Pembroke College gown 20
25. St Catharine's College gown 20
26. St John's College gown 20
27. Selwyn College gown 20
28. Sidney Sussex College gown 20
29. Trinity College gown 20
30. Trinity Hall gown 20
31. Cambridge M.B. gown 21
32. Cambridge Vet.M.B. gown 21
33. Cambridge LL.B. gown 21
34. Cambridge B.Chir. gown 21
35. Cambridge B.Ed. gown 21

36.	Cambridge Mus.B. gown	21
37.	Cambridge B.A. gown	22
38.	Oxford B.A. gown	22
39.	Belfast bachelors' gown	22
40.	Dublin bachelors' gown	22
41.	Durham and Newcastle bachelors' gown	22
42.	London bachelors' gown	22
43.	Reading bachelors' gown	23
44.	Sussex bachelors' gown	23
45.	Wales bachelors' gown	23
46.	Newcastle M.B. gown	23
47.	London M.B. gown	23
48.	Cambridge M.A. gown	24
49.	Oxford M.A. gown	24
50.	Aberdeen, all graduates' gown	24
51.	Bristol masters' gown	24
52.	Dublin masters' gown	24
53.	Glasgow masters' and St Andrews bachelors', masters' and Ph.D gown	24
54.	Leeds masters' gown	25
55.	Leicester masters' gown	25
56.	London masters' gown	25
57.	Manchester masters' gown	25
58.	Sussex masters' gown	25
59.	Wales masters' and doctors' gown	25
60.	Cambridge doctors' gown	26
61.	Cambridge Mus.D. robe	26
62.	Oxford doctors' robe	26
63.	London doctors' robe	26
64.	Sussex doctors' robe	26
65.	Cambridge masters' sleeve decorations	27
66.	Full shaped hood with square corners	28
67.	Full shaped hood with rounded corners	28
68.	Full shaped hood with cape and cowl edged	28
69.	Burgon shaped hood	28
70.	Oxford Burgon, flat hood	29
71.	Oxford Burgon, folded and hanging hood	29
72.	Oxford simple shape, flat hood	29
73.	Oxford doctors', flat hood	29
74.	Oxford doctors', folded and hanging hood	29
75.	Cambridge, flat hood	30
76.	Cambridge, folded and hanging hood	30
77.	Aberdeen, flat hood	30
78.	Aberdeen, folded and hanging hood	30
79.	Dublin, flat hood	30
80.	Dublin, folded and hanging hood	30
81.	Leicester, flat hood	31
82.	Leicester, folded and hanging hood	31
83.	Wales, flat hood	31

LIST OF ILLUSTRATIONS

84. Durham and Newcastle, flat hood 31
85. Belfast, bachelors' and masters', flat hood 31
86. Edinburgh, flat hood 31
87. London, flat hood 31
88. Mortar board or trencher 32
89. Doctors' Tudor bonnet 32
90. John Knox cap 32
91. Bishop Andrewes cap 32
92. Pileus cap 32
93. Oxford ladies' soft cap 32

Colour Plates

Between pages 16 and 17

I	Lambeth Degree
II	Greenwich University
III	Manchester Metropolitan University
IV	Manchester B.Sc.
V	Exeter bachelors'
VI	Wolverhampton bachelors'
VII	London B.Sc.
VIII	London B.Mus.
IX	Portsmouth M.Phil., front view
X	Portsmouth M.Phil., rear view
XI	Southampton M.A.
XII	Warwick M.A.
XIII	Durham M.A.
XIV	Leeds M.Ed.
XV	Portsmouth Ph.D.
XVI	Manchester all doctors'
XVII	London Arts
XVIII	Lancaster Ph.D.
XIX	Durham Ph.D.
XX	Wolverhampton Ph.D.
XXI	Warwick Ph.D.
XXII	Open University Ph.D.
XXIII	Brighton Ph.D.
XXIV	Lancaster Ph.D.
XXV	Lancaster Ph.D.
XXVI	University of Hertfordshire
XXVIII	Staffordshire and Hertfordshire

Acknowledgements

I am indebted to the Registrars of the following universities for permission to reproduce information from their university calendars: Aberdeen, Aston, Bath, Belfast, Birmingham, Bournemouth, Bradford, Bristol, Brookes, Brunel, Buckingham, Central England, Central Lancashire, City, Coventry, Cranfield, Derby, Dundee, East Anglia, East London, Edinburgh, Essex, Glamorgan, Glasgow, Greenwich, Guildhall, Hallam, Heriot-Watt, Hertfordshire, Hull, Humberside, Keele, Kent, John Moores, Lancaster, Leeds, Leicester, Liverpool, London, Loughborough, Manchester, Manchester Metropolitan, Middlesex, Napier, Newcastle, Nottingham, Open, Paisley, Plymouth, Portsmouth, Reading, Robert Gordon, Salford, Sheffield, Southampton, St Andrews, Stafford, Stirling, Strathclyde, Sunderland, Surrey, Sussex, Thames Valley, Ulster, Wales, Warwick, West of England, Westminster, Wolverhampton, York.

I am also greatly indebted to the following Official Robemakers for more detailed information: Messrs. Wippell of Exeter for details fo the universities of Brighton, Exeter, Hertfordshire, Lancaster, Manchester, Portsmouth, Stafford, Southampton, Warwick and Wolverhampton; Messrs. Ryder & Amies (Cambridge); Messrs. Ridley & Co. Norwich (East Anglia); Messrs. Gray & Co. (Durham & Newcastle); Messrs. Phelan Conan Associates (Dublin City, Dublin Institute of Technology, Trinity College Dublin, Limerick and St Patrick's College, Maynooth); Messrs. Northam & Co. of Oxford (Bolton Institute, de Montford, Huddersfield, Humberside, Kingston, and Leeds Metropolitan); Messrs. Ede & Ravenscroft (Abertay, Anglia, Caledonian, Teesside, Trent, Queen Margaret College, Nene, Northumbria, North London and South Bank). Dr. David Avery kindly provided details of Westminster University.

I would like to give my particular thanks to Mr. Robin Richardson of Messrs. J. Wippell of Exeter and to Miss Carol Amies of Messrs. Ryder & Amies of Cambridge who gave me access to their photographic collections.

I must also thank the Registrars of Manchester Metropolitan University and Greenwich University for allowing me to reproduce photographs from their Newsletters, and to Mr. John Venables of Messrs. Shepherd & Woodward, Oxford, for the reproduction from Academic Dress of the University of Oxford. The photograph of the Lambeth ceremony was taken by Mr. Keith Ellis, and of the Open University by Dr. Martin Thompson, and for that of Dr. Mary Archer I must thank Dr. Bruce Christianson of the University of Hertfordshire.

Introduction

INTRODUCTION

Each university in Great Britain and Ireland has a system of academical dress which is used by its graduates to indicate their degree (i.e. bachelor, master or doctor) and often also the faculty in which they took the degree.

Academical dress arose by a process of evolution and modification of ordinary wear. The gown or robe was the topcoat or cloak of the medieval scholar, and the hood was a headcover. Academical dress has been worn by graduates and students for hundreds of years and even in this modern world there is no obvious sign of such garments becoming obsolete. Each new university on receiving its charter adopts a set of robes of its own which are distinctive and peculiar to that institution. The styles of dress used by our two ancient universities of Oxford and Cambridge have been modified from time to time but have now reached a point of stability, and it is from these two august bodies that the newer universities have derived their inspiration; most of them have managed to evolve a sane and logical system.

In this country the three professions which make daily use of gowns and hoods are lawyers, clergy and teachers. Unfortunately with the demise of the grammar schools, it is left to the public schools to maintain the tradition, and even Oxford and Cambridge now require them only for formal hall. By most other graduates—medical men, research workers, for example—academical dress is worn only on rare occasions. Such people would tend to hire rather than purchase their outfits.

Within the last few years, we have seen the conversion of the polytechnics into universities, hence the necessity to update the 1966 edition containing 28 universities to the present total of around the hundred mark.

It has been necessary to add remarkably little to the line drawings from the first edition, since almost nothing new has been added to the range of gowns, and only minor alterations to the basic simple, full, Burgon and Aberdeen shapes of hood.

The design of academical dress is in the hands of the robemakers far more than the universities themselves and the former seem to have abandoned their flair for innovation on the gown front and plumped for standardised styles. The basic bachelors' gown is used by most of the newer institutions as is the basic masters' gown. Unfortunately no undress gown for doctors seems to have been provided, yet this would have been so simple, by following the example of most of the older universities and adding lace, braid or gimp above or around the armholes of the masters' gown.

It is also remarkable that none of the new universities have used fur in their hoods, no doubt fearing the wrath of the so-called 'animal rights' activists: and the use of artificial or nylon fur is to be deplored, as it in no way resembles real fur.

Most of the new universities have not included faculty colours in their schemes, the hood indicating only the university and the level of the degree. This can only be regarded as a progressive step, since the proliferation of faculties, covering every possible subject, would make impossible demands on resources as well as creating major headaches for the robemakers! The simplest scheme of all is seen at the University of Teesside, where a single hood (the 'University hood') is used to cover all degrees, whereas the National University of Ireland has over 66 hoods!

Materials

The regulations laid down by individual universities usually specify the materials from which their academical robes are to be made. For gowns and hoods, 'stuff' or 'silk' are often specified. Stuff can generally be taken to mean spun rayon or Russell cord. The former is somewhat bodyless material, the only merit of which lies in its cheapness. It is often used for undergraduates, gowns but any gown made from it rapidly loses its shape with wear, and its use is to be avoided wherever possible. Russell cord is used extensively for black graduate gowns. It stands up to hard wear, and a gown made from a good quality Russell cord will last for years. When silk is specified for gowns and the outer part of hoods it can be taken to mean either real corded silk, or one of the materials resembling silk, such as ribbed rayon. A gown of real corded Ottoman silk might cost several hundred pounds and such garments are rarely made nowadays, when a gown of almost identical appearance, but made from artificial fibres, can be obtained for about one hundred pounds. For the linings of hoods, taffetas are often used in place of genuine silks. They are cheap and have the required shiny surface.

There are at least seven types of lace, braid or gimp which are used to trim black gowns, perhaps the most extensively used being Oxford gimp (as illustrated in the frontispiece, f and i). This form is used by Durham and Hull for music gowns, by Sheffield for doctors' undress gowns and by Oxford for all graduates other than B.A., B.F.A., B.Theol., B.D. and M.A. The next most extensively used braid is that worn at Birmingham, Leicester, Nottingham and Reading for doctors' undress gowns. Cambridge doctors' lace (illustrated in the frontispiece, g and h) is used by doctors at Cambridge, Bath and Exeter for undress gowns. Cambridge miniature lace appears on all graduate gowns at Leeds and on all doctors' undress gowns at Hull. Newcastle uses two forms of lace for its medical graduates. Doctors of Medicine, Surgery, Hygiene and Dental Surgery have lace with a Greek key pattern, whilst the corresponding bachelors use a lace similar to but not identical with Cambridge miniature lace. Southampton has yet another style of lace, with three vertical bars alternating with a lozenge shape.

Gowns

The basic article of academical dress is the gown. This is an open fronted garment made of stuff or silk. The back of the gown is gathered or rouched to give a definite yoke below the collar (figs. 5 and 6). The fronts are turned back to form facings about two inches wide. Some universities (e.g. Cambridge) have silk ribbons ('strings') attached to the inside of the facings (fig. 1 and 2). Some universities also add a cord and button to the yoke.

The alternative style is the flap collar gown. This has glove sleeves which are not gathered at the top, nor is the body of the gown gathered into a yoke. It is less full than the standard gown, and far less dignified in its appearance. It is used mainly by solicitors and Q.C.s, and decorated with lace for many Oxford degrees.

Except for undergraduates, gowns have traditionally been black. With the first wave of new universities in the 1960s, coloured gowns for graduates made their appearance. The University of East Anglia left the design of robes to a dressmaker—Cecil Beaton. He introduced a dull indigo coloured gown, which was not gathered into a yoke but roughly rouched like a surplice. Other universities, including The Open University, Anglia Polytechnic University, the University of Central England and many more use coloured gowns for all graduates. Nearly all have opted for some shade of blue, although York has chosen grey for all graduates. In several other universities (e.g. Derby, Hallam and London), the black gowns are used with the exception of the M.Phil. degree which has been picked out for special treatment, usually by adding coloured facings.

Undergraduates
The undergraduate gown of most universities is based on either the Oxford scholars' gown or the London undergraduates' gown. In all cases the undergraduate gown is short, reaching to just above the knee. In the former case, the sleeves are short and bell-shaped. In the latter case the sleeves are a very much reduced version of the Oxford B.A. sleeve. In both cases the sleeves are gathered at the shoulders into a yoke.

There are two forms of undergraduate gown at Oxford: the scholars' gown already mentioned, which is worn by those undergraduates holding a scholarship of any of the constituent colleges, or an exhibition of certain colleges; and the commoners' gown, worn by all undergraduates except those mentioned above, and by all graduates of other universities who are not reading for a D.Phil. This gown is a short, sleeveless, and a very undignified relic of its former self. The true commoners' gown, which is much longer than the one in present use, is worn by advanced students, i.e. graduates who are reading for a D.Phil.

In no other university (except perhaps Belfast, Manchester, the N.U.I. and most of the new universities where they have no gown at all!) are undergraduates so badly served in the matter of gowns as they are at Oxford.

The commoners' gown at Trinity College, Dublin, is of the same shape as the Oxford advanced students' gown, i.e. with a flap collar and sleeveless, but with the addition of three rows of tassels to the shoulder flaps, three rows of tassels at the sides and a Q.C. type of slit at the back.

Black is not the only colour used for undergraduates. Two Cambridge colleges—Trinity and Caius—wear a dark blue gown. Selwyn has a black gown with dark blue facings, and a similar one is worn at Reading University. In the four ancient Scottish universities undergraduates are even more brightly attired, wearing a scarlet gown.

A strange anomaly is found at Liverpool University, where undergraduates wear the bachelors' gown without, of course, a hood; and since the bachelors' gown at Liverpool is the Cambridge M.A. gown, the Liverpool undergraduate appears arrayed as an M.A. at Cambridge! A similar situation is found at the University of Hertfordshire where undergraduates are entitled to use the bachelors' gown.

Bachelors
There are two basic shapes for the sleeves of graduate gowns, both of them derived from the sleeves of everyday medieval garments. These are the open sleeve, and the closed or glove sleeve. The former, of Norman origin, is in effect a greatly exaggerated coat sleeve, usually long enough for the lower border to hang down as a point.

We can again take the Oxford gown as basic, and note how it has been modified by other universities. The B.A. Oxford sleeve is open, wing-like and pointed. The same sleeve has been taken for bachelors, without any modification other than of size, by most universities. Cambridge has taken the sleeve and opened the forearm seam from the shoulder almost to the wrist, and the slit so formed is often used as an armhole, the sleeve itself hanging behind the arm. This gown has been adopted unmodified by such universities as Birmingham, Bristol, Exeter and Nottingham, and slightly modified by rounding off the point of the sleeve at Reading.

At London University, a smaller version of the Oxford B.A. sleeve is used. It is gathered at the lower end of the forearm seam and held by a cord and button, sewn vertically over the pleats. The same sleeve is used at Hull and Southampton, but here the cords and buttons are blue. Three of the four ancient Scottish universities (Aberdeen, St Andrews and Edinburgh) together with Bradford and Liverpool use the masters' gown for all their bachelors' degrees, whilst several universities (Cambridge, Durham, Hull, Nottingham and Oxford) regard the B.D. as a higher degree, and use the masters' gown. At N.U.I. the LL.B. wears a masters' gown, whilst at Manchester the M.B. is chosen for this privilege.

At Oxford, all bachelors' degrees other than B.A., B.F.A. and B.Theol. are 'higher' degrees in that they can only be taken by people who are already graduates, and the gown used for these degrees is a very elaborate version of a doctors' undress gown, with a flap collar and heavily decorated with broad black gimp. Some other universities have also adopted the practice of using the doctors' undress gown for bachelors. Thus at London, the M.B., B.D.S., B.Pharm and B.Mus. use the flap-collar gown with the London sleeve ending, and the LL.B. wears the same gown with a square-ended sleeve and a slit at the back like the Q.C. gown. At Hull the B.Mus. wears a flap collar gown decorated with Oxford gimp, and gimp is also worn at Newcastle by M.B., B.S., B.Hy., B.D.S. and B.Mus.

In addition to its B.A. gown, Cambridge has a special gown for each of its bachelors' degrees. These are described elsewhere.

Masters

Just as the open wing-like sleeve is traditional for bachelors' gowns, so with masters can the closed or glove sleeve be regarded as typical. The glove-sleeve, which is of Tudor origin, consists of a tube-like appendage, usually reaching to the hem of the gown. The distal end is closed and there is a slit at elbow level to free the arm. The sleeve end often has a cut-out section, the boot of the sleeve, the shape of the boot being indicative of the university. However, practically all the newer universities have opted for a square cut sleeve ending.

The Oxford M.A. sleeve can be taken as our basic pattern. Here there is a crescent shape cut on the inner margin of the sleeve at the foot. This leaves two points facing inwards. This same gown is used by masters at Belfast, Edinburgh, N.U.I. and Sheffield. The same, with the addition of a black cord and button on the yoke, is used at Durham and Newcastle, and with a blue cord and button at Hull and Southampton. At Cambridge, M.A.s wear the Oxford sleeve with the upper point removed by rounding off. This Cambridge gown is used at Exeter, Nottingham, Reading etc. and with a cord and button on the yoke at Aberdeen and Liverpool. At Glasgow and St Andrews the masters' gown has a boot of the Oxford shape, but this is on the outer edge of the sleeve, so that the two points face backwards. Leeds have an Oxford-shaped cut both on the inner and outer borders. At London the two points are rounded off to give a double ogee curve, whilst at Wales and Birmingham the masters' gown has an inverted-T armhole to prevent overlap with Oxford and Cambridge respectively.

Doctors' Undress
In about half of the older universities and in all the new ones except Westminster, doctors do not have a special undress gown, but wear the masters' gown. Again Cambridge takes the lead in having a special undress gown for each doctorate. The Ph.D. has four inches of Cambridge lace placed horizontally above the armhole, the Sc.D. has lace horizontally right across the armhole, and the Litt.D. has lace vertically from armhole to shoulder. The three other doctorates have a flap collar gown, the M.D. having lace round and vertically above the armhole, round the flap collar and across the foot of the sleeve. The Mus.D. adds an extra row of lace to the collar, and the LL.D. has the same gown without lace, thus making it suitable for wear in court. Oxford takes the gimp gown and adds an extra (more or less invisible) panel of gimp under the arm.

The other 17 universities which have special doctors' undress gowns have simple patterns, none differentiating between individual doctorates, but nonetheless indicating the degree to be of higher status than a master.

Doctors' Full Dress Robes
Traditionally doctors wear scarlet cloth when in full dress. However, many institutions have moved away from tradition and wear practically every colour imaginable. In many cases the Ph.D. has worn a robe of claret, crimson or maroon, to differentiate them from a higher doctorate, but many institutions have followed the unfortunate practice adopted by Cambridge of adding loose facings to the masters' gown.

The full dress robe is of the same basic pattern as the black gown, with the sleeves and back gathered into a yoke. The facings are usually covered with silk of the faculty colour or the university colour. There are three basic shapes for sleeves: the Oxford pattern which is an open bell shape, covered to within inches of the shoulder with silk. This can be modified to having only the cuffs covered in silk, say, five inches or so. The second pattern is the open pointed sleeve with the elbow region turned back, as in London, or with the point removed to round off the bottom as in Cambridge. There is an intermediate stage between the Oxford and the Cambridge sleeve which is seen in the Cambridge Mus.D. and in some of the Scottish universities. The third pattern is the glove sleeve, as in City and Manchester universities. Here the armhole is often edged with silk, or even the front of the sleeve can be so covered.

Oxford doctors have another scarlet robe. This is the convocation habit, a sleeveless garment which can be worn over a black gown or surplice. The habit is essentially an ecclesiastical garment, and is worn by bishops as a chimere (frontispiece, f).

Hoods
As the name indicates, the hood was originally a head covering. The Cambridge or full shape hood consists of a cape which covers the shoulders, and a cowl—the original headgear (figs. 66-69). The cowl has a liripipe or tail which at one time

was long enough to be used as a scarf. The hood is held in position by a neckband which joins the two sides together at the throat. The neckband is usually fitted with a cord loop which can be used to anchor it to a button or brooch.

Hoods are usually made of a specific material such as stuff or corded silk, and lined with another material, frequently silk or taffeta. The outer part should always be of a heavier material than the lining, otherwise a very clumsy effect is obtained. In many cases the hood is not fully lined, but only bordered with silk. This is seen particularly in non-graduate hoods, such as those of theological colleges.

The Oxford or simple-shaped hood consists of the cowl part only, without the cape. In Oxford, two forms of this hood are in use. The first is the basic simple shape (fig. 72). This form reveals little of the lining. The second and by far the commonest is the Dean Burgon shape—a larger hood which it is possible to fold in such a way as to show the silk lining (figs. 70-71).

A more recent development has been the Aberdeen shape—a symmetrical hood, unlike the full (and Burgon) shapes which tend to have the cowl falling to one side or the other (figs. 77-78). This hood has the lining turned out to show to the best advantage.

Hoods are sometimes edged, bound or bordered with silk or fur. An edging consists of a narrow strip of material on the outside of the cowl and perhaps also round the cape (fig. 68). A bound hood has a strip of the material both inside and outside the cowl. A border is present on the inside edge of the cowl only. Thus the Cambridge M.A. hood is lined with white silk which ends at the edge of the cowl, whereas the blood crimson silk lining of the Oxford M.A. hood is carried over to form an edging about half an inch wide. A hood might also be piped, i.e. have a coloured cord or very narrow ribbon at the junction of two other materials.

Hoods are normally worn with the cowl turned inside out for part of its width, thus showing some of the lining material, except as on certain occasions at Cambridge when the hood is worn 'squared', i.e. with none of the lining showing.

Degrees

Nowadays, in an increasing number of subjects, a three-year first degree is not a sufficient introduction to form a sound basis for research. This has led to four-year undergraduate courses, or to post-graduate taught courses in specialised branches, the latter usually being rewarded with an M.A. or M.Sc. Formerly these were introductory research degrees, probably preceding a Ph.D. Since the introduction in 1964 of the degree of M.Phil. by Sussex University, practically every university now awards it as a first research degree. Unfortunately it is also used as a one- or two-year taught degrees by some universities.

Oxford and Cambridge have recently introduced the degree of Master of Studies (M.St.) and many others are considering the introduction of a Master of Research (M.Res.). Cambridge now have a Master of Natural Science (M.Sci.) for four-year undergraduate courses, whilst others are thinking of creating Master of Physics (M.Phys.) and Master of Mathematics (M.Math.) to cover the extended course.

This proliferation of degrees is leading to confusion (e.g. who can say what M.T.P. or M.U.R.P. stand for?) especially since there seems to be no standardisation of requirements for these degrees. We must expect increasing entropy in the world of academe!

Abbreviation of Degrees

ABBREVIATION OF DEGREES

Agr.B.	Bachelor in Agriculture
Agr.M.	Master in Agriculture
Agr.(Forest)B	Bachelor in Agriculture (Forestry)
Agr.(Forest)M	Master in Agriculture (Forestry)
B.A.	Bachelor of Arts
B.A.Admin.	Bachelor of Arts in Administration
B.A.Com.	Bachelor of Arts in Commerce
B.A.Econ.	Bachelor of Arts in Economics
B.A.Law	Bachelor of Arts in Law
B.A.Soc.	Bachelor of Arts in Social Studies
B.A.Theol.	Bachelor of Arts in Theology
B.Acc.	Bachelor of Accountancy
B.Admin.	Bachelor of Administration
B.Agr.	Bachelor of Agriculture
B.Arch.	Bachelor of Architecture
B.A.I.	Bachelor of Civil Engineering
B.A.I.Elect.& Mech.	Bachelor of Electrical & Mechanical Engineering
B.A.O.	Bachelor of Obstetrics
B.B.S.	Bachelor of Business Studies
B.Ch.	Bachelor of Surgery
B.Chir.	Bachelor of Surgery
B.Ch.D.	Bachelor of Dental Surgery
B.C.L.	Bachelor of Civil Law
B.Com.	Bachelor of Commerce
B.Com.Sc.	Bachelor of Commercial Science
B.D.	Bachelor of Divinity
B.D.S.	Bachelor of Dental Surgery
B.Dent.Sc.	Bachelor of Dental Science
B.Des.	Bachelor of Design
B.Ed.	Bachelor of Education
B.Eng.	Bachelor of Engineering
B.F.A.	Bachelor of Fine Art
B.H.	Bachelor of Humanities
B.Health Sc.	Bachelor of Health Science
B.Hy.	Bachelor of Hygiene
B.Jur.	Bachelor of Jurisprudence
B.L.	Bachelor of Law
B.Lib.	Bachelor of Librarianship
B.Litt.	Bachelor of Letters
B.M.	Bachelor of Medicine
B.Med.Sc.	Bachelor of Medical Science

B.Met.	Bachelor of Metallurgy
B.Mus.	Bachelor of Music
B.Nurs.	Bachelor of Nursing
B.Pharm.	Bachelor of Pharmacy
B.Phil.	Bachelor of Philosophy
B.Physioth.	Bachelor of Physiotherapy
B.S.	Bachelor of Surgery
B.Sc.	Bachelor of Science
B.Sc.Agr.	Bachelor of Science in Agriculture
B.Sc.Dairying	Bachelor of Science in Dairying
B.Sc.(Dom.Sc.)	Bachelor of Science in Domestic Science
B.Sc.Econ.	Bachelor of Science in Economics
B.Sc.Eng.	Bachelor of Science in Engineering
B.Sc.For.	Bachelor of Science in Forestry
B.Sc.Health Sc.	Bachelor of Science in Heath Science
B.Sc.Hort.	Bachelor of Science in Horticulture
B.Sc.Med.	Bachelor of Medical Science
B.Sc.Min.	Bachelor of Science in Mining
B.Sc.Mar.Res.Man.	Bachelor of Science in Marine Research & Management
B.Sc.P.H.	Bachelor of Science in Public Health
B.Sc.Tech.	Bachelor of Science in Technology
B.Soc.Sc.	Bachelor of Social Science
B.S.S.	Bachelor of Social Studies
B.Tech.	Bachelor of Technology
B.Theol.	Bachelor of Theology
B.V.Sc.	Bachelor of Veterinary Science
B.Vet.M.	Bachelor of Veterinary Medicine
B.Vet.Med.	Bachelor of Veterinary Medicine
B.V.M.&S.	Bachelor of Veterinary Medicine and Surgery
Ch.B.	Bachelor of Surgery
Ch.M.	Master of Surgery
Clin.Psych.M.	Master of Clinical Psychology
D.B.A.	Doctor of Business Administration
D.Ch.	Doctor of Surgery
D.C.L.	Doctor of Civil Law
D.D.	Doctor of Divinity
D.D.Sc.	Doctor of Dental Science
D.Econ.Sc.	Doctor of Science in Economics
D.Ed.	Doctor of Education
D.Eng.	Doctor of Engineering
D.Hy.	Doctor of Hygiene
D.Lit.	Doctor of Literature
D.Litt.	Doctor of Letters
D.Litt.Celt.	Doctor of Celtic Literature
D.M.	Doctor of Medicine
D.Med.Sc.	Doctor of Medical Science
D.Met.	Doctor of Metallurgy
D.Mus.	Doctor of Music
D.Phil.	Doctor of Philosophy

ABBREVIATION OF DEGREES

D.Sc.	Doctor of Science
D.S.Sc.	Doctor of Social Science
D.Sc.Agr.	Doctor of Science in Agriculture
D.Sc.Econ.	Doctor of Science in Economics
D.Sc.Eng.	Doctor of Science in Engineering
D.Sc.Hort.	Doctor of Science in Horticulture
D.Sc.Min.	Doctor of Science in Mining
D.Sc.P.H.	Doctor of Science in Public Health
D.Sc.Tech.	Doctor of Science in Technology
D.Tech.	Doctor of Technology
D.V.Sc.	Doctor of Veterinary Science
D.Vet.Med.	Doctor of Veterinary Medicine
D.V.M.& S.	Doctor of Veterinary Medicine and Surgery
Ed.B.	Bachelor of Education
LL.B.	Bachelor of Laws
LL.D.	Doctor of Laws
LL.M.	Master of Laws
Litt.D.	Doctor of Letters
M.A.	Master of Arts
M.A.Ed.	Master of Arts in Education
M.Agr.	Master of Agriculture
M.A.I.	Master of Civil Engineering
M.Arch.	Master of Architecture
M.A.Econ.	Master of Arts in Economics
M.A.Com.	Master of Arts in Commerce
M.A.O.	Master of Obstetrics
M.A.Soc.	Master of Arts in Social Studies
M.A.Soc.Sc.	Master of Arts in Social Science
M.A.Admin.	Master of Arts in Administration
M.Acc.	Master of Accountancy
M.App.Psy.	Master of Applied Psychology
M.B.	Bachelor of Medicine
M.B.A.	Master of Business Administration
M.B.S.	Master of Business Studies
M.B.Sc.	Master of Business Science
M.C.C.	Master of Community Care
M.C.D.	Master of Civic Design
M.Ch.	Master of Surgery
M.Chir.	Master of Surgery
M.Ch.D.	Master of Dental Surgery
M.Ch.Orth.	Master of Orthopaedic Surgery
M.Com.	Master of Commerce
M.Com.Sc.	Master of Commercial Science
M.D.	Doctor of Medicine
M.Des.	Master of Design
M.D.S.	Master of Dental Surgery
M.Dent.Sc.	Master of Dental Science
M.E.B.A.	Master of European Business Administration
M.Econ.Sc.	Master of Science in Economics

M.Ed.	Master of Education
M.Eng.	Master of Engineering
M.Jur.	Master of Jurisprudence
M.Lib.	Master of Librarianship
M.L.A.	Master of Landscape Architecture
M.L.D.	Master of Landscape Design
M.Litt.	Master of Letters
M.Litt.Ct.	Master of Celtic Literature
M.Math.	Master of Mathematics
M.M.Sc.	Master of Medical Science
M.Met.	Master of Metallurgy
M.Mus.	Master of Music
M.N.	Master of Nursing
M.P.A.	Master of Public Administration
M.P.H.	Master of Public Health
M.Pharm.	Master of Pharmacy
M.Phil.	Master of Philosophy
M.Phys.	Master of Physics
M.Psych.	Master of Psychology
M.Rad.	Master of Radiology
M.S.	Master of Surgery
M.S.Sc.	Master of Social Science
M.S.W.	Master of Social Work
M.Sc.	Master of Science
M.Sc.Econ.	Master of Science in Economics
M.Sc.Eng.	Master of Science in Engineering
M.Sc.Hort.	Master of Science in Horticulture
M.Sc.Min.	Master of Science in Mining
M.Sc.Tech.	Master of Science in Technology
M.Sc.P.H.	Master of Science in Public Heath
M.Sci.	Master of Natural Science
M.St.	Master of Studies
M.Th. or M.Theol.	Master of Theology
M.Trop.Med.	Master of Tropical Medicine
M.T.P.	Master of Town Planning
M.U.R.P.	Master of Urban and Rural Planning
Mus.B.	Bachelor of Music
Mus.D.	Doctor of Music
Mus.M.	Master of Music
M.Univ.	Master of the University
M.Univ.Admin.	Master of University Administration
M.V.B.	Bachelor of Vetinerary Medicine
M.V.M.	Master of Veterinary Medicine
M.V.Sc.	Master of Vetinerary Science
M.Vet.Med.	Master of Veterinary Medicine
Ph.D.	Doctor of Philosophy
Sc.B.Tech.	Bachelor of Science in Technology
Sc.D.	Doctor of Science

Illustrations

I Lambeth Degrees

The Archbishop of Canterbury has the privilege of awarding Lambeth degrees. The recipients wear the academical dress of the Archbishop's own university, which has always, until now, been Oxford or Cambridge. The present Archbishop, Dr. George Carey, is a London graduate, but has decided to carry on with the traditional practice, and in this case all the graduates are wearing Oxford gowns. Here we see the Archbishop seated, wearing a Cambridge D.D. gown, flanked by Stephen Dykes Bower (D.Litt) and Lady Helen Oppenheimer (D.D.). Standing are, *left to right*, Brian Pearce (M.Litt.), the Rev. George Lings (M.Litt.), Peter Lowater (M.A.), Sir John Owen (D.C.L.), Canon Eric James (D.D.), the Right Rev. Colin Buchanan (D.D.) and Canon Richard Buck (M.A.).

II Greenwich University gowns

III   Manchester Metropolitan University gowns

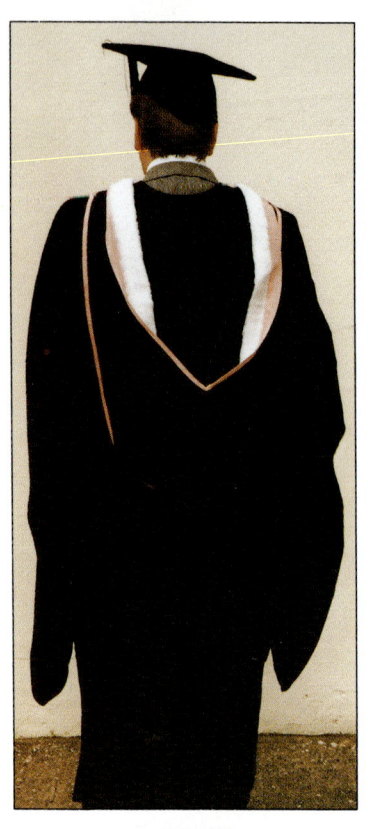

IV Manchester B.Sc. gown, *far left*

V Exeter bachelors' gown, *left*

VI Wolverhampton bachelors' gown, *below left*

VII London B.Sc. gown, *below centre*

VIII London B.Mus. gown, *below right*

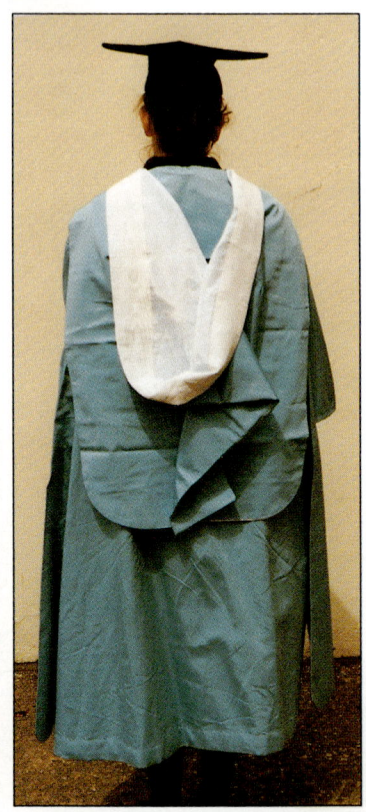

IX Portsmouth M.Phil. gown, front view, *above left*

X Portsmouth M.Phil. gown, rear view, *above centre*

XI Southampton M.A. gown, *above right*

XII Warwick M.A. gown, *below left*

XIII Durham M.A. gown, *below centre*

XIV Leeds M.Ed. gown, *below right*

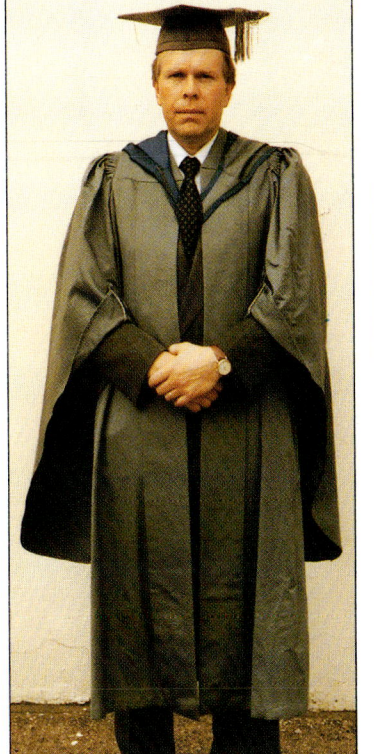

XV Portsmouth Ph.D. gown

XVI Manchester doctors' gown

XVII London Arts gown

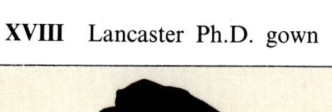

XVIII Lancaster Ph.D. gown

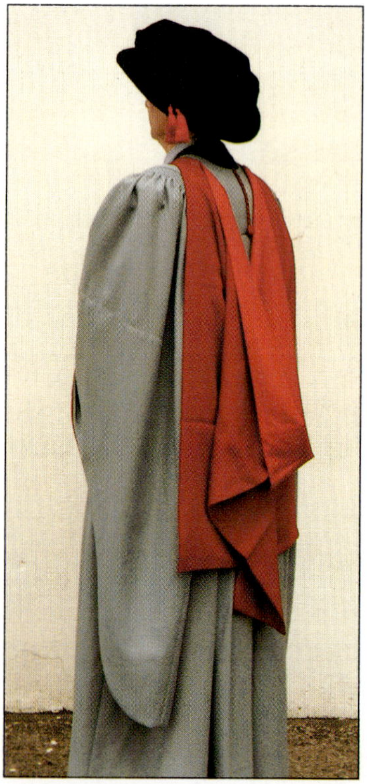

XIX Durham Ph.D. gown

XX Wolverhampton Ph.D. gown

left to right

XXI Warwick Ph.D. gown
XXII Open University Ph.D. gown
XXIII Brighton Ph.D. gown

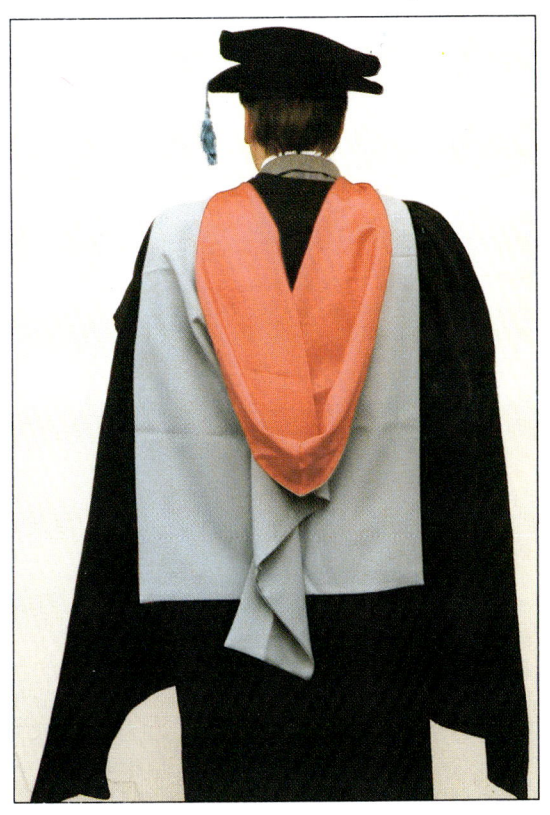

XXIV & XXV Lancaster Ph.D. gown: back and front views

XXVI Dr. Mary Archer modelling the higher doctors' gown of the University of Hertfordshire.

XXVIII *Right to left:* Staffordshire Ph.D gown, Hertfordshire bachelors' gown and Hertfordshire Ph.D. gown.

ILLUSTRATIONS

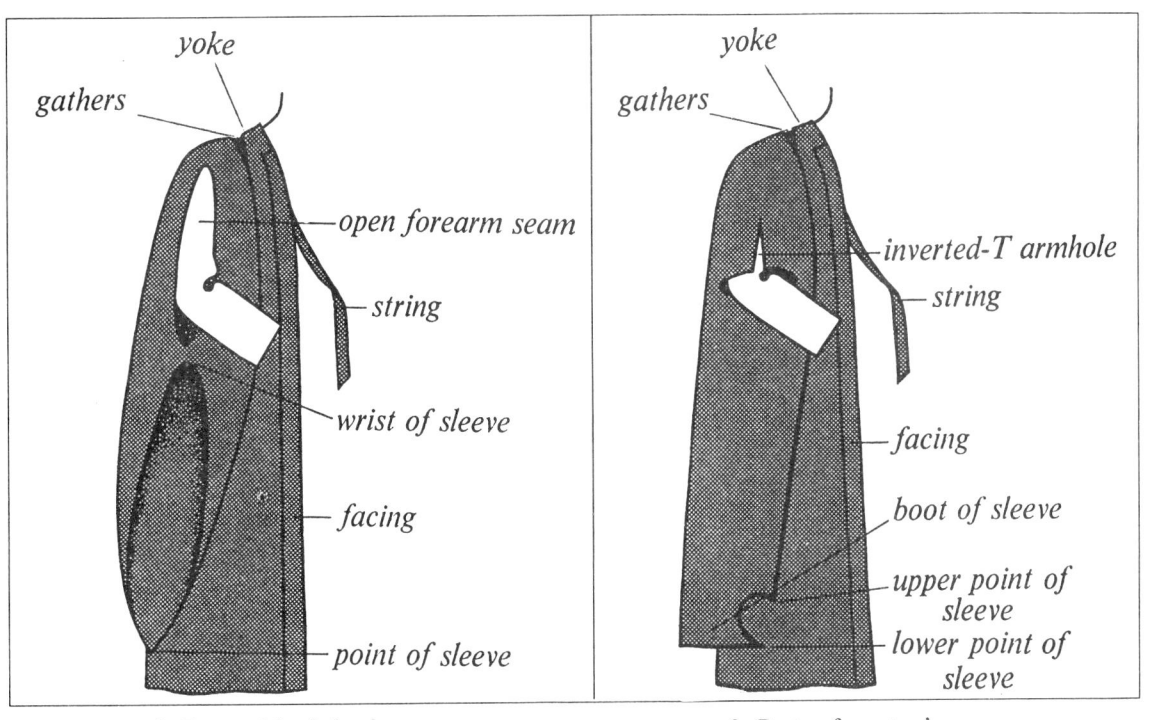

1. Parts of bachelors' gown.

2. Parts of masters' gown.

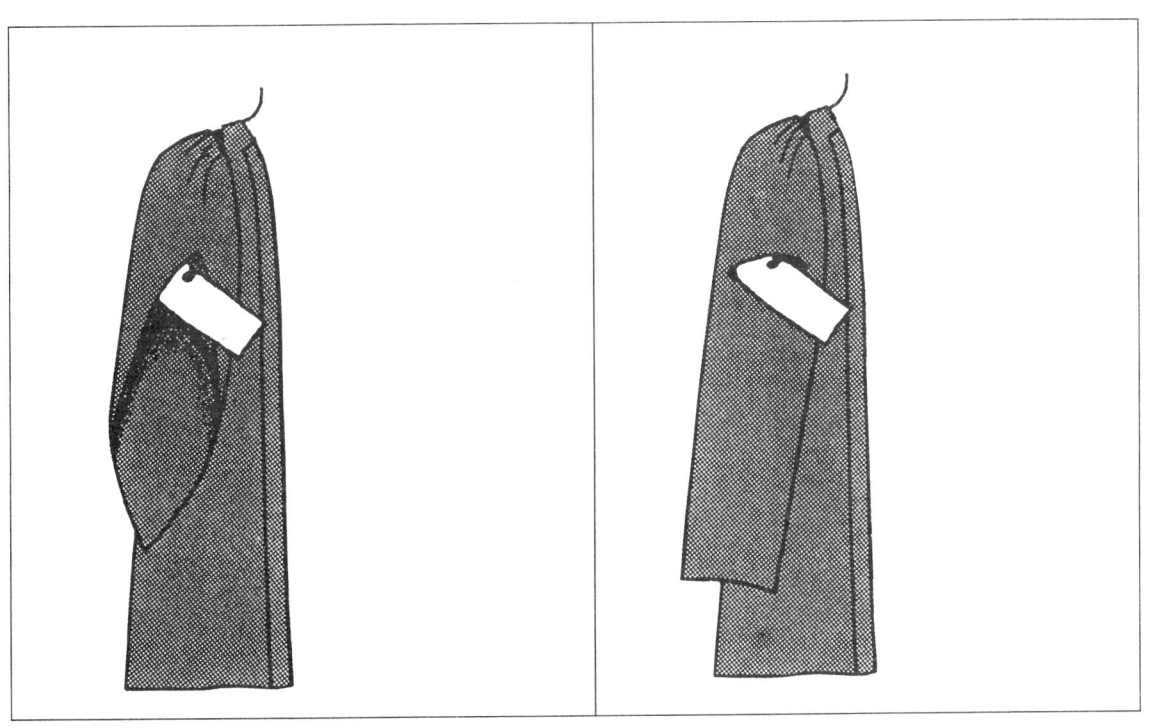

3. The basic bachelors' gown.

4. The basic masters' gown.

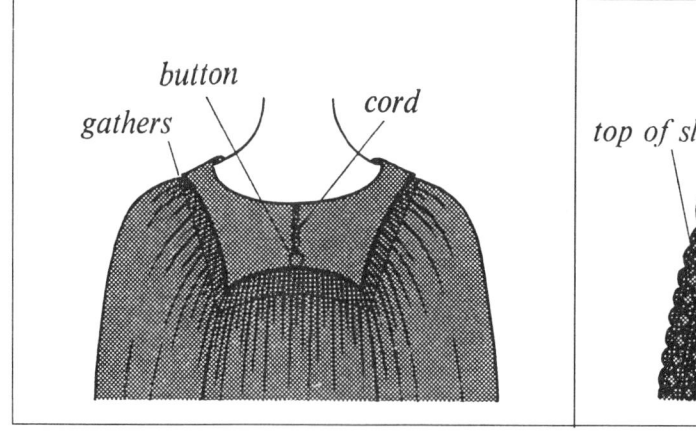

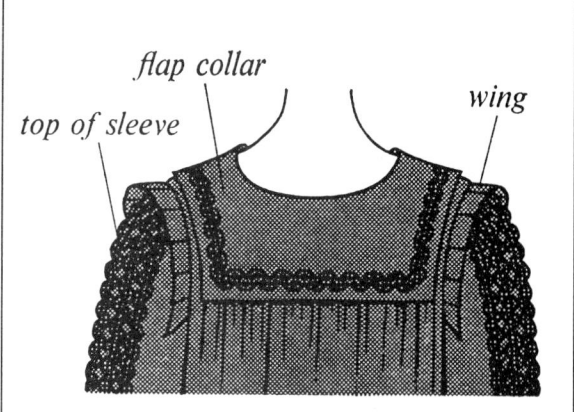

5. The standard yoke.

6. The flap collar yoke.

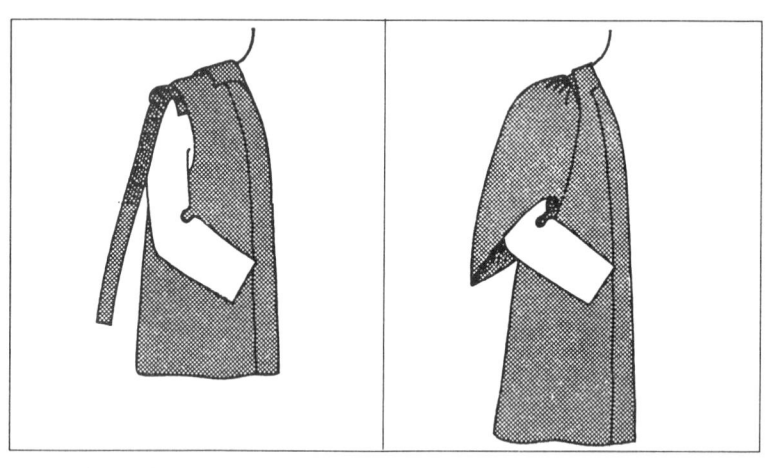

7. Oxford: the commoners' gown.

8. Oxford: the scholars' gown.

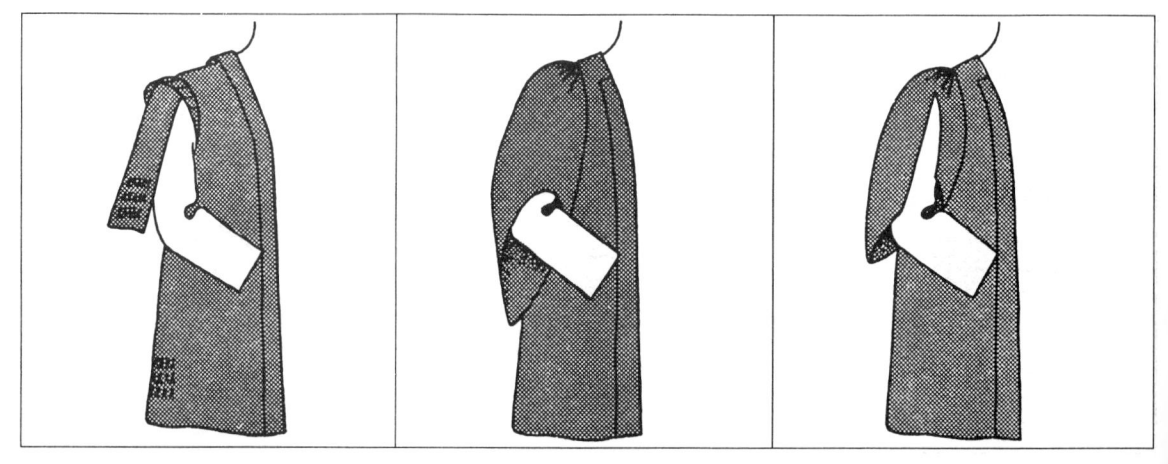

9. Trinity College, Dublin: the undergraduate gown.

10. London: the undergraduate gown.

11. Scottish universities: the undergraduate gown.

ILLUSTRATIONS

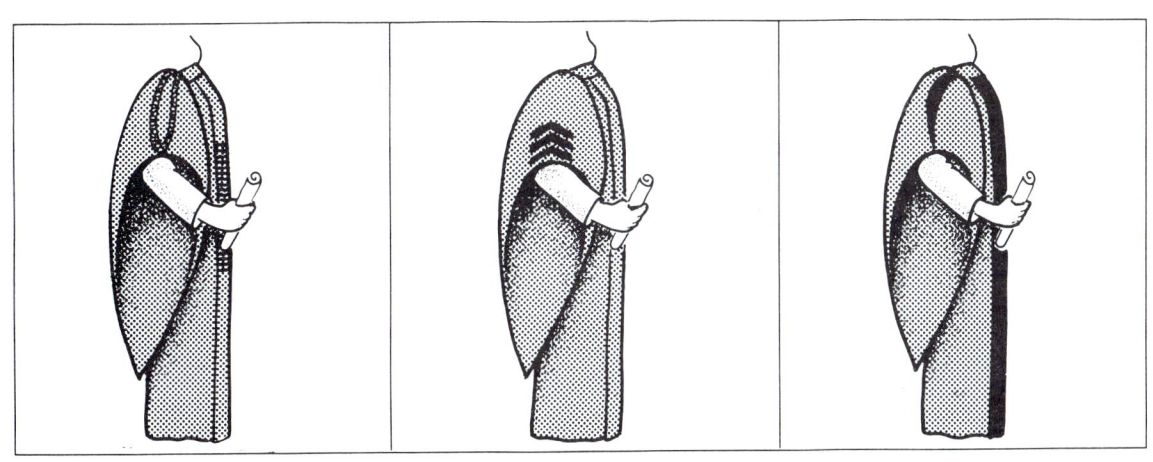

12. Christ's College gown.

13. Clare College gown.

14. Corpus Christi College gown.

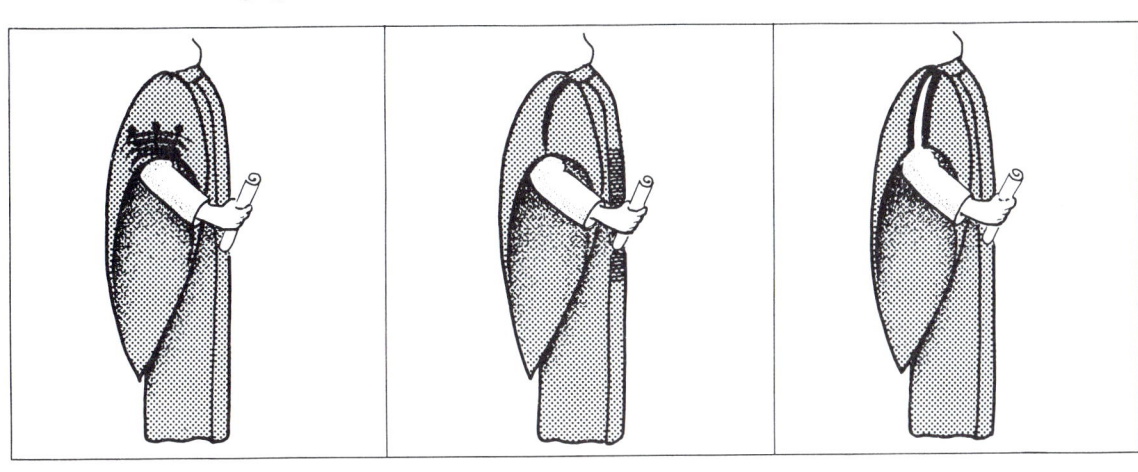

15. Downing College gown.

16. Emmanuel College gown.

17. Fitzwilliam College gown.

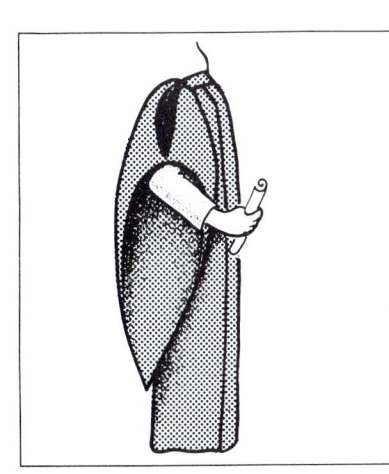

18. Churchill, King's, Peterhouse, Queens' and Robinson, gowns.

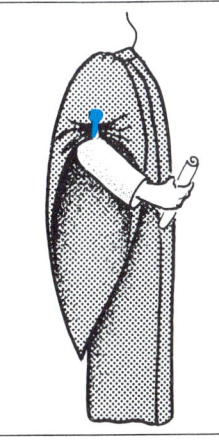

19. Clare Hall, Hughes Hall, St Edmunds College, Lucy Cavendish and Wolfson, gowns.

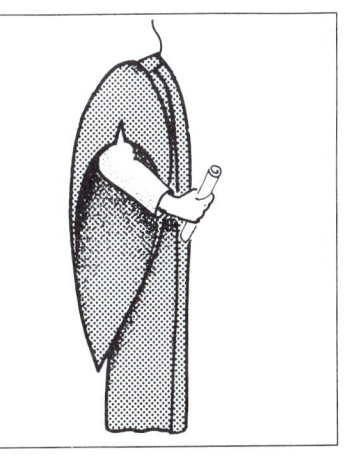

20. Girton, Homerton, Newnham and New Hall, gowns.

20   ACADEMICAL DRESS OF BRITISH AND IRISH UNIVERSITIES

21. Gonville & Caius College gown.

22. Jesus College gown.

23. Magdalene College gown.

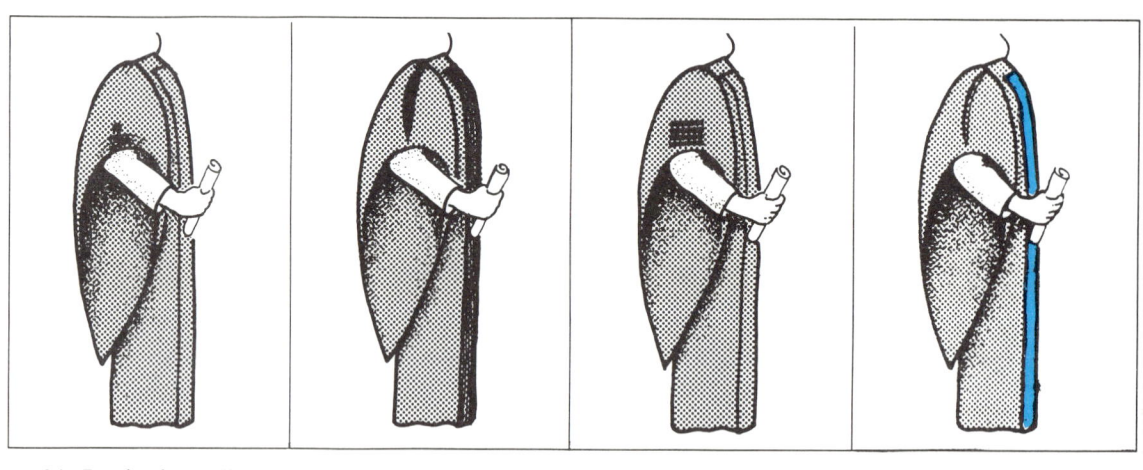

24. Pembroke College gown.

25. St Catharine's College gown.

26. St John's College gown.

27. Selwyn College gown.

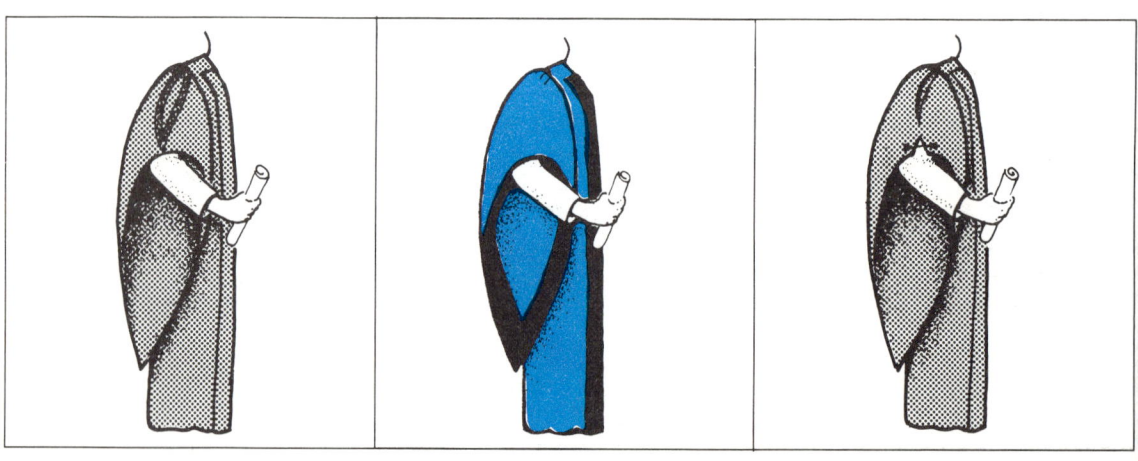

28. Sidney Sussex College gown.

29. Trinity College gown.

30. Trinity Hall gown.

ILLUSTRATIONS

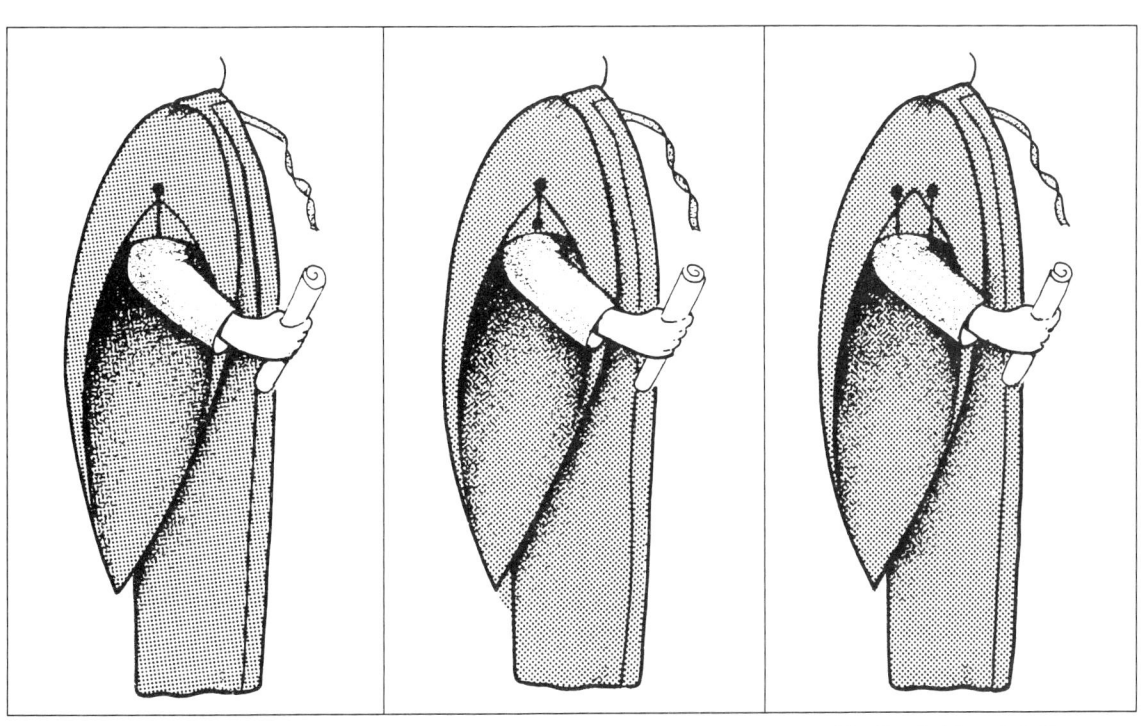

31. Cambridge, M.B.

32. Cambridge, Vet.M.B.

33. Cambridge, L.L.B. (discontinued).

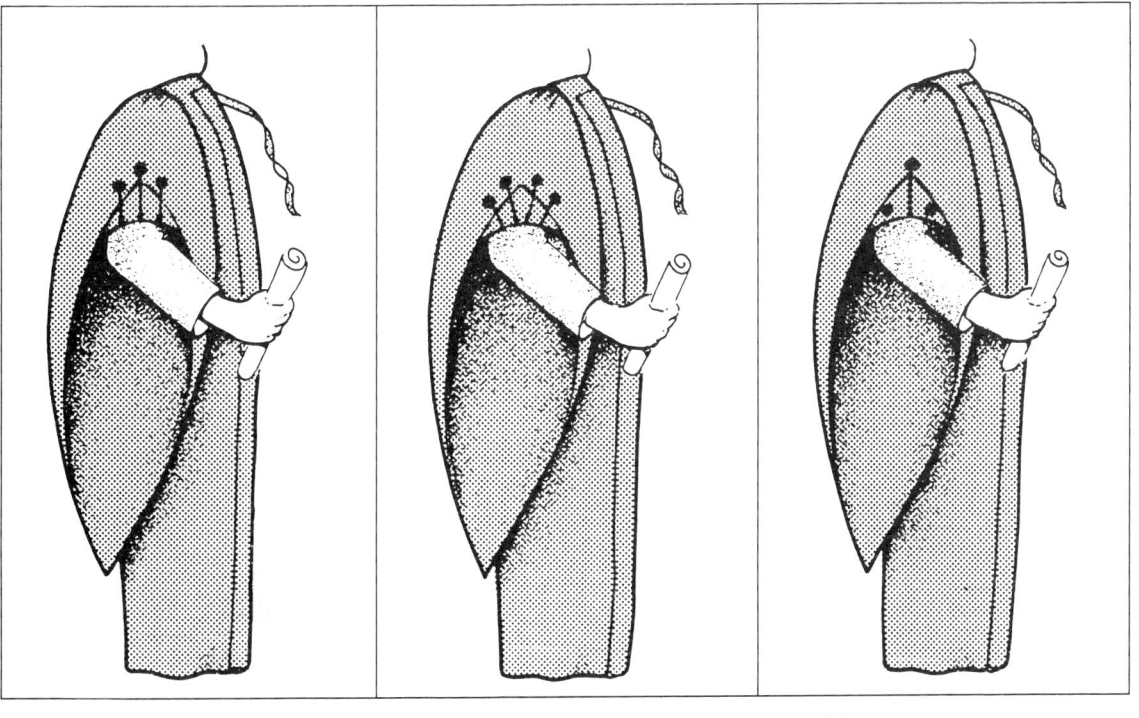

34. Cambridge, B.Chir.

35. Cambridge, B.Ed.

36. Cambridge, Mus.B.

22   ACADEMICAL DRESS OF BRITISH AND IRISH UNIVERSITIES

37. Cambridge B.A. gown.

38. Oxford B.A. gown.

39. Belfast bachelors' gown.

40. Dublin bachelors' gown.

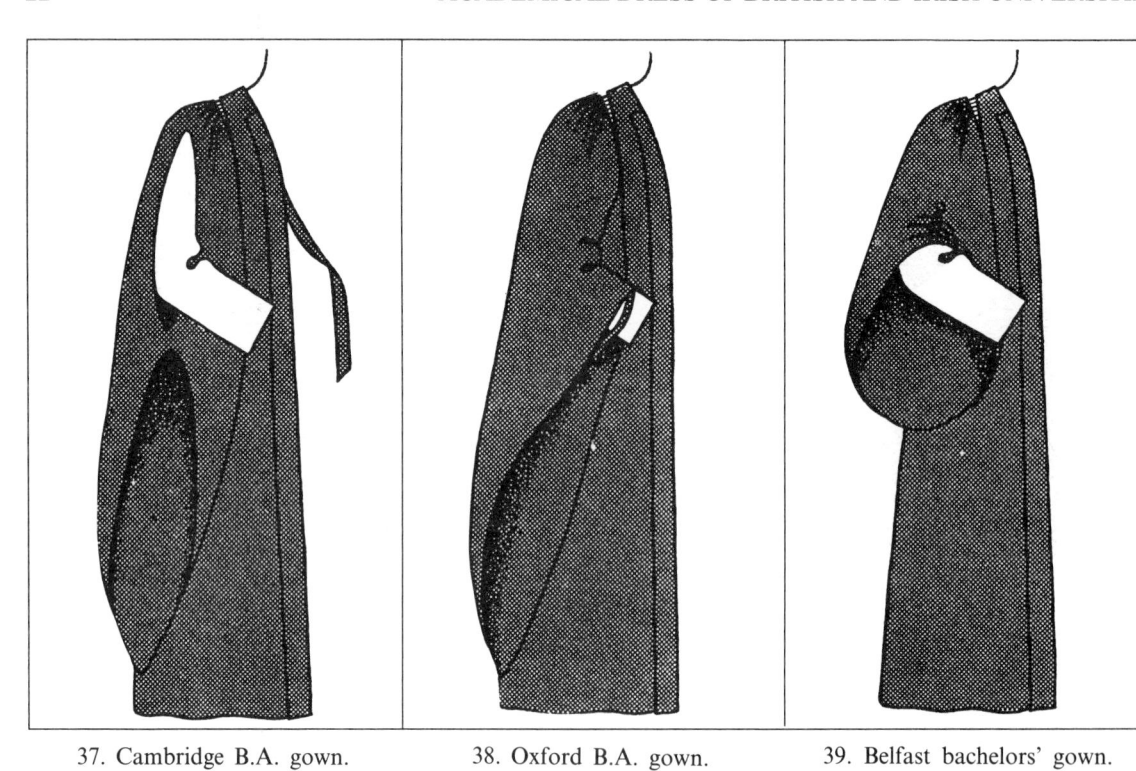

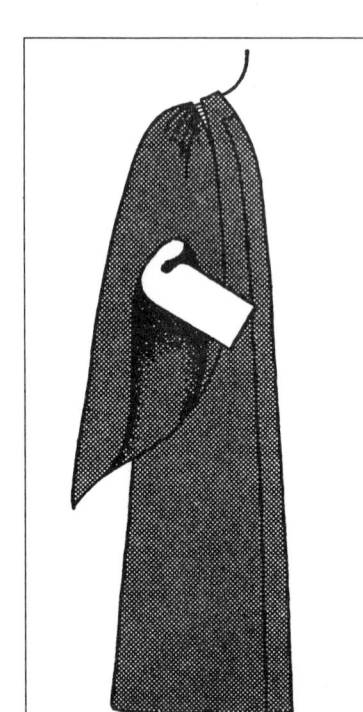

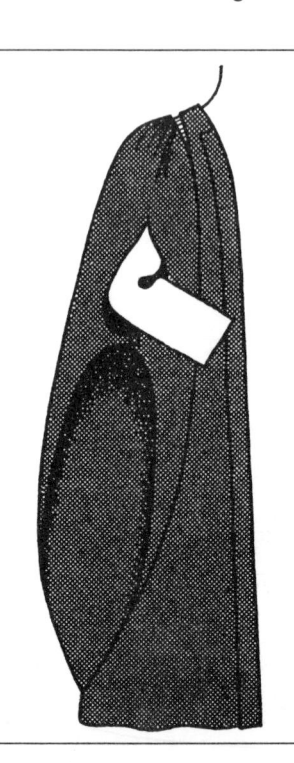

41. Durham and Newcastle bachelors' gown.

42. London bachelors' gown.

ILLUSTRATIONS

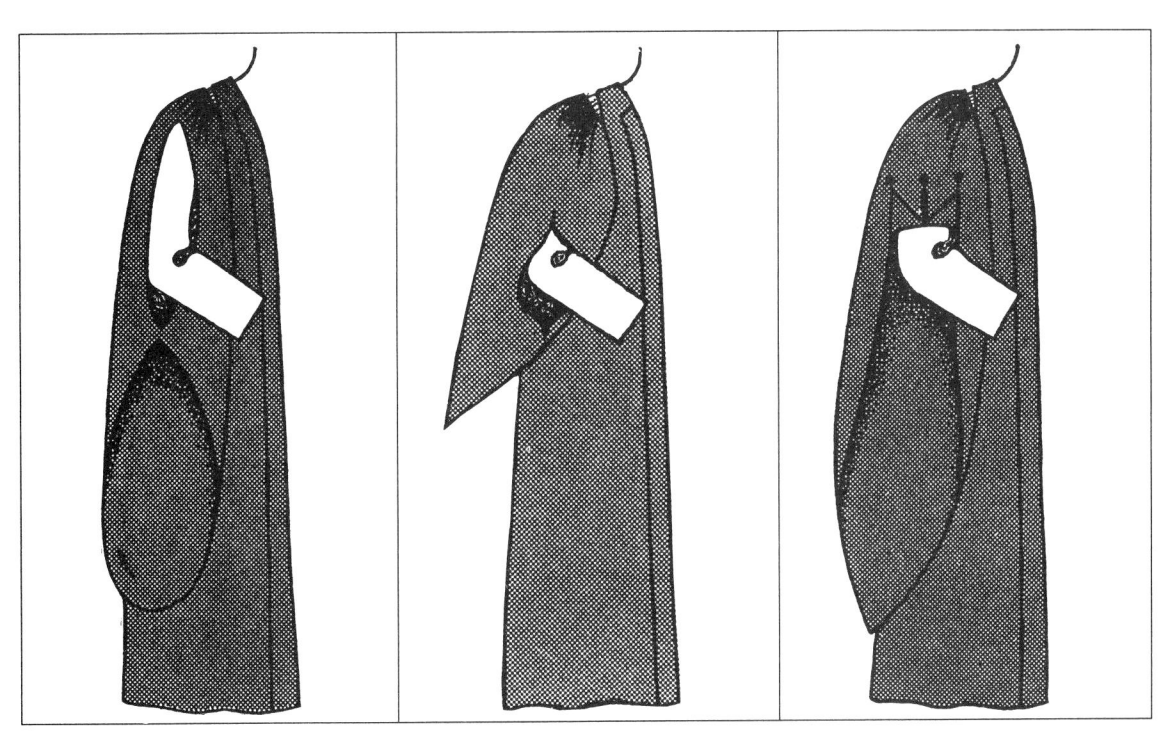

43. Reading bachelors' gown.

44. Sussex bachelors' gown.

45. Wales bachelors' gown.

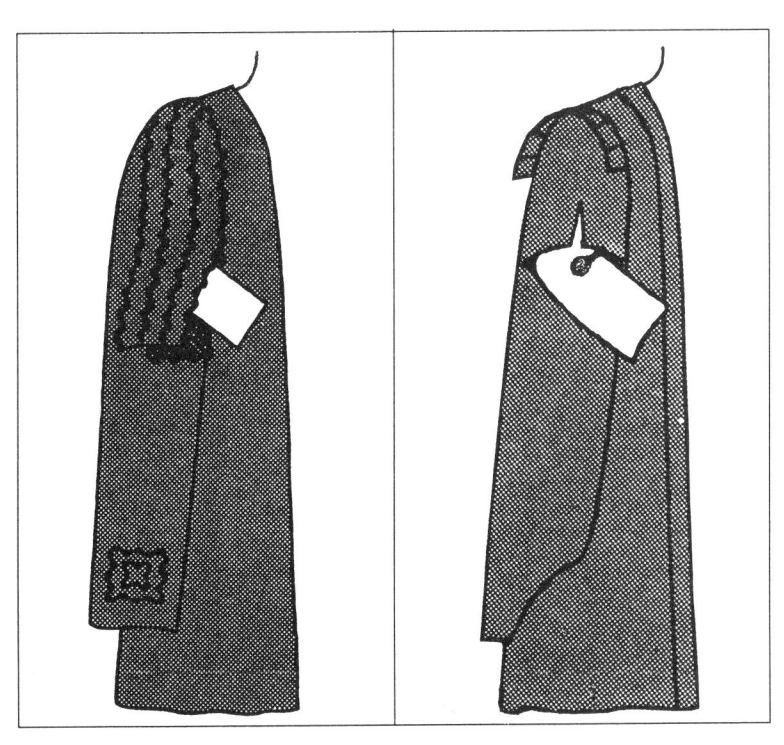

46. Newcastle M.B. gown.

47. London M.B. gown.

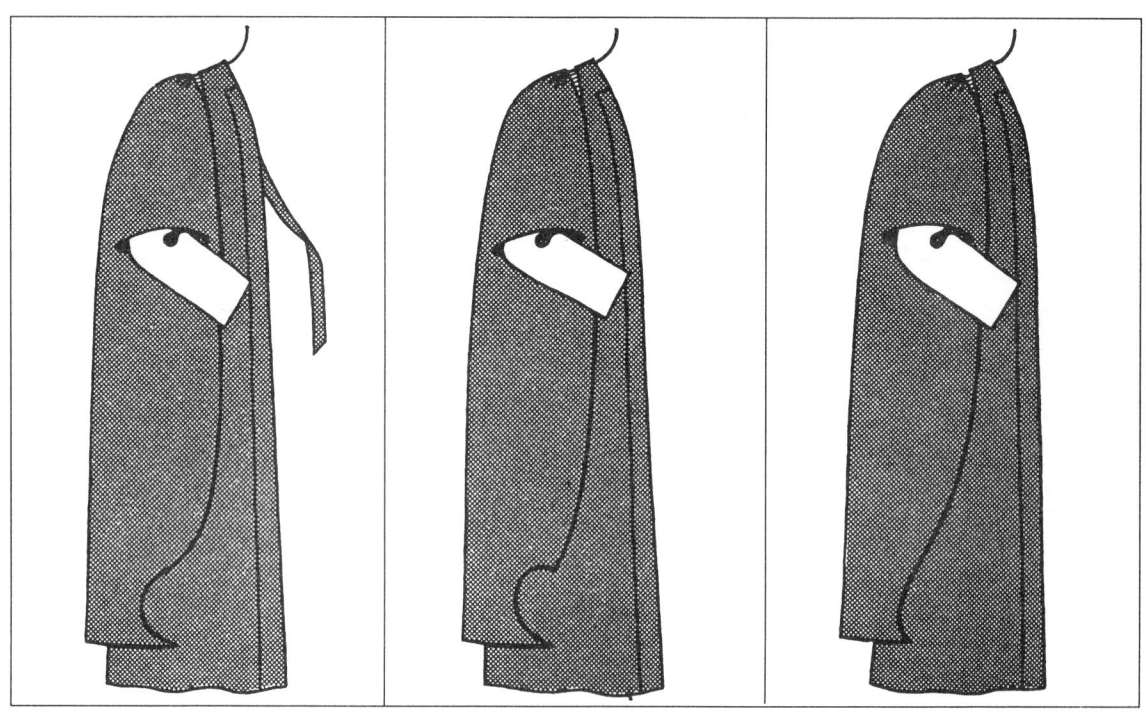

48. Cambridge M.A. gown.

49. Oxford M.A. gown.

50. Aberdeen: all graduates gown.

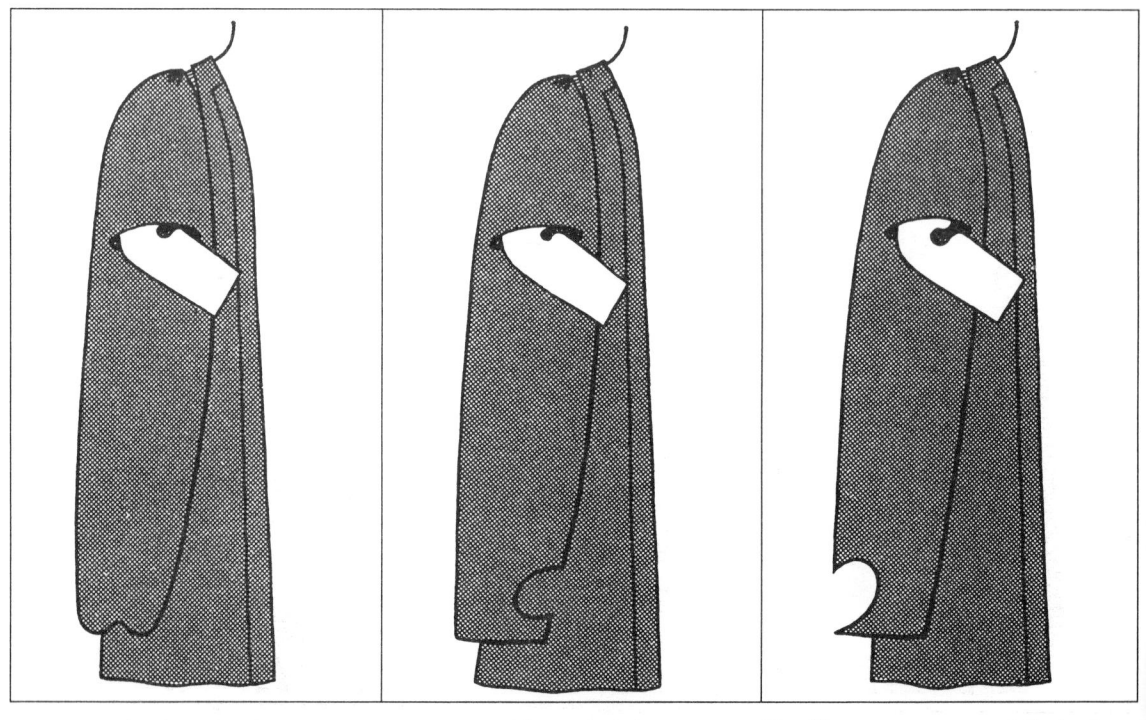

51. Bristol masters' gown.

52. Dublin masters' gown.

53. Glasgow masters and St Andrews bachelors', masters', Ph.D. gown.

ILLUSTRATIONS

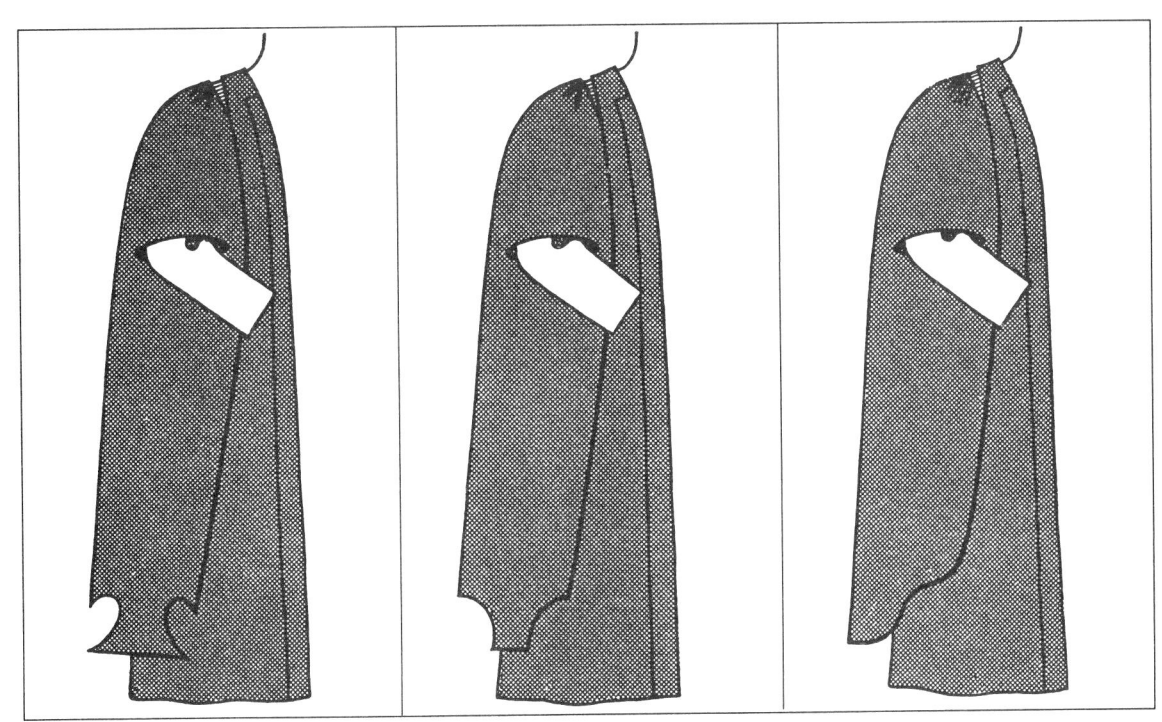

54. Leeds masters' gown.

55. Leicester masters' gown.

56. London masters' gown.

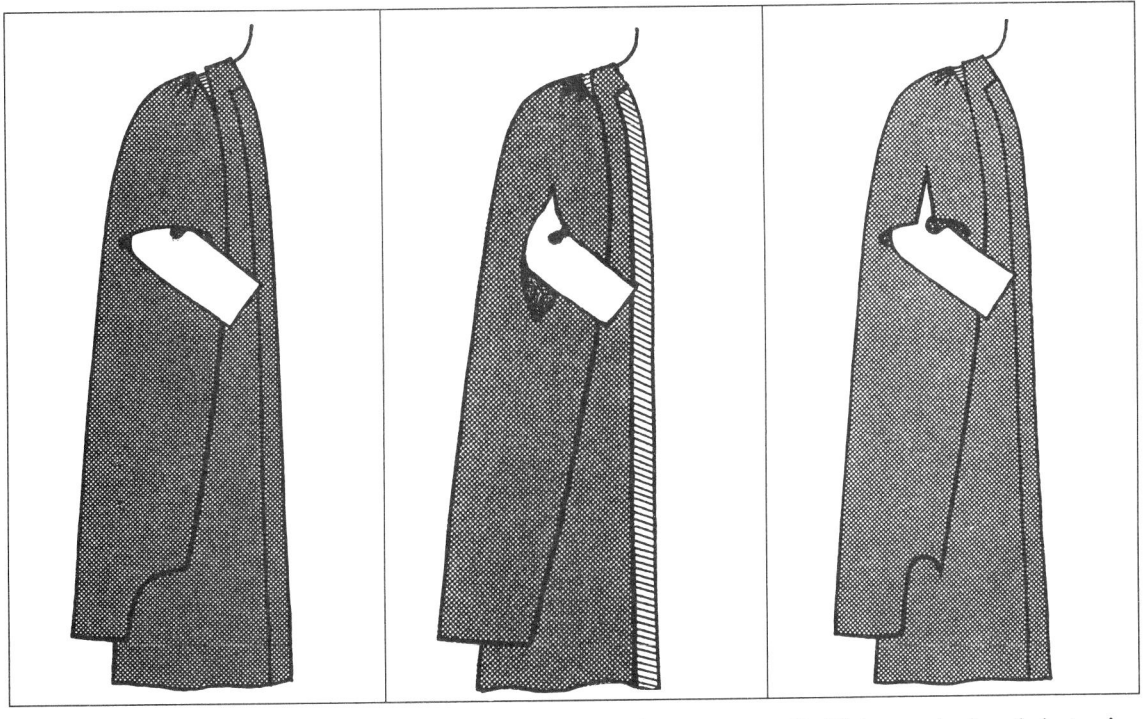

57. Manchester masters' gown.

58. Sussex masters' gown.

59. Wales masters' and doctors' gown.

26   ACADEMICAL DRESS OF BRITISH AND IRISH UNIVERSITIES

60. Cambridge doctors' robe.

61. Cambridge Mus.D. robe.

62. Oxford doctors' robe.

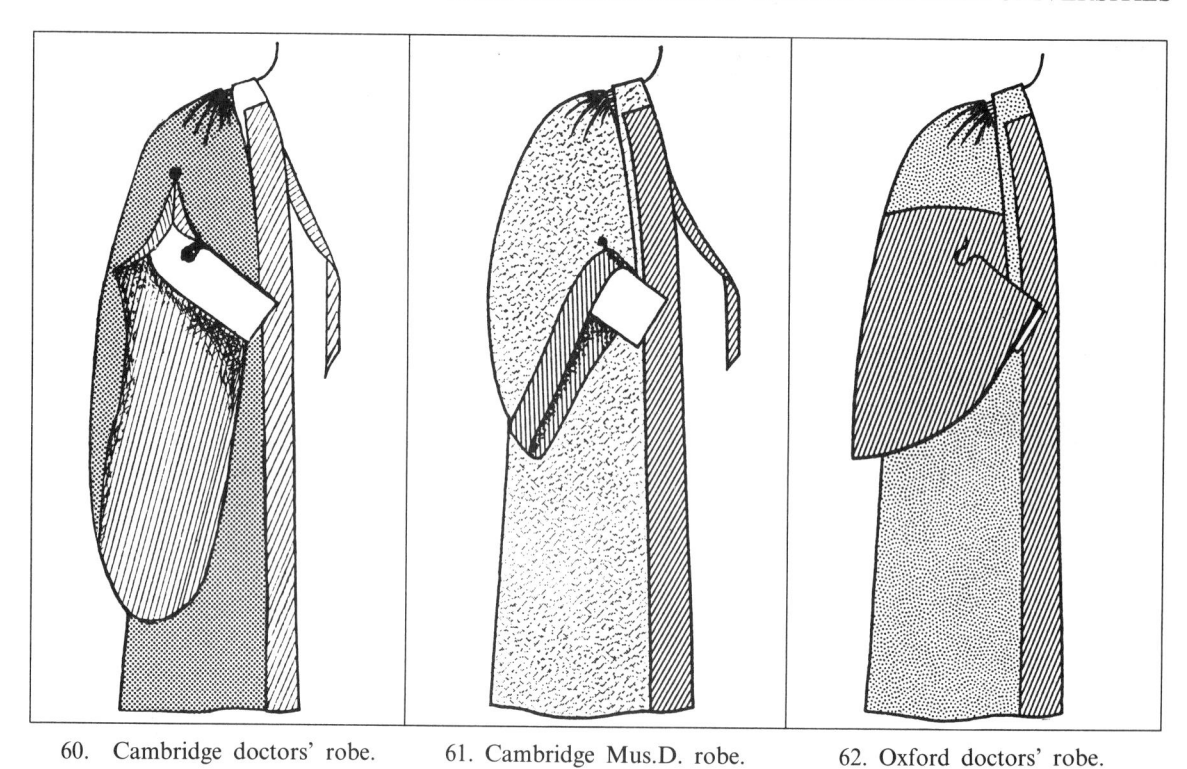

63. London doctors' robe.

64. Sussex doctors' robe.

ILLUSTRATIONS

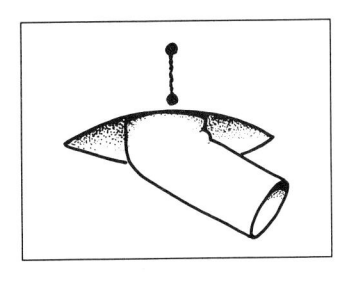

65a. Cambridge, M.Phil. sleeve decoration (left).

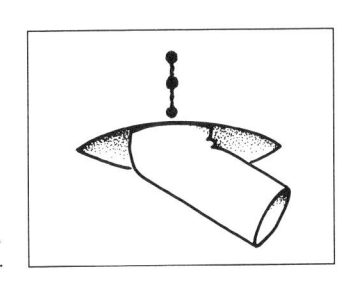

65b. Cambridge, M.Litt. sleeve decoration (right).

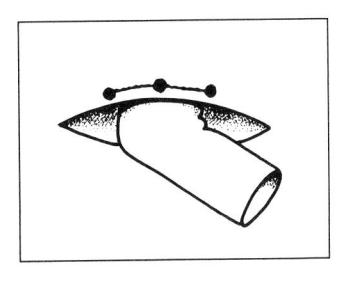

65c. Cambridge, M.Sc. sleeve decoration (left).

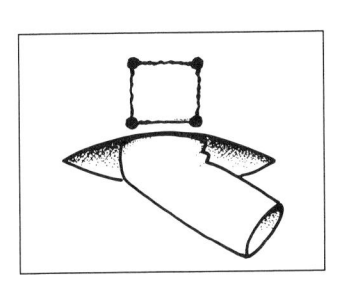

65d. Cambridge, M.B.A. sleeve decoration (right).

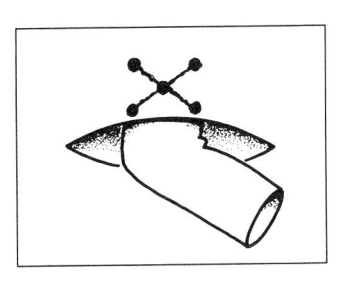

65e. Cambridge, M.Ed. sleeve decoration (left).

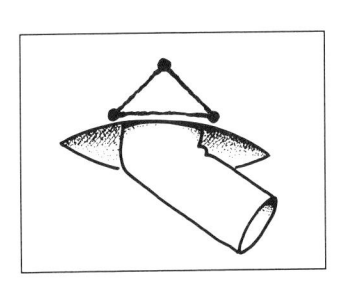

65f. Cambridge, M.Mus. sleeve decoration (right).

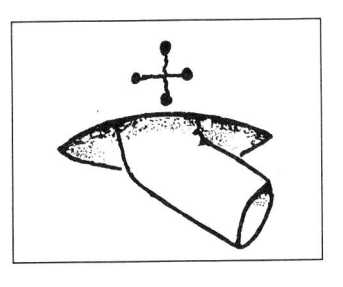

65g. Cambridge, M.St. sleeve decoration (left).

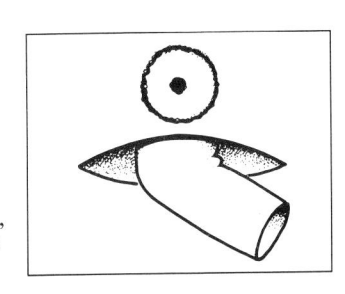

65h. Cambridge, M.Eng., M.Sci. sleeve decoration (right).

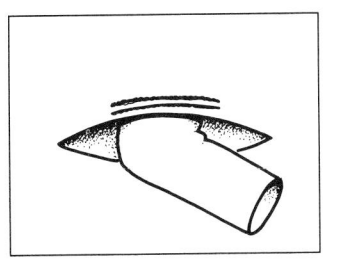

65i. Cambridge, LL.M. sleeve decoration (left).

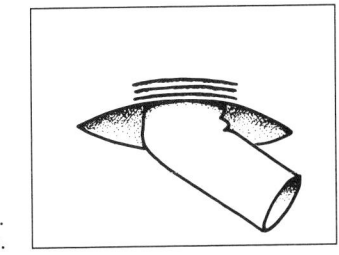

65j. Cambridge, M.Chir. sleeve decoration (right).

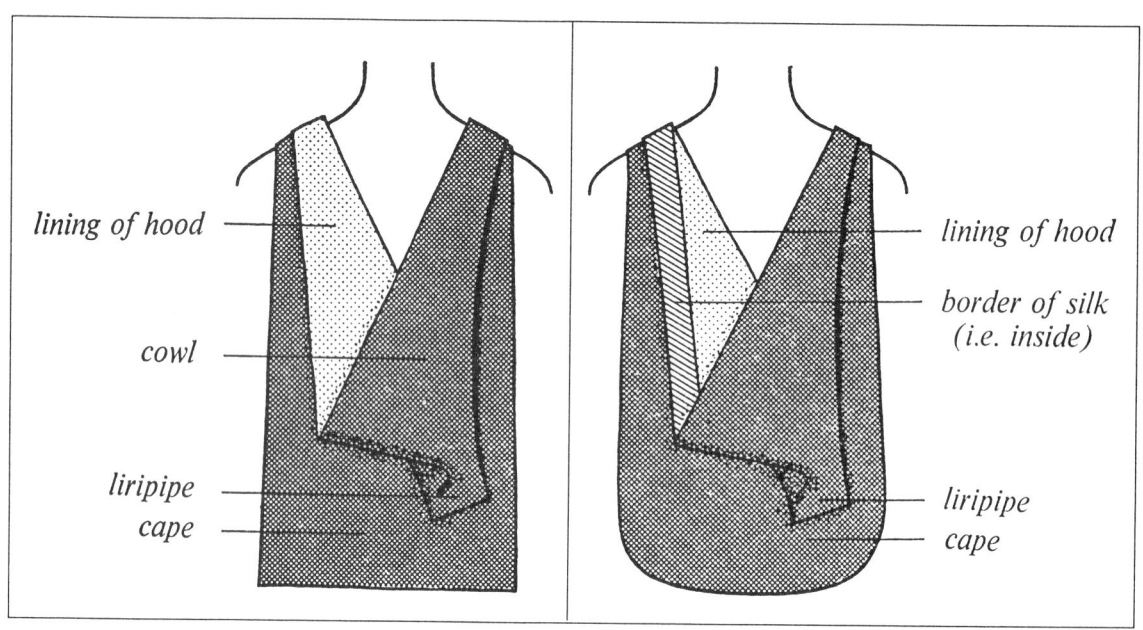

28 ACADEMICAL DRESS OF BRITISH AND IRISH UNIVERSITIES

lining of hood

cowl

liripipe
cape

66. Full shaped hood with square corners.

lining of hood

border of silk (i.e. inside)

liripipe
cape

67. Full shaped hood with rounded corners.

68. Full shaped hood with cape and cowl edged.

69. Burgon shaped hood.

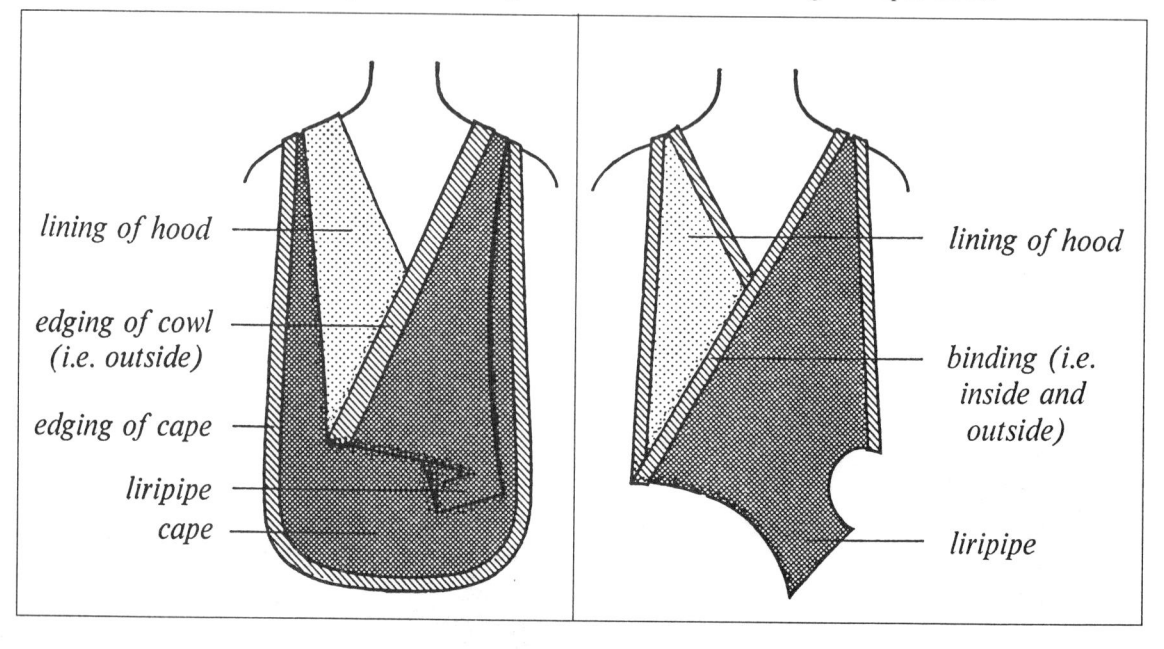

lining of hood

edging of cowl (i.e. outside)

edging of cape

liripipe
cape

lining of hood

binding (i.e. inside and outside)

liripipe

ILLUSTRATIONS

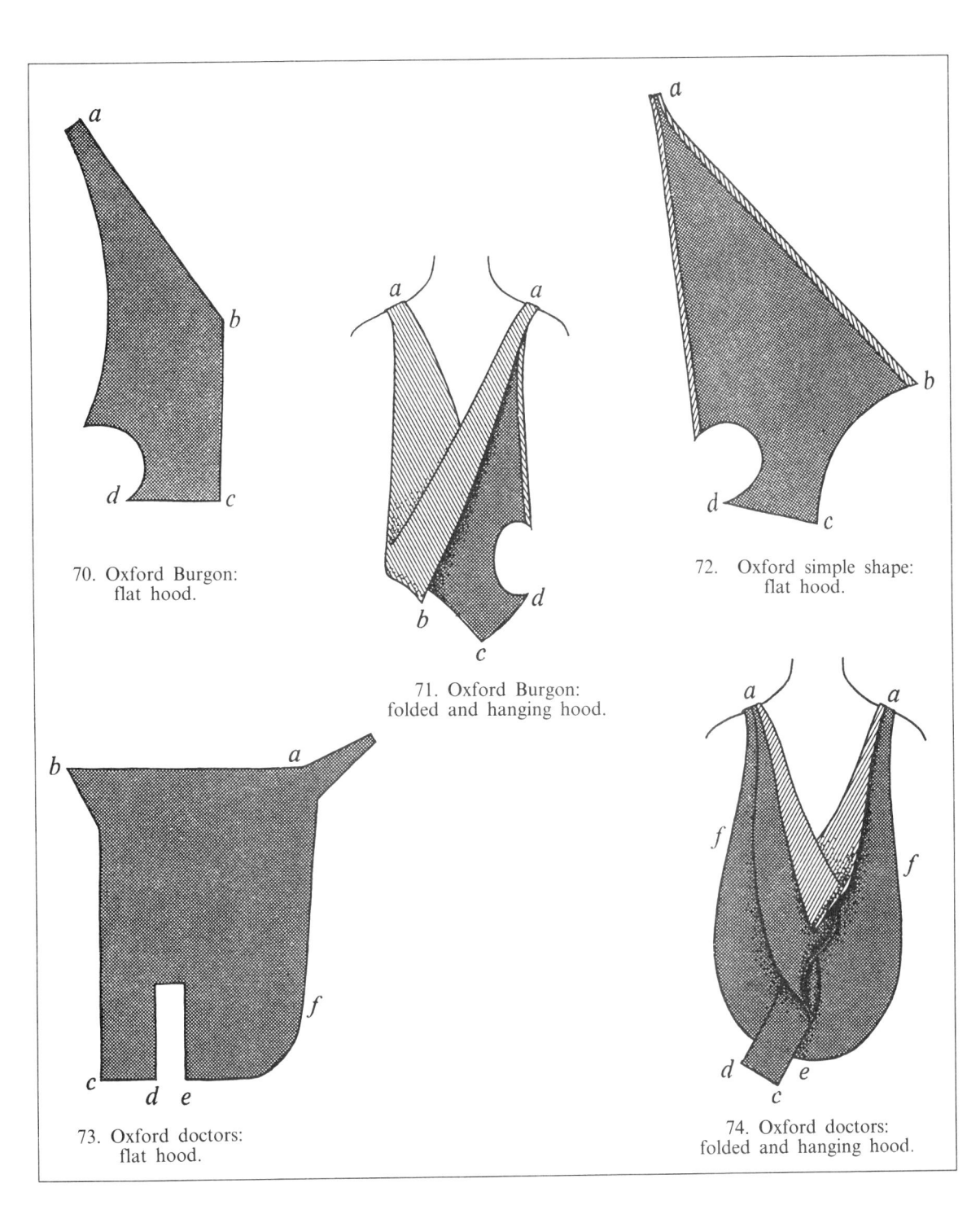

70. Oxford Burgon: flat hood.

71. Oxford Burgon: folded and hanging hood.

72. Oxford simple shape: flat hood.

73. Oxford doctors: flat hood.

74. Oxford doctors: folded and hanging hood.

75. Cambridge: folded and hanging hood (*far left*).

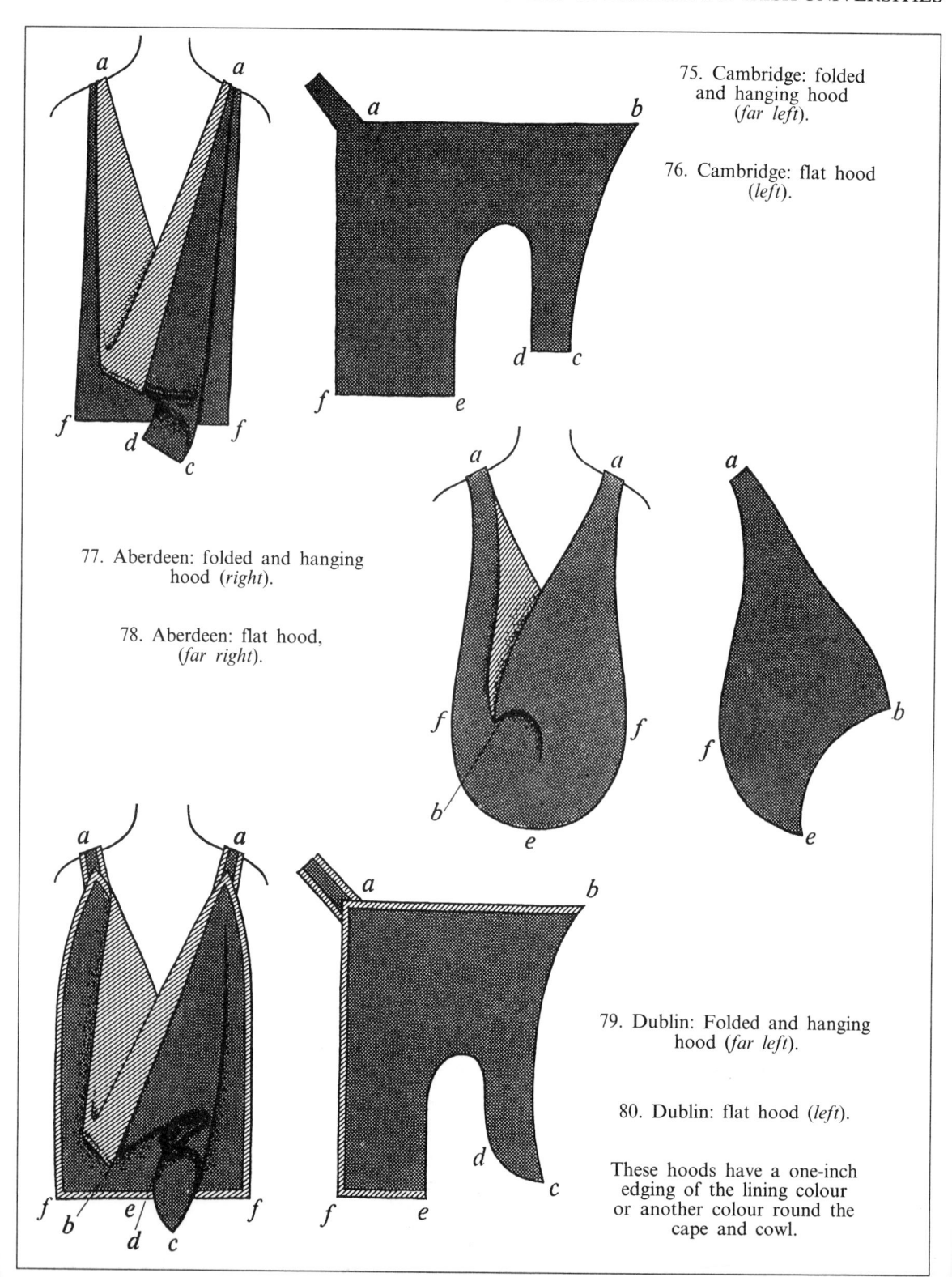

76. Cambridge: flat hood (*left*).

77. Aberdeen: folded and hanging hood (*right*).

78. Aberdeen: flat hood, (*far right*).

79. Dublin: Folded and hanging hood (*far left*).

80. Dublin: flat hood (*left*).

These hoods have a one-inch edging of the lining colour or another colour round the cape and cowl.

ILLUSTRATIONS

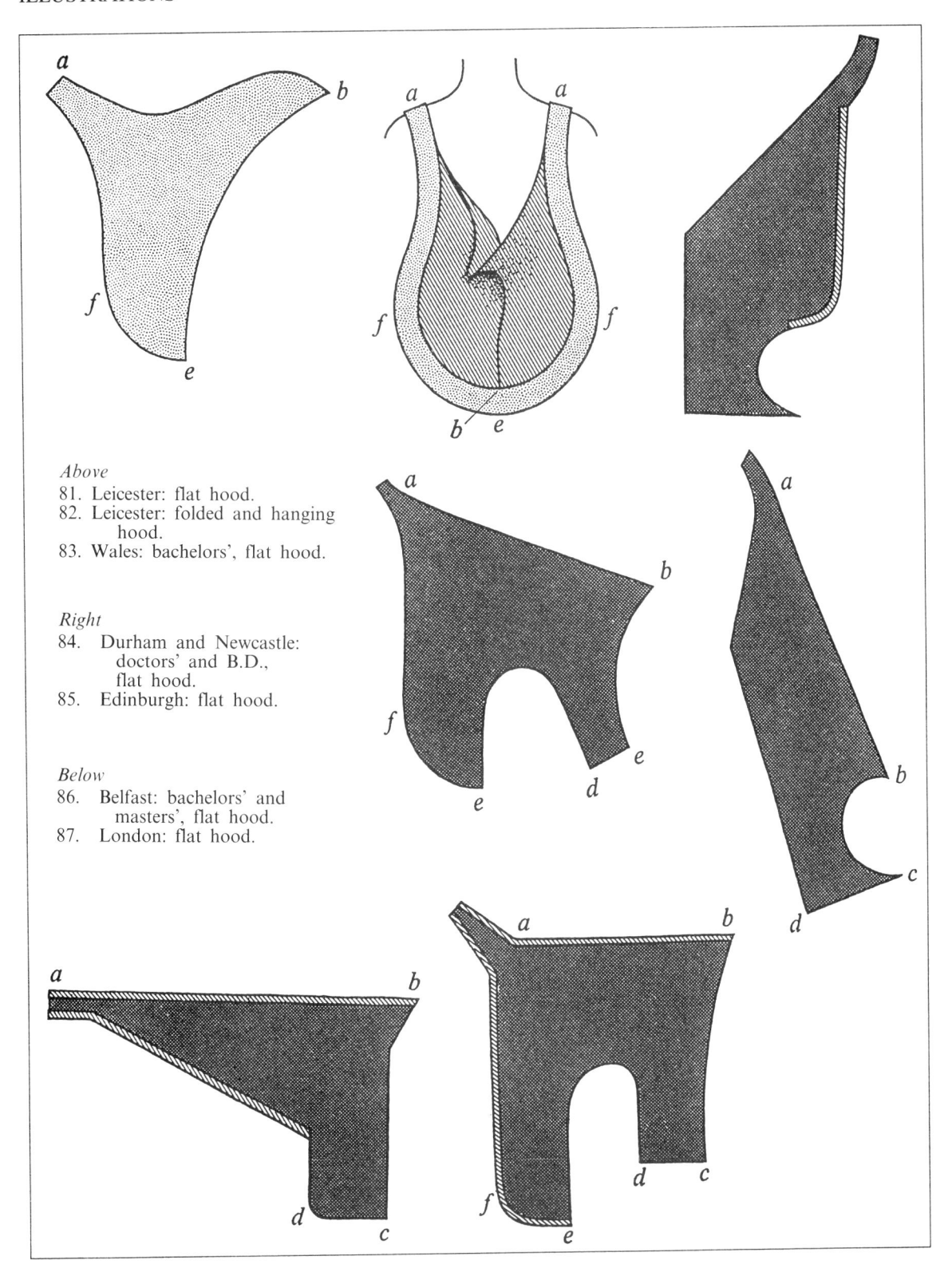

Above
81. Leicester: flat hood.
82. Leicester: folded and hanging hood.
83. Wales: bachelors', flat hood.

Right
84. Durham and Newcastle: doctors' and B.D., flat hood.
85. Edinburgh: flat hood.

Below
86. Belfast: bachelors' and masters', flat hood.
87. London: flat hood.

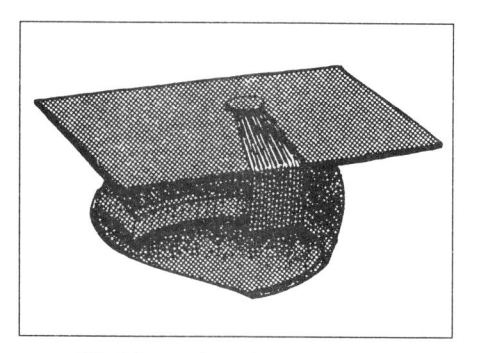

88. Mortar-board or trencher.

89. Doctors' Tudor bonnet.

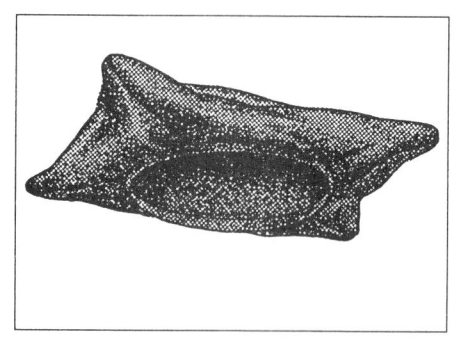

90. John Knox cap.

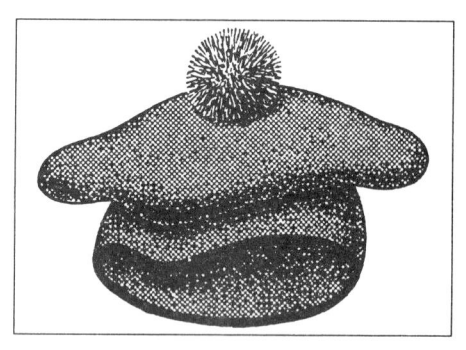

91. Bishop Andrewes cap.

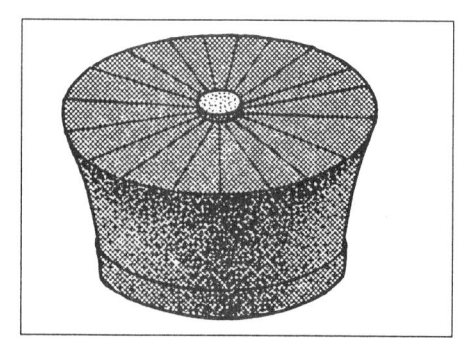

92. Pileus cap.

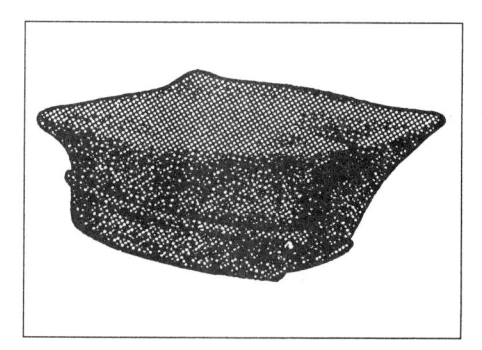

93. Oxford ladies' soft cap.

Specifications

University of Cambridge
(early 13th century)

Cambridge University has the most comprehensive system of academical dress of any university in the world, and for this reason only it will be described first.

Each degree—bachelor, master or doctor—in each faculty, in addition to having its own hood, also has its own gown (with the exception of M.Sci.) which enables one to identify the wearers' degree when hoods are not being worn.

There are 20 different undergraduate gowns among the 30 colleges, which means that almost all of the colleges have their own distinctive gown. Two of the newer colleges (Churchill and Robinson) have opted for the same basic gown as worn by Peterhouse and Queens'. The post-graduate colleges (Clare Hall, St Edmund's, Darwin, Hughes Hall and Wolfson) all use the same gown, and the women's colleges (Newnham and New Hall) together with the former women's colleges (Girton and Homerton) share a common gown. All bachelors' degrees other than B.A. and B.Ed. are postgraduate awards and for them the hood is made of silk in the faculty colour, half lined with white fur. For the B.A. and B.Ed.— the first degrees—the hood is of black stuff, half lined with fur. The B.Ed. also has a half lining of dark blue silk. The B.D. is exceptional being of black silk lined with black silk. The same hood, in slightly differing shapes, is also used by their B.D.s at Oxford, Trinity College Dublin and Durham Universities.

Masters' hoods (except M.A.—black lined with white)—are of black cloth or silk lined with the faculty colour. Some confusion has arisen with the introduction of M.Ed., using light blue. The B.Ed. uses a dark blue lining, but this shade has already been given to the M.Phil. The obvious solution would be to exchange the M.Ed. and M.Phil. colours, thus giving dark blue to the faculty of Education and light blue, i.e. Cambridge blue, to philosophy.

Until the recent advent of the newer degrees—i.e. business administration, engineering, education, philosophy and studies, only two basic colours had been used in hoods, namely various shades of red or cherry, and white or grey. The light and mid cherry silks used by laws and medicine are often difficult to separate when seen together and even harder to pinpoint when seen singly. Likewise the greyish silks used by divinity and science tend to be confused especially when faded by age.

Another unfortunate feature of the system is the treatment of Ph.D.s. They are denied the use of a scarlet doctors' robe and unfortunately allowed to attach scarlet cloth facings to their undress gowns by means of paper clips! To add insult to injury they are then given only a masters' hood to wear (black, no fur, lined with a colour). The M.Litt. and Ph.D. hoods are identical in colour (black lined with scarlet) and only a careful observer will notice the difference in materials. A suitable doctoral hood for Ph.D.s would be scarlet cloth lined with dark blue or lined with light blue, after the exchange suggested above.

Undergraduates

The basic undergraduate gown is essentially a miniature version of the B.A. gown. It reaches down to the mid thigh and has an open pointed sleeve with the forearm seam left open (fig. 18). This basic gown is modified by most colleges in a way specific to that college.

Christ's College: As for the basic gown with the facings box pleated horizontally from lapel to waist. There is also a pleated strip round the armhole (fig. 12).

Churchill College: As for the basic gown unmodified (fig. 18).

Clare College: As for the basic gown with three black velvet chevrons across the forearm seam (fig. 13).

Clare Hall: As for the basic gown with the sleeves gathered above the elbow and held by a blue cord and button (fig. 19).

Corpus Christi College: As for the basic gown but with facings of black velvet (fig. 14).

Darwin College: As for Clare Hall (fig. 19).

Downing College: As for the basic gown with the sleeves gathered into six broad pleats above the elbow and held by three cords and buttons (fig. 15).

Emmanuel College: As for the basic gown with facings box pleated from breast to waist (fig. 16).

Fitzwilliam College: As for the basic gown with the addition of two stripes of black velvet along the slit from shoulder to elbow (fig. 17).

Girton College: As for the basic gown with the forearm seam closed except for the last 4" (fig. 20).

Gonville & Caius College: A dark blue gown with black velvet facings and yoke and with a black velvet stripe down each side of the open forearm seam (fig. 21).

Homerton College: As for Girton (fig. 20).

Hughes Hall: As for Clare Hall (fig. 19).

Jesus College: As for the basic gown with the forearm seam gathered into six pleats and with a black velvet stripe over the forearm seam (fig. 22).

King's College: As for the basic gown but made of costume cloth (fig. 18).

Lucy Cavendish College: As for Clare Hall (fig. 19).

SPECIFICATIONS: CAMBRIDGE

Magdalene College: As for the basic gown with the sleeves gathered above the elbow and held by a cord and button. The forearm seam is left open above the gathers (fig. 23).

New Hall: As for Girton (fig. 20).

Newnham College: As for Girton (fig. 20).

Pembroke College: As for Magdalene, buit without the slit above the gathers (fig. 24).

Peterhouse: As for the basic gown (fig. 18).

Queens' College: As for the basic gown (fig. 18).

Robinson College: As for the basic gown (fig. 18).

St Catharine's College: As for the basic gown but with the facings machined in vertical rows (fig. 25).

St Edmund's College: As for Clare Hall (fig. 19).

St John's College: As for the basic gown with four black velvet bars across the forearm seam (fig. 26).

Selwyn College: As for the basic gown with dark blue rayon facings (fig. 27).

Sidney Sussex College: As for the basic gown with the addition of two rows of tiny chevrons from the shoulder to 4" above the elbow (fig. 28).

Trinity College: A dark blue gown with black cloth facings and with a black edging 2" wide inside the sleeve (fig. 29).

Trinity Hall: As for the basic gown with the forearm seam left open and the two edges held by a cord and two buttons (fig. 30).

Wolfson College: As for Clare Hall (fig. 19).

Undergraduates: Wear, when required to do so, a black cloth square topped cap (mortar board) with a black tassel.

Bachelors

Gowns
B.A.: A black stuff gown with open pointed sleeves. The forearm seam is left open, except at the bottom, and is ofen used as an armhole. There are strings attached to the facings inside (fig. 1).

M.B.: A black silk or stuff gown of the open sleeve pattern, the front of the sleeve being turned back to form a triangle, and held by a cord about 5" long with

a button at the top (fig. 31).
Vet.M.B.: As for the M.B. gown with an extra button at the bottom of the cord (fig. 32).
B.Chir.: As for the M.B. gown but with three cords ½" apart, with a button at the top of each one (fig. 34).
LL.B.: As for the M.B. gown but with two parallel cords with buttons (fig. 33). (Note: this degree is no longer awarded.)
B.Chir.: As for the M.B. gown but with three parallel twisted cords each with a button at the top (fig. 34).
B.Ed.: As for the M.B. gown but with four parallel cords each with a button at the top (fig. 35).
Mus.B.: As for the M.B. gown but with the addition of an extra button on each side of the triangle (fig. 36).
B.D.: As for the M.A. gown with a cord and button on the yoke.

Research Students (who are not Cambridge graduates and do not have senior status): As for the B.A. gown without the strings.
Bachelors: A black cloth mortar board.

Hoods

All hoods used by the University of Cambridge are of the same full shape, and consist of a square-cornered cape, a cowl with liripipe and a plain, i.e. unedged, neckband.

Bachelors' hoods (except B.D.) are half lined with white fur and (except for B.Chir. and B.D.) bound round the cape with fur.

B.A.: Black stuff (i.e. not silk), half lined with white fur and the cape bound 1" inside and outside with fur.
M.B.: Mid-cherry silk partly lined with fur and with the cape edged with fur 1" each side.
Vet.M.B.: As for the M.B. hood but the cape bound with fur 2" on each side.
B.Chir.: As for the M.B. hood but the cape is not bound with fur.
LL.B.: Light cherry silk half lined with fur and with the cape edged 1" with fur.
Mus.B.: Dark cherry satin half lined with fur and the cape edged 1" with fur.
B.Ed.: Black stuff lined with Royal blue silk and half lined and bound with fur.

Masters

Gowns

Masters: A black stuff or silk gown with a glove sleeve, that is a closed, Tudor bag sleeve with a horizontal slit at elbow level to free the arm. The bottom of the sleeve is cut on the inner side to form the 'boot', which has a single point (fig. 48). There are strings behind the facings.
All Masters (other than M.A.s): The sleeve is decorated with cords or buttons and cords above the armhole.
M.A.: Wear the gown described above (fig. 48).
M.Phil.: As for the M.A. gown but with two buttons placed vertically above the armhole, 2½" apart and joined by a double twisted cord (fig. 65a).
M.Litt.: As for the M.A. gown but with three buttons placed vertically above the

SPECIFICATIONS: CAMBRIDGE

armhole, and joined by a double twisted cord (fig. 65b).

M.Sc.: As for the M.A. gown with three buttons placed horizontally above the armhole, 2½" apart and joined by a double twisted cord (fig. 65c).

M.Sci.: As for the M.Eng. gown (fig. 65b).

M.B.A.: As for the M.A. gown with four buttons in the form of a square and joined by a double twisted cord (fig. 65d).

M.Ed.: As for the M.B.A. gown but with a fifth button in the centre and the buttons joined crosswise by a double twisted cord (fig. 65e).

M.Mus.: As for the M.A. gown with three buttons forming a triangle, each 5" apart and joined by double twisted cords (fig. 65f).

M.St.: As for the M.A. gown but with five buttons joined by cords forming a cross on the upper edge of each arm slit (fig. 65g).

M.Eng.: As for the M.A. gown with a circle, 5" in diameter of double twisted cord, with a button in the centre (fig. 65h).

LL.M.: As for the M.A. gown with two rows of single black silk cord, 5" long and ½" apart, sewn horizontally above the armhole (fig. 65i).

M.Chir.: As for the LL.M. gown but with three rows of single black silk cord above the armhole (fig. 65j).

Research Students (who are not Cambridge graduates, but who hold senior status): the M.A. gown without the strings.

Masters: A black cloth mortar board.

Doctors

Undress Gowns

These (except for LL.D.) are distinguished by having Cambridge doctors' lace, in various patterns.

Sc.D.: As for the M.A. gown with a row of doctors' lace sewn horizontally above the armhole (fig. 48).

Litt.D.: As for the M.A. gown with a row of doctor's lace sewn vertically above the armhole.

Ph.D.: As for the M.A. gown with 4" of doctors' lace sewn horizontally 3" above the armhole (frontispiece, g).

D.D.: A black silk gown with bell-shaped sleeves which are folded under and rouched round the elbow. There is a black cord and button on the yoke, and a black silk scarf is worn with this gown. More often the M.A. gown with cord and button on the yoke and a black silk scarf is worn.

LL.D.: This gown is of a different pattern to all the above, being of the form used by Queen's Council (with or without the slit at the back). It is of black silk with square-ended sleeves and with an inverted-T armhole. The sleeves are not gathered but have 1" wings round the head. The facings are carried round to join a flap-collar.

M.D.: As for the LL.D. gown decorated with doctors' lace round the armhole and carried up to the shoulder. There is a row of lace across the sleeve bottom and a row down the facings and carried round the flap-collar (frontispiece h).

Mus.D.: As for the M.D. gown but with an additional row of lace across the bottom of the flap collar.

Doctors: In undress wear a black mortar board.

Full Dress Robes

These (except for Ph.D. and Mus.D.) are of scarlet cloth with long open sleeves, the ends of which are rounded off. The front of the sleeve above the elbow is turned back revealing the lining of the sleeve, the turned back piece being held by a cord and button (fig. 60). The sleeves are lined and the robe is faced with the faculty silk as follows:

D.D.: Dove coloured silk (turquoise blue shot with rose pink). The sleeve buttons (22-line flat silk) and the cord (one-eighth black twisted) are black. There is a similar cord and button on the yoke. The strings are black silk, and a black silk cassock is worn under this robe.

LL.D.: Light cherry silk. Scarlet cords and buttons.

M.D.: Mid-cherry silk. Scarlet cords and buttons.

Sc.D.: Pink shot light blue silk. Scarlet cords and buttons.

Litt.D.: Scarlet silk, cords and buttons.

Mus.D.: A robe of cream damask. The sleeves are shorter than for other doctorates, and are turned back all round the edge for 3" to 4" showing the lining which is of dark cherry satin. The buttons, cords and strings are of the same colour.

Ph.D.: A black silk robe of the M.A. shape, with facings of scarlet cloth 4" wide. There is no doctors' lace over the armhole.

Hoods

These (except Ph.D. and Mus.D.) are of scarlet cloth, of the usual Cambridge shape. They are fully lined with the same silk as the full dress robe.

Ph.D.: Black silk lined with scarlet cloth.

Mus.D.: Cream damask lined with dark cherry satin.

Academical caps

Undergraduates, Bachelors, Masters: In undress wear a black cloth mortar board.

Doctors of Divinity: In full dress wear a soft square cap with a black tuft in place of the more usual tassel. This is the Bishop Andrewes cap (fig. 91).

Other Doctors: In full dress wear a round black velvet bonnet with a gold cord and tassels (fig. 89).

University of Oxford
(12th century)

The academical dress of Oxford, like that of Cambridge, forms the basic pattern from which all other universities have evolved their individual systems. The present Oxford system is, however, far less logical than that of Cambridge both in hood colours and gown shapes. Thus the colours of doctors' robes and hoods bear no relation whatsoever to those used by bachelors or masters in the same faculties. There is considerable ambiguity as for example when a B.M., B.Ch., B.C.L. and M.Jur. wear the same hood (light blue half lined with fur) and the corresponding doctors (D.M. and D.C.L.) both wear scarlet lined blood crimson—the same shade as the M.A. hood lining.

With the introduction of several new degrees, a more rational and systematic approach has been possible. Specific faculty colours have been introduced for Education and Theology but the M.Jur. has been added to the now long list of degrees using the B.M. hood. It is also the first time in the history of the University (except for the proctors and now the M.Eng.) that a master has had a hood with fur!

The M.Eng. is a first degree, engineering being a four-year course, and for the purpose of academical dress is treated as a B.A. degree. When the degree is first taken, the B.A. dress is worn. If he or she so wishes, after 21 terms from matriculation, the recipient may become a member of convocation, when the M.A. gown and hood are worn.

The same gimp-trimmed gown is used by all graduates—bachelor, master and doctor other than B.A., B.F.A., B.Theol., M.A., B.D. and D.D., the only difference being, for doctors, a small and practically invisible panel of gimp under the arm.

Undergraduates

Commoners Gowns
A sleeveless waist-length gown with a flap collar. There are facings of the usual type, formed by the front edges of the gown being turned back about 2". Attached to the top of each armhole is a ribbon about 18" long with a squared pattern on the outside, and surrounding each armhole is a small wing about ½" wide (fig. 7).

Scholars' Gowns
A gown of knee length which is gathered at the yoke in the usual way. The sleeves are open, bell-shaped and of elbow length only (fig. 8).

Advanced Students' Gowns
The gown is exactly like the commoners' gown except that it is made on a much

larger scale. It reaches below the knee, is sleeveless with a flap collar, with streamers about 2 ft. long and 5" wide. There are small 1" wings surrounding the armholes.

Bachelors

Gowns

B.A., B.F.A., B.Ed., B.Theol.: A Russell cord or polyester, full sleeved gown. The sleeves are open and pointed reaching to the hem of the gown. The sleeve has no slit or other decoration. Most robemakers attach a loop of tape at the wrist through which the hand can be slipped to control the sleeve (fig. 38).

B.M., B.Ch., B.C.L., B.Mus. (B.Sc., B.Litt.): This gown has a flap collar and closed square-ended sleeves, the armholes of which are of the inverted-T type. It is trimmed with black silk gimp round the collar, round and above each armhole to the shoulder, on the bottom front face of each sleeve, and near the foot of the gown on each side and at the back. This gown is sometimes called the lay or gimp gown (frontispiece, i).

B.D.: As for the M.A. gown with the addition of a black silk scarf which is held in position by a cord and button on the yoke.

Hoods

There are two possible shapes of hood—the Oxford plain shape which has a single row of fur and the Dean Burgon shape which is edged and half lined with fur. The former is hardly ever seen nowadays.

B.A.: Black corded silk half lined and edged with white fur.
(B.Sc., B.Litt.): Light blue ribbed silk with fur. (No longer awarded).
B.C.L., B.M., B.Ch.: Mid-blue corded silk with fur.
B.Mus.: Lilac ribbed silk with fur.
B.D.: Black corded silk lined with fine black ribbed silk.
B.Phil.: Dark blue silk lined with white silk.
B.F.A.: Black silk with a narrow band of gold silk inside the cowl.
B.Ed.: Black silk with a narrow band of green silk inside the cowl.
B.Theol.: Black silk with a narrow band of magenta inside the cowl.

Masters

Gowns

M.A.: A gown with closed or glove sleeves with an oval opening at the elbow to free the arm. The foot of the sleeve has a crescent-shaped cut on the inner border, so forming two points (fig. 49).

M.Ch., M.Sc., M.Litt., M.Phil., M.St., M.Theol., M.Ed., M.Jur.: The lay, or gimp gown, as for B.C.L.

Hoods

These are of the Burgon shape (fig. 70 and 71).

M.A.: A black corded silk hood lined and edged with blood crimson shot silk.
M.Ch.: A black corded silk hood lined and edged with royal blue silk.

SPECIFICATIONS: OXFORD

M.Sc., M.Litt.: A light blue silk hood lined and edged with grey silk.
M.Phil.: As for the B.Phil. hood.
M.St.: A deep green silk hood lined and edged with white silk.
M.Theol.: A black corded silk hood lined and edged with magenta silk.
M.Ed.: A black corded silk hood lined and edged with mid green silk.
M.Eng.: As for the B.A. hood. If a member of convocation, the M.A. hood.

Doctors

Undress Gowns
D.D.: As for the M.A. gown with a black silk scarf held at the yoke by a button and cord.
Other Doctors: The gimp gown, as for the B.C.L. but with the addition of an extra gimp panel under the arm at elbow level.

Full Dress Robes
D.C.L., D.M.: A scarlet cloth robe with bell shaped sleeves (the Oxford shape, fig. 62). The sleeves and facings of the robe are of blood crimson silk.
D.Sc., D.Litt.: A scarlet cloth robe of the Oxford shape with sleeves and facings of grey silk.
D.D.: A scarlet cloth robe of the Oxford shape with sleeves and facings of black velvet.
D.Phil.: A scarlet cloth robe of the Oxford shape with sleeves and facings of blue silk.
D.Mus.: A robe of cream silk brocade with apple blossom design, and with sleeves and facings of cherry crimson silk.

Hoods
These are of a special full shape hood with a well rounded cape, made of scarlet cloth (except Music) and lined with the same silk as the full dress robe. In the case of music, the hood is of cream brocade and lined with cherry crimson silk (figs. 73 and 74).

Convocation Habits
These are sleeveless scarlet cloth robes, with a gathered yoke. They are lined to a depth of about 6" with silk of the same shade as the hood. They fasten with two buttons below the chin. The convocation habit is worn over the black undress gown, the sleeves of which are pulled through the armholes of the habit (frontispiece, f).

Academical Caps
Undergraduates, Bachelors, Masters, Doctors: In undress wear a black cloth mortar board.
D.Mus., D.C.L., D.M.: In full dress, wear a round velvet Tudor bonnet with a black silk ribbon in place of the more usual gold cord and tassels.
D.Sc., D.Litt., D.Phil.: In full dress wear black velvet mortar board. With convocation habit a mortar board is worn. Women may opt for the soft Oxford cap (fig. 93).

University of Aberdeen
(1495)

The undergraduates of Aberdeen, like those of the other ancient Scottish universities, wear a scarlet undergraduate gown. Only one black gown is used for graduates, whether bachelors, masters or doctors. This is a special Cambridge M.A. shape with a cord and button on the yoke. Hoods are of a shape peculiar to Aberdeen, having only a very small cowl, and showing very little of the lining.

With the full dress robe, no hoods are worn. This follows the Oxford tradition. The robes are, however, of the Cambridge shape.

Undergraduates

Undergraduates wear a short scarlet cloth gown called a toga. This has a red velveteen flap collar and epaulettes. The sleeves are of elbow length, straight round the bottom like the Oxford scholars' gown, but not much wider than a coat sleeve.

Bachelors

Gowns
A black stuff gown of the special Cambridge M.A. shape (fig. 50) with a cord and button on the yoke.

Hoods
These are of a special shape—a rounded cape with almost no cowl (figs. 77 and 78). They are of black silk and either lined or bound with the faculty colour, ½" inside and outside the small cowl.

Faculty Colours
B.Sc.: Lined with green silk.
B.Sc.Agric.: Bound with green silk.
B.Sc.Biomed.Sc.: Lined with green silk and bound with waived white silk.
B.Sc.Eng.: Bound with green silk and bordered with white cloth ½" within the green silk.
B.Sc.For.: Edged with waived green silk.
B.Sc.Health Sc.: Bound with crimson silk and bordered inside the crimson with white cloth ½" wide.
B.Sc.Med.Sc.: Lined with crimson silk, and bound with waived white silk.

SPECIFICATIONS: ABERDEEN

B.Sc.Mar.Res.Man.: Bound with pale blue silk.
B.Eng.: Lined with pale yellow silk.
B.Technol.Agr.Bus.Man.: Lined with russet brown silk.
B.Technol.Aquacult.: Lined with russet brown silk bordered inside with white cloth ½" wide.
B.D.: Lined with purple silk and bordered inside with white silk 1" wide.
B.Th.: Lined with purple silk and bound with waived white silk ½" wide.
LL.B.: Lined with pale blue silk.
M.B., Ch.B.: Lined with crimson silk.

Masters

Gowns

As for the bachelors' gown.

Hoods

A white (except for the M.A.) silk hood of the bachelors' shape, lined or bound with the faculty colour.

Faculty Colours

Ch.M.: Lined with crimson silk.
M.A.: A black silk hood, lined with white silk.
M.B.A.: Lined with lilac silk.
M.B.A.C.C.: Lined with lilac silk bordered inside with white cloth ½" wide.
M.Ed.: Lined with orange silk.
M.L.E.: Lined with pale blue silk, bordered inside with white cloth ½" wide.
M.Litt.: Lined with violet silk.
M.Med.Sc.: Lined with crimson silk, and bordered inside with white cloth ½" wide.
M.Phil.: Lined with black silk and bordered inside with white cloth ½" wide.
M.Sc.: Lined with green silk.
M.Th.: Lined with purple silk.
LL.M.: Lined with pale blue silk.

Doctors

Undress Gowns

As for the bachelors' gown.

Full Dress Robes

A scarlet cloth robe of the Cambridge doctors' shape. The facings and sleeve linings are of the faculty colour. The facings are continued round as an added flap collar. With this robe no hoods are worn.

Hoods

A scarlet cloth hood of the bachelors' shape, lined with the faculty colour.

Faculty Colours

D.D.: Purple silk.
D.Litt.: White silk.
D.Mus.: Light brown silk.
D.Sc.: Green silk.
LL.D.: Pale blue silk.
M.D.: Crimson silk.
Ph.D.: Black ribbed silk, the ribs running horizontally.

Academical Caps

Undergraduates, Bachelors, Masters, Doctors: In undress wear a black cloth mortar board.
Doctors: In full dress wear a black velvet 'John Knox' cap (fig. 90).

University of Abertay, Dundee
(1994)

Diplomas and Certificates

Gowns
As for the bachelors' gown with cord and button on the yoke.

Hoods
A blue hood of the Aberdeen shaped and fully lined in red.

Post-graduate Diplomas

Gowns
As for the masters' gown with cord and button on the yoke.

Hoods
A blue hood of the Aberdeen shape and fully lined with the cape bound 1" in red.

Diplomas in Higher Education

Gowns
As for the post-graduates gown.

Hoods
A blue hood of the Aberdeen shape and fully lined in gold.

Bachelors

Gowns
The basic bachelors' gown with cord and button on the yoke.

Hoods
All bachelors' hoods are of the full shape in blue, lined with the faculty colour.

Faculty Colours
B.Eng.: Sky blue.
B.Sc.Eng.: Silver satin.
B.A.(Management): Yellow.

B.Sc. (Management): Yellow.
B.Sc.(Science): Green.
B.A.: Pink.

Masters

Gowns
As for the basic masters' gown with cord and button on the yoke.

Hoods
All masters' hoods are full shaped, blue lined and bound 1" round the cape as follows:
M.Sc.(Eng): Silver satin.
M.Sc.(Management): Yellow.
M.Sc.: Green.
M.B.A.: White.

Masters of Philosophy

Gowns
As for the masters' gown with facings 2½" wide in gold.

Hoods
A full shaped green hood, fully lined and bound with gold.

Doctors

Full Dress Robes
Ph.D.: A maroon robe of the St Andrews style with facings and cuffs of gold 2½" wide and with a collar of gold.
Higher Doctors: As for the Ph.D. but of blue panama in place of maroon.

Hoods
Ph.D.: A full shaped maroon hood, fully lined in gold and with a gold neckband.
Higher Doctors: A blue hood fully lined and bound with 1" gold on the cape, and with a gold neckband.

Academical Caps
All Graduates: Wear a black cloth mortar board.
Ph.D.: In full dress wear a black Tudor bonnet with gold cord and tassel.
Higher Doctors: In full dress wear a blue Tudor bonnet with a gold cord and tassel.

Anglia Polytechnic University
(1993)

HNC/HND College Awards

Gowns
A blue gown of the masters' shape.

Hoods
A blue hood of the simple shape, lined gold and the cowl bound with narrow blue binding.

Bachelors

Gowns
As for the basic bachelors' gown (fig. 3).

Hoods
A blue hood of the full shape, part lined with gold and bound with a narrow blue silk binding.

Masters

Gowns
A blue gown of the basic masters' shape (fig. 4).

Hoods
A blue hood of the full shape, fully lined with gold and bound with a wide binding of blue silk.

Doctors of Philosophy

Full Dress Robes
A blue robe of the London doctors' shape with facings and sleeve linings of gold.

Hoods
A blue hood of the full shape, fully lined with gold and piped with gold.

Higher Doctors and Honorary Doctors

Full Dress Robes
As for the Ph.D. robe but with the addition of a blue cord and button on the sleeve.

Hoods
As for the Ph.D. robe but bound with wider gold.

Academical Caps
All Graduates: Wear a blue mortar board.
Ph.D.: In full dress wear a blue cloth bonnet with gold tassels.
Higher Doctors: Wear a blue velvet bonnet with gold tassels.

University of Aston
(1966)

Aston University has adopted gowns and robes similar to those used by Continental universities.

Undergraduates

No academical dress is worn.

Bachelors

Gowns
A black stuff gown, with sleeves of the same shape as a coat, but slightly wider. They are not gathered at the top. The body of the gown itself is gathered into an extra wide straight yoke. The narrow facings of the gown are carried up round the neck as a collar, but are sewn down.

Hoods
B.Sc., B.Eng.: A black stuff hood of a special simple shape, bordered inside for 3" with the university lining. There are four crests on each border.

Masters

Gowns
As for the bachelors' gown.

Hoods
M.Eng.: As for the bachelors' hood.
M.Sc.: A black hood of the same shape as for the bachelors but fully lined with the university silk.
M.Phil: A blue stuff hood of the same shape as for the bachelors but fully lined with the university silk.

Doctors

Undress Gowns
As for the bachelors' gown.

Full Dress Robes
Ph.D.: A claret coloured cloth robe of the same shape as for the bachelors.

DSc.: A university red robe of the same shape as for the bachelors, but with facings of the university silk, and with gold cuffs to the sleeves.

Hoods

Ph.D.: A university red hood of the same shape as for the bachelors, bordered for 3" with the university silk.

D.Sc.: A gold silk hood of the same shape as for the bachelors and fully lined with the university silk.

Academical Caps

Bachelors, Masters, Doctors: In undress wear a black mortar board.
Ph.D.: In full dress wear a black cloth bonnet with university red cord and tassels.
D.Sc.: In full dress wear a black velvet bonnet with gold cord and tassels.

The university silk lining is a blood crimson silk shot with the shield of the university crest in colour at 5" intervals.

SPECIFICATIONS: BATH

University of Bath
(1966)

The hoods of this university are of old gold grosgrain, to represent Bath stone.

Undergraduates
A black stuff gown of the Oxford scholars' shape but with the forearm seam left open for 6" and with a black button at the top of the slit.

Bachelors

Gowns

A black stuff gown of the basic bachelors' shape but with the forearm seam left open for 6" from the wrist and with a black button at the top of the slit.

Hoods

B.Sc., B.Pharm., B.Eng.: An old gold grosgrain hood of the Oxford simple shape, lined with light olive green taffeta.
B.A.: As for the B.Sc. hood but with a binding of yellow silk round the cowl.
B.Arch.: As for B.Sc. hood but with a binding of light crimson silk.
B.Ed.: As for the B.Sc. hood but with a binding of orange silk.
B.Mus.: As for B.Sc. but with a binding of cream damask.

Masters

Gowns

A black stuff gown is worn having glove sleeves and an inverted-T armhole. The 6" upright sleeve slit is surmounted by a black button, and the bottom of the bag sleeve is cut on the oblique (frontispiece, b).
M.Ch.: Wear the doctors' undress gown.

Hoods

M.Sc.: An old gold grosgrain hood of the same shape as for bachelors, lined with pale blue taffeta.
M.A.: As for the M.Sc. hood with the addition of a binding of yellow silk.
M.Arch.: As for the M.Sc. hood with the addition of a binding of medium crimson.
M.Ed.: As for the M.Sc. hood with the addition of a binding of orange silk.
M.Eng.: As for the M.Sc. hood with the addition of a binding of purple silk.
M.Phil.: As for the M.Sc. hood with the addition of a binding of red silk.
M.B.A.: As for the M.Sc. hood with the addition of a binding of dark blue silk.
Ch.M.: An old gold grosgrain hood of the Oxford simple shape, lined with medium crimson taffeta and bound with pale blue silk.

Doctors

Undress Gowns

All Doctors, Masters of Surgery: In undress wear the masters' gown with the addition of Cambridge doctors' lace round the armhole.

Full Dress Robes

Ph.D.: A lightweight medium crimson cloth robe of the Oxford doctors' shape with old gold grosgrain facings 5" wide and with sleeve cuffs 9" deep.

M.D.: As for the Ph.D. robe with the addition of 1" wide deep crimson edging on the facings and cuffs.

Ch.M.: As for the Ph.D. robe with 1" edging of pale blue silk to the facings and cuffs.

D.Sc.: A lightweight scarlet cloth robe of the Oxford doctors' shape, with old gold grosgrain facings and cuffs.

LL.D.: As for the D.Sc. robe with the addition of 1" wide white silk edging to the facings and cuffs.

D.Litt.: As for the D.Sc. robe with the addition of 1" wide yellow silk edging to the sleeves and cuffs.

D.Mus.: A lightweight cream damask robe of the Oxford doctors' shape with old gold grosgrain facings and cuffs.

Hoods

Ph.D.: An old gold grosgrain hood of the Oxford simple shape, lined with medium crimson taffeta.

M.D.: An old gold grosgrain hood lined with medium crimson taffeta and bound with deep crimson taffeta.

Ch.M.: An old gold grosgrain hood lined with medium crimson taffeta and bound with pale blue taffeta.

D.Sc.: An old gold grosgrain hood lined with scarlet taffeta.

LL.D.: An old gold grosgrain hood lined scarlet and bound with white silk.

D.Litt.: An old gold grosgrain hood lined scarlet and bound with yellow silk.

D.Mus: An old gold grosgrain hood lined with cream damask.

Academical Caps

Undergraduates, Bachelors, Masters, Doctors: In undress wear a black mortar board for men, and a plain black soft square for women.

Ph.D., M.D. or Ch.M.: In full dress, men wear a black cloth bonnet with silver cord and tassels.

D.Sc., LL.D., D.Litt. or D.Mus.: In full dress, men wear a black velvet bonnet with gold cord and tassels.

Women holding any *Doctorate* or *Ch.M.*: Wear a partially soft black velvet square.

# The Queen's University, Belfast
(1909)

The system of academical dress used at Belfast is a semi-logical one. The hoods of all graduates have the diagnostic feature of a binding, ½" wide inside and outside the cowl, of blue watered silk. Bachelors' hoods are of black silk (except B.Mus.) lined with the faculty colour (except B.A.), and masters' hoods are of red silk lined with the faculty colour (except M.A., M.Eng. and M.Arch.).

Doctors' full dress robes are also distinguished by having a blue watered silk binding down the facings.

Undergraduates

No academical dress is worn.

Bachelors

Gowns
An open sleeved gown of stuff or silk. The front seam is gathered at the elbow and held by a cord and button. The back of the sleeve is rounded off (fig. 39).

Hoods
A black silk hood (except B.Mus.), of a special simple shape (fig. 85), bound ½" inside and outside the cowl with blue watered silk, and lined with the faculty colour (except the B.A.):

Faculty Colours
B.A.: White fur.
B.Sc.: Light green.
LL.B.: Pink.
B.Sc. (Econ., Acc., Inf., Inf.Mgt.): Light rose pink.
B.S.Sc.: Dark rose pink.
M.B., B.Ch., B.A.O.: Scarlet silk.
B.D.S.: Dove grey.
B.Med.Sc.: Purple.
B.Sc.Eng.: Dark green.
B.Eng.: Eau-de-Nil pale green.
B.Agr.: Light primrose.
B.Sc.(Food Science): Dark primrose.
B.D.: White silk.
B.Ed.: Mauve.
B.Mus.: Blue silk lined with white silk.

Masters

Gowns

A black silk gown of the Oxford M.A. shape (fig. 49).

Hoods

These are of the same shape as for bachelors, made of red silk (except M.A., M.Eng., M.Arch.). They too are bound with blue watered silk round the cowl and lined with the faculty colour:

Faculty Colours

M.Sc.: Light green.
LL.M.: Pink.
M.Sc.(Econ), M.Acc., M.Sc.(Mgt.), M.Sc. (Corp.Fin & Cont., Inf.Mgt.): Light rose.
M.S.Sc.(Social Work), M.S.W.: Dark rose.
M.Ch.: Scarlet.
M.Med.Sc.: Purple.
M.D.Sc.: Dove grey.
M.Sc.Eng.: Dark green.
M.Agr.: Light primrose.
M.Sc.(Food Sc.): Dark primrose.
M.Th.: White.
M.A.Ed.: Blue.
M.Ed.: Mauve.
M.A.: Black silk lined with blue silk.
M.Eng.: Black lined Eau-de-Nil bordered inside with red silk.
M.Arch.: White silk lined with dark green.

Doctors

Undress gowns

As for the masters' gown.

Full Dress Robes

A scarlet cloth robe of the Oxford doctors' shape. The sleeves and facings are of the faculty colour, and there is a binding down the facings 1" wide of blue watered silk:

Faculty Colours

D.Lit.: White silk sleeves and facings.
D.Mus.: Blue silk.
D.Sc.: Light green silk.
LL.D.: Pink silk.
D.Sc.(Econ.): Light rose pink silk.
D.S.Sc.: Dark rose pink silk.
M.D.: Scarlet silk.
D.Med.Sc.: Purple silk.

D.Sc.(Eng.): Dark green silk.
D.Sc.(Agric. & Food Sc.): Dark primrose silk.
D.D.: Black silk facings only.
D.Sc.(Ed.): Mauve silk.
Ph.D.: Violet silk.

Hoods
A scarlet cloth hood of the full Dublin shape (figs. 79 and 80), bound with blue watered silk and lined with the same silk as the facings of the full dress robe.

Academical Caps
Bachelors, Masters, Doctors: In undress wear a black cloth mortar board.
Doctors: In full dress wear a black velvet bonnet.

University of Birmingham
(1900)

Birmingham University has a completely logical system of academical dress, which uses distinctive bird's eye watered silks for its faculty colours. Due to the proliferation of new degrees over the years, the system now includes over sixty different hoods.

Undergraduates

A black stuff gown of the Oxford scholars' shape with the forearm seam left open.

Bachelors

Gowns

A black stuff gown of the Cambridge B.A. shape but without the strings (fig. 37).

Hoods

A black stuff or silk hood of the full shape with rounded corners to the cape, i.e. of the London hood shape (fig. 87) edged a ¼" outside and bordered 4" inside the cowl with the faculty colour, of bird's eye watered silks. In some cases there is an additional binding of another colour. The first colour then becomes a border inside the cowl.

B.A.: Bordered and edged with electric blue.
B.Litt.: Bordered inside with electric blue and bound round the cowl with white.
B.Mus.: Bordered and edged with tangerine.
B.D.: Bordered and edged with cobalt blue.
B.Theol.: Bordered with electric blue and bound with cobalt blue.
B.Com.: Bordered and edged with terracotta.
B.Soc.Sc.: Bordered with terracotta and bound with grey.
B.Phil.(Ed.): Bordered primrose yellow and bound with white.
B.Ed.: Bordered and edged with primrose yellow.
B.Eng. & B.Com.: Bordered with purple and bound terracotta.
B.Eng.: Bordered and edged with purple.
B.Eng. & Com.: Bordered with purple and bound with cobalt blue.
LL.B.: Bordered and edged with bronze green.
M.B., Ch.: Bordered and edged with cardinal red.
B.Med.Sc.: Bordered with cardinal red and bound with dark grey.

SPECIFICATIONS: BIRMINGHAM

B.D.S.: Bordered and edged with dark red (Grenat).
B.Nurs.: Bordered and edged with rose red.
B.Physiotherapy: Bordered with rose red and bound with white.
B.Sc.: Bordered and edged with silver grey.
B.Hum.: Not decided.

Masters

Gowns

A black stuff or silk gown of the Cambridge M.A. shape but with an inverted-T armhole, and with strings.

Holders of the M.Eng. and M.Eng. & Man. wear the bachelors' gown.

Hoods

A black silk hood (except for M.Eng., M.Eng. & Man.), fully lined with the faculty colour. In some cases there is also a border or a binding of another colour.

M.A.: Lined electric blue watered silk.
M.Phil.(Arts): Lined electric blue and bound with white.
M.Litt.: Lined electric blue and bound with crimson.
M.Mus.: Lined with tangerine.
M.Com.: Lined with terracotta.
M.Soc.Sc.: Lined terracotta and bordered with grey.
M.B.A.: Lined terracotta and bordered with white.
M.I.S.: Lined terracotta and bordered with mid-blue.
M.Phil.(Com. & Soc.Sc.): Lined terracotta and bordered with crimson.
M.Ed.: Lined with primrose yellow.
M.Phil.(Ed.): Lined primrose yellow and bordered with white.
M.Sc.(Eng.): Lined with purple.
M.Phil.(Eng.): Llined purple and bordered with crimson.
M.Eng.: A black stuff or silk hood bordered with purple and bound with white.
M.Eng. & Man.: A black stuff or silk hood edged and bordered with white watered silk.
LL.M.: Black silk lined with bronze.
M.Jur.: Lined with bronze and bordered with grey.
M.Med.Sc.: Lined cardinal and bordered with dark grey.
M.C.D.H.: Lined dark red and bordered with white.
M.Dent.Sc.: Lined dark red and bordered dark grey.
M.Sc.: Lined silver grey.
M.Phil.(Sc.), M.App.Psy.: Lined silver grey and bordered crimson.
Clin.Psy.M.: Lined with grey and bordered with white.

Doctors

Undress Gowns

Ph.D.: As for the masters' gown.
Other Doctors: As for the masters' gown, but the special narrow facings have a row of braid (of the type in frontispiece, d) down their length.

Full Dress Robes
These are of the same shape as the Cambridge doctors' robe with facings and sleeve linings of the faculty colour. The Ph.D.s wear a robe of crimson cloth and other doctors wear a robe of scarlet cloth (fig. 60).

Hoods
These are of the same shape as for the bachelors' hood, lined with the faculty colour. The Ph.D. hood is of crimson cloth and other doctors of scarlet cloth.

Ph.D.: Lined with the faculty colour.
D.Litt.: Lined with electric blue.
D.Mus.: Lined with tangerine.
D.D.: Lined cobalt blue.
D.Soc.Sc.: Lined terracotta and bound with grey.
LL.D.: Lined with bronze green.
D.Eng.: Lined with purple.
M.D.: Lined with cardinal.
D.D.S.: Lined with dark red.
D.Sc.: Lined with silver grey.

Academical Caps

Undergraduates, Bachelors, Masters, Doctors: In undress wear a black cloth mortar board.

Doctors: In full dress wear a black velvet bonnet with gold cord and tassels, and lined with the faculty colour.

Women wear the soft Oxford cap.

Bolton Institute of Higher Education
(1993)

Undergraduates

No academical dress is worn.

Degree Certificates

Gowns
A black gown of the bachelors' shape.

Hoods
A Cardinal red silk hood of the Leeds simple shape, lined and turned back 2" with yellow. The neckband is yellow, and lined in cardinal red.

Bachelors

Gowns
A black gown of the basic bachelors' shape (fig. 3).

Hoods
A cardinal red silk hood of the simple shape, lined and turned back 2" in yellow and with green tape down the centre of the turnback. This continues onto the neckband.

Post-graduate Diplomas

Gowns
As for the bachelors' gown.

Hoods
A cardinal red hood of the simple shape, lined and turned back 2" in yellow. The turnback has green tape on each edge which continues onto the neckband.

Masters

Gowns
A black gown of the basic masters' shape (fig. 4).

Hoods
M.A., M.Sc. etc.: A cardinal red silk hood of the full Cambridge shape, lined with yellow. The cowl is bordered inside with green tape. The neckband is lined and edged top and bottom with yellow.

Honorary Masters, M.Univ.: As for the M.A. etc. but the cape is also edged with green. The neckband is lined and bound (top and bottom) with yellow.

Doctors

Honorary Doctors, D.Univ.: A cardinal red robe of the Cambridge shape with sleeve linings and facings of yellow, the sleeves being looped up with a green cord and button. The facings are edged on the outer side with green. The yoke has a green cord with yellow button.

Hoods
Doctors: Wear the same hood as for the Hon. Masters and M.Univ.

Academical Caps
Sub-degrees, Bachelors, Post-graduates, Masters: Wear a black mortar board.
Honorary Doctors: Wear a black velvet bonnet with green cord and tassels.

University of Bournemouth
(1993)

Undergraduates

No academical dress is worn.

Subdegrees HNC/HND & University Diplomas

Gowns
As for the bachelors' gown.

Hoods
A university blue hood of the Aberdeen shape lined in black and bound with white.

Bachelors

Gowns
As for the basic bachelors' gown (fig. 3).

Hoods
A university blue hood of the Cambridge full shape, half lined with university gold and the cowl bound with white.

Masters

Gowns
As for the basic masters' gown (fig. 4).

Hoods
A university blue hood of the Cambridge full shape, lined with gold and the cowl bound with white.

Post-graduate Awards

Gowns
As for the bachelors' gown.

Hoods
As for the masters' hood.

Doctors

Undress Gowns
As for the masters' gown.

Full Dress Robes
Ph.D.: A university blue robe of the Cambridge doctors' style with facings and sleeve linings of university gold silk.
Higher Doctors: As for the Ph.D. robe but with the sleeves bound in white.

Hoods
Ph.D.: A university blue hood of the Cambridge full shape, lined with university gold and bound all round with white.
Higher Doctors: As for the Ph.D. hood but with a wider white binding.

Academical Caps
With black gowns a black cloth mortar board is worn.
Doctors: In full dress wear a black velvet bonnet with gold cord and tassels.

University of Bradford
(1966)

The robes for the Chancellor, Vice-Chancellor and other Officials were designed by students of the university, and hence are somewhat unusual. The system of academical dress for graduates follows a more conventional pathway.

Undergraduates

No academical dress is worn.

Bachelors

Gowns
A black gown of the Cambridge M.A. shape.

Hoods
B.A., B.Sc., B.Tech., B.Eng.: A black hood of the full shape with the cowl bordered 3" inside with saffron silk.

Masters

Gowns
As for the bachelors' gown.

Hoods
A black stuff hood of the full shape and fully lined with saffron silk.

Doctors

Undress Gowns
As for the bachelors' gown.

Full Dress Robes
Ph.D.: A scarlet robe of the Cambridge shape with sleeve linings and facings of saffron silk.
Other Doctors: The same scarlet robe as for Ph.D.

Hoods
As for the Ph.D. hood but with the addition of a binding as follows:
D.Eng.: Green.
D.Litt.: White.

D.Sc.: Blue.
D.Tech.: Violet.
D.Univ.: Silver.

Academical Caps
Bachelors, Masters, Doctors: In undress wear a black cloth mortar board.
Doctors: In full dress wear a black velvet bonnet.

University of Brighton
(1993)

The University of Brighton has adopted a simple and logical system of academical dress.

Sub-Degree Certificates and Diplomas
(including BTEC, HND and HNC)

Gowns
A black polyester panama gown of the bachelors' shape.

Hoods
A black polyester panama hood of the C.N.A.A. shape (fig. 77 and 78), lined with light blue leaf damask.

Bachelors
(and M.Eng.)

Gowns
As for the basic bachelors' gown (fig. 3).

Hoods
A black polyester panama hood of the full shape, with rounded corners to the cape, lined with reflex blue leaf damask. The neckband is also lined and edged ³/₈" with the reflex blue damask.

Post-graduate Certificates and Diplomas

Gowns
As for the bachelors' gown.

Hoods
A black stuff full shaped hood with rounded cape, fully lined with reflex blue leaf damask, and with a border 1" wide inside the cowl of light blue leaf damask.

Masters

Gowns
A black stuff gown with Tudor bag sleeves, the end of the sleeve to be square cut (fig. 4).
M.Phil.: In full dress wear the masters' gown with 1" purple ribbon down the outside of the facings.

Hoods
A black stuff hood of the full shape with rounded cape, fully lined with purple leaf damask.

M.Eng.: A black stuff hood of the full shape with rounded cape, fully lined with reflex blue leaf damask. There is a border 1" wide of purple leaf damask inside the cowl.

M.Phil.: A black stuff hood of the full shape with rounded cape, lined with purple leaf damask, and with a border 1" wide of reflex blue leaf damask inside the cowl.

Doctors

Undress Gowns

As for the masters' gown.

Full Dress Robes

Ph.D.: A claret wool panama robe of the Oxford doctors' shape with 5" facings and sleeve cuffs of reflex blue leaf damask.

Higher Doctors: A scarlet wool panama robe of the Oxford doctors' shape with 5" facings and sleeve cuffs of reflex blue leaf damask.

Hoods

Ph.D.: A claret wool hood of the full shape with rounded corners and lined with reflex blue leaf damask.

Higher Doctors: A scarlet wool hood of the full shape with rounded corners and lined with reflex blue leaf damask.

Honorary Fellows

Fellows of the new university wear a black masters' gown, or the robes of their own degree. Fellows of the old polytechnic wear the black masters' gown with the Fellows' hood. This is a black hood of the full shape, lined with red and with a 2" edging of gold round the cowl.

Official Robes

Chairman of the Board of Governors wears a blue robe of the Cambridge doctors' shape. Sleeve linings and facings are of purple leaf damask. Each facing is edged outside with ½" gold oak leaf lace. The open sleeves are gathered and held by a gold cord and button at the elbow. There is a gold cord and button on the yoke.

The Director wears a similar robe to that of the Chairman but with silver oak leaf in place of the gold lace.

Academical Caps

Certificates, Diplomas, Bachelors, Masters, Doctors: In undress wear a black cloth mortar board with black button and tassel.

Ph.D.: In full dress wear a black cloth Tudor bonnet with reflex blue cord and tassels.

Higher Doctors: In full dress wear a black velvet Tudor bonnet with reflex blue cord and tassels.

University of Bristol
(1909)

The Bristol system of academical dress is very simple and quite logical. All hoods—bachelors, masters and doctors—are of the same full shape and of the same shade of red. Faculty colours are not used, and all bachelors' hoods (except M.B., LL.B. and B.Mus.) are lined with a lighter shade of red, masters hoods are lined with white and those of doctors (except Ph.D. and D.Ed.) with salmon pink.

Undergraduates

A black stuff gown of the Oxford scholars' shape (fig. 8).

Bachelors

Gowns
A black stuff gown of the Cambridge B.A. shape (fig. 37). The M.B. gown may be of stuff or silk.

Hoods
A university red silk or stuff hood of the full shape with square corners to the cape (fig. 66), and lined with a lighter shade of the same red.
M.B.: In addition has a binding ¾" in white round the cowl.
LL.B.: Bound with violet silk.
B.Mus.: Lined throughout with lavender silk.

Masters

A black stuff or silk gown of the Oxford M.A. shape, except that the sleeves are ended with rounded corners, and there is a slight concavity in the lower border (fig. 57).

Hoods
A university red silk hood of the bachelors' shape, lined with white.

Doctors

Undress Gowns
Ph.D., D.Ed.: As for the masters' gown.
Other Doctors: The same gown with the addition of a triangular area of scroll work in black braid above each armhole.

Full Dress Robes

Ph.D., D.Ed.: A scarlet cloth robe of the Oxford doctors' shape. The facings (3½") and the sleeves are covered in dark violet silk.

Other Doctors: A similar scarlet robe with facings of salmon pink silk. The sleeves are not faced with silk.

Hoods

Ph.D., D.Ed.: A university red hood of the bachelors' shape, lined with dark violet silk.

Other Doctors: As for the Ph.D. hood but lined with salmon pink silk.

Academical Caps

Undergraduates, Bachelors, Masters, Doctors: In undress wear a black cloth mortar board.

Ph.D. or *D.Ed.*: In full dress wear a black velvet mortar board.

Other Doctors: In full dress wear a black velvet Tudor bonnet with gold cord and tassels.

Brookes University, Oxford
(1993)

Undergraduates

No academical dress is worn.

BTEC

Gowns
As for the Oxford B.A. gown without the tapes and buttons at the wrist (fig. 38).

Hoods
A black C.N.A.A. shaped hood partly lined with cream silk piped with blue.

Bachelors

Gowns
As for the BTEC gown.

Hoods
A black silk hood of the full shape, partly lined with dark blue and with the cowl bound ½" in cream. The top of the neckband is also in cream.

Post-graduate Diplomas

Gowns
As for the bachelors' gown.

Hoods
A black silk hood of the full shape, fully lined with cream silk and edged ¾" outside only with blue silk. The neckband is edged top and bottom with cream silk.

Masters

Gowns
As for the basic masters' gown, i.e. glove sleeve straight cut end (fig. 4). The facings are of blue silk.

Hoods
A black silk hood of the full shape, fully lined with the university blue silk and edged ¾" in cream. The neckband is black, lined with blue and edged ⅜" top and bottom with cream.

Doctors

Undress Gowns
As for the masters' gown.

Full Dress Robes
Ph.D.: A maroon cloth robe of the Oxford doctors' shape with facings and sleeves of blue embossed silk. The facings also have 1" of cream silk on the outer edge.
Other Doctors: A maroon cloth robe of the Cambridge doctors' shape with facings and sleeves of blue embossed silk. The facings also have 1¼" of cream silk on the outer edge. The cord and button on each sleeve is cream.

Hoods
Ph.D.: A maroon cloth hood of the full shape, fully lined with blue embossed silk and edged with 1" of cream silk.
Other Doctors: As for the Ph.D. hood but edged with 1½" of cream silk.

Academical Caps
With black gowns, black cloth mortar boards are worn.
Ph.D.: In full dress wear a black velvet bonnet with a blue cord and tassels.
Other Doctors: In full dress wear a black velvet bonnet with a maroon cord and tassels.

Brunel University, West London
(1966)

Brunel University uses a special blue velvet to distinguish its hoods. The system is simple and involves only five hoods.

Undergraduates

No academical dress is worn.

Bachelors

Gowns
A black stuff gown of the basic bachelors' shape (fig. 3).

Hoods
A black stuff hood of the special simple shape, lined with white silk and bordered inside the cowl with 1½" of Brunel blue velvet. The neckband is blue.

Masters

Gowns
A black stuff gown of the basic masters' shape (fig. 4).

M.Univ. (Honorary only): A black gown of the Oxford doctors' full dress robe with a 5" facing and 5" cuffs of Brunel blue velvet.

Hoods
A Brunel blue hood of the Cambridge full shape, lined with silver and bordered inside with 2½" of Brunel blue velvet.

M.Univ. (Honorary only): A black full shaped hood lined with silver and bordered inside with 3½" of Brunel blue velvet.

Doctors

Undress Gowns
As for the masters' gown.

Full Dress Robes
Ph.D., D.B.A.: A mushroom cloth robe of the Oxford doctors' shape with 4" facings and 4" cuffs of Brunel blue velvet.

D. Univ. (Honorary only), *D. Litt., D. Sc., D. Tech.*: A cardinal red robe of the Oxford doctors' shape with 6" facings and 7" cuffs of Brunel blue velvet.

Academical Caps
Bachelors, Masters, Doctors: In undress wear a black cloth mortar board.
Ph.D., D.B.A.: In full dress wear a black cloth Tudor bonnet with cardinal red cord and tassels.
Other Doctors: Wear a black velvet bonnet with gold cord and tassels.

University of Buckingham
(1983)

This is a small, independent university with two-year courses. These originally ended with a Licence of the University, but now terminate with a degree. A simple logical system of academical dress is used.

Undergraduates

No academical dress is worn.

Bachelors

Gowns
A black stuff gown of the London B.A. shape (fig. 42).

Hoods
A blue stuff hood of the simple shape, lined with white silk and bordered inside the cowl with 1" coloured ribbon as follows:

B.A.: Pink.
LL.B.: Red.
B.Sc.: Maroon.
B.Sc.(Econ.): Lemon.

Masters

Gowns
A black cord gown of the Oxford M.A. shape.

Hoods
A blue silk hood of the full shape, lined (except M.Phil.) with white silk and bordered inside the cowl with 2" of coloured ribbon as follows:

M.A.: Pink.
LL.M.: Red.
M.Sc.: (in the School of Science): Maroon.
M.Sc.: (in the School of ABE): Lemon.
M.Phil.: Blue silk ribbon lined with blue silk bordered by 2" of white ribbon.
M.L.S.: To be determined.

Doctors

Undress Gowns
As for the masters' gown.

Full Dress Robes
D.Phil.: A maroon wool panama robe of the Oxford doctors' shape with 4" cuffs and 4" facings and a yoke of dark blue silk.
D.Univ., D.Litt., LL.D., D.Sc.: A scarlet wool panama robe of the Oxford doctors' shape with dark blue silk facings, cuffs and yoke.

Hoods
D.Phil.: A maroon silk hood of the full shape, lined with dark blue silk.
Other Doctors: A scarlet wool panama hood of the full shape, lined with dark blue silk and with a 2" ribbon inside the cowl of the following colours:

D.Univ. (Honorary): Gold.
D.Litt.: Pink.
D.Sc.: Maroon.
LL.D.: Red.

Academical Caps
Bachelors, Masters, Doctors: In undress wear a black cloth mortar board.
D.Phil.: In full dress wear a black cloth Tudor bonnet with dark blue cord and tassels.
Other Doctors: In full dress wear a black velvet bonnet with old gold cord and tassels.

Caledonian University, Glasgow
(1993)

University Certificates

Gowns

A black gown of the Oxford B.A. style, the sleeves reaching the hem. There is a cord and button on the yoke.

Hoods

A black hood of the 'special shape', fully lined in university blue satin.

Undergraduate Diplomas, SCOTVECE HND

Gowns

As for the certificate gown.

Hoods

A black hood of the 'special shape', fully lined in university blue satin and edged with ½" of white ribbon on the top edge.

Bachelors

Gowns

As for the certificate gown.

Hoods

A black hood of the 'special shape', fully lined in university blue satin and edged with 1" of white ribbon on the top edge.

Post-graduate Diplomas

Gowns

A black gown of the Glasgow masters' shape (fig. 53). There is a cord and button on the yoke.

Hoods

A black hood of the 'special shape', fully lined in university blue satin and edged with ½" of gold ribbon on the top edge.

Masters

Gowns
As for the post-graduate gown.

Hoods
A black hood of the 'special shape', fully lined in university blue satin and edged with 1" of gold ribbon on the top edge.

Masters of Philosophy

Gowns
As for the masters' gown with blue satin facings.

Hoods
A black hood of the 'special shape', fully lined in university blue satin and edged with 1" of gold ribbon.

Doctors of Philosophy

Full Dress Robes
As for the masters' gown in pale blue panama, with inverted-T armhole. The outer edge of the facings and round the armholes is trimmed with 1" of gold. The facings also have six gold chevrons piped with red—three near the top and three near the bottom.

Hoods
A blue panama hood of the 'special shape', fully lined in blue satin with the top edge trimmed with 1" gold and piped on the inner edge with red. There are three gold buttons on the cowl seam.

Academical Caps
These do not seem to be used.

University of Central England, Birmingham
(1993)

BTEC Awards (HND, HNC)

Gowns
As for the basic bachelors' gown in black stuff (fig. 3).

Hoods
Dark blue stuff hood of the simple shape, lined with scarlet silk.

Graduate Diplomas and Certificates
(Dip.Higher Ed., Dip.Prof.St., Cert.Higher Ed., Cert.Management, Cert.Professional Studies)

Gowns
As for the bachelors' gown in dark blue cloth.

Hoods
A dark blue hood of the simple shape, lined with cream silk.

Bachelors

Gowns
As for the basic bachelors' gown in dark blue cloth.

Hoods
A dark blue cloth hood of the full shape, partly lined with cream silk and edged with ½" of gold ribbon.

Post-graduate Diplomas and Certificates

Gowns
As for the bachelors' gown in dark blue cloth.

Hoods
A dark blue cloth hood of the full shape, fully lined with cream silk and edged with 1" of gold ribbon.

Masters

Gowns
A dark blue cloth gown of the basic masters' shape (fig. 4) i.e. with glove sleeves square cut at the bottom and with facings of cream silk.

Hoods

M.A., M.B.A., M.Sc.: A dark blue cloth of the full shape, fully lined with cream silk and edged with 1½" of gold silk.

M.Phil.: A dark blue cloth of the full shape, fully lined with gold silk and edged with 1½" of cream silk.

Doctors

Undress Gowns

As for the masters' gown.

Full Dress Robes

Ph.D.: A scarlet panama robe of the Oxford doctors' shape with facings and sleeves of cream silk with 1" of cream ribbon down the facings.

D.Univ. (Honorary award): A gold panama robe of the same shape as for the Ph.D. with facings and sleeves of cream silk.

Higher Doctors: Robes have not yet been specified.

Hoods

Ph.D.: A scarlet hood of the full shaped, lined and edged 1" with cream silk.

D.Univ.: A gold panama hood of the full shape, lined and edged 1" with cream silk.

University of Central Lancashire, Preston
(1993)

Undergraduates

No academical dress is worn.

HND/HNC

Gowns
As for the bachelors' gown.

Hoods
A grey hood of the simple shape, part lined with the university's red embossed silk.

Bachelors

Gowns
A black stuff gown with the basic bachelors' style sleeves (fig. 3).

Hoods
A grey hood of the simple shape, fully lined with the university's red embossed silk.

Masters

Gowns
A black stuff gown of the basic masters' shape (fig. 4).

Hoods
A grey cloth hood of the full shape, fully lined with the university's red embossed silk.

Other University Awards

Gowns
As for the bachelors' gown.

Hoods
A grey cloth hood of the simple shape, part-lined with the university's red embossed silk, and with 1" black ribbon inside the cowl between the red and grey.

Doctors

Undress Gowns
As for the masters' gown.

Full Dress Robes
Ph.D.: A grey cloth robe of the Cambridge doctors' style, with facings and sleeve linings in the university's red embossed silk.
Other Doctorates: Not yet approved.

Hoods
Ph.D: A grey cloth hood of the full shape, fully lined with the university's red embossed silk.
Other Doctorates: Not yet approved.

Honorary Awards

Honorary Fellows
A light grey cloth robe of the doctors' shape, with the university logo on each sleeve. The hood is that prescribed for bachelors.

Honorary Masters
A light grey cloth gown in the masters' shape, with facings of the university's red embossed silk. The hood is that prescribed for bachelors.

Honorary Doctors
A light grey cloth robe as for the Ph.D. but with a grey cord and button at the sleeve turnback. The hood is of grey cloth, full shaped and fully lined with the university's red embossed silk and edged 2" outside the cowl.

Academical Caps
Certificates, Diploma holders, Bachelors, Masters, Doctors: In undress wear a black cloth mortar board.
Ph.D.: In full dress wear a grey cloth Tudor bonnet with red cord and tassels.
Honorary Fellows and *Honorary Masters:* Wear a grey cloth mortar board.
Honorary Doctors: Wear a grey Tudor bonnet with red tassels.

City University, London
(1966)

Undergraduates

As for the Oxford scholars' gown.

Bachelors and Holders of all Diplomas

Gowns

As for the Cambridge B.A. gown without the strings.

Hoods

Post-graduate Diplomas: A maroon silk hood of the full shape with no lining, but the neckband is of the discipline (faculty) colour.
Bachelors: A maroon cloth hood of the simple shape lined with gold taffeta. The neckband is of the discipline colour.

Masters

Gowns

As for the Cambridge M.A. without the strings and with an inverted-T armhole.

Hoods

M.Sc., M.Eng., M.B.A., M.A., M.H.M.: A maroon silk hood of the full shape, fully lined and edged with ½" gold taffeta. The neckband is of the discipline colour.
M.Phil.: As for the masters' hood, above, with the addition of a 1" ribbon in maroon bordering the cowl.

Doctors

Undress Gowns

As for the masters' gown.

Full Dress Robes

Ph.D.: A maroon cloth robe of the masters' shape with facings of 2" of gold taffeta and ¼" of gold taffeta round the armholes.
Higher Doctors: As for the Ph.D. robe but with facings of gold taffeta 5" wide, and on the bottom of the bag sleeve.

Hoods

Ph.D.: A maroon cloth hood of the full shape, half lined with maroon and half with gold taffeta. The neckband is of the discipline colour, see below.

Higher Doctors: A cardinal red cloth hood of the full shape, lined half with maroon and half with gold taffeta. The neckband is of the following discipline colour:

Engineering: Blue.
Science: Grey.
Arts (including *Social Science, Business & Management Studies*): Green.
Music: Gold.
Law: Scarlet.
Divinity: Purple.

Validated Courses: For those who graduate with a degree or diploma in a course validated by the University, any hood may be differenced by a 1½" chevron across the inside of the hood. The colour of the chevron depends upon the institution involved.
Ashridge Management College: Green.

Academical Caps

Undergraduates, Bachelors, Diplomas, Masters, Doctors: In undress wear a black cloth mortar board.
Ph.D.: In full dress wear a black cloth bonnet with maroon cord and tassels.
Higher Doctors: In full dress wear a black velvet bonnet with cord and tassels of maroon and gold.

Council for National Academic Awards
(1964)

Until 1993 when Polytechnics became Universities in their own right, the degrees taken at these colleges were validated and awarded by the Council for National Academic Awards (C.N.A.A.). Since the creation of the 33 new Universities, each conferring their own degrees, the C.N.A.A. has become almost redundant. Nonetheless, during its active life, the C.N.A.A. must have awarded many thousands of degrees, and the academical dress involved will be seen for many years to come.

Undergraduates

No academical dress is worn.

Bachelors

Gowns
A black stuff gown of the basic bachelors' shape, i.e. an open pointed sleeve with no decoration (fig. 3). This gown is worn 12" off the ground.

Hoods
A gold panama hood of the special Aberdeen shape, lined with blue.

Masters

Gowns
A black stuff gown of the basic masters' shape, i.e. with a glove sleeve which is cut square across the bottom. This gown is worn 8" off the ground (fig. 4).

Hoods
A gold panama hood of the special Aberdeen shape, lined with white.

Doctors

Undress Gowns
As for the masters' gown.

Full Dress Robes
Ph.D.: As for the masters' black gown with 5" facings and the yoke covered in maroon silk.
Other Doctors: A gold panama robe of the same shape as for the masters' gown, but with a vertical armhole and with facings of cream brocade.

Hoods

Ph.D.: A gold panama hood of the special Aberdeen shape, lined with maroon silk.
Other Doctors: A gold panama hood of the special Aberdeen shape, lined and edged with cream brocade.

Academical Caps

Bachelors, Masters, Doctors: In undress wear a black cloth mortar board.
Ph.D.: In full dress wear a black cloth bonnet with maroon cord and tassels.
Other Doctors: In full dress wear a black velvet bonnet with gold cord and tassels.

Coventry University
(1993)

This university uses special silks embossed with the Coventry Phoenix for hood linings, so giving a feature distinctive to the university.

Undergraduates

No academical dress is worn.

Certificates and Undergraduate Diplomas

Gowns
A black gown of the basic bachelors' shape.

Hoods
A black hood of the simple shape partly lined with blue and with gold silk.

Bachelors

Gowns
The basic bachelors' gown in black stuff (fig. 3).

Hoods
A gold art silk hood of the full shape, bordered inside with blue silk embossed with the phoenix.

Masters, Post-graduate Diplomas and Certifcates

Gowns
M.Phil.: As for the basic masters' gown, i.e .with Tudor bag sleeves straight cut across the foot. The facings are in blue embossed silk.
Other Masters, Post-graduate Diplomas: As for the M.Phil. gown but without the blue silk facings.

Hoods
All Masters (including *M.Phil.*)*, Post-graduate Diplomas*: Wear a gold art silk hood of the full shape, fully lined with blue embossed silk.

Doctors

Undress Gowns
As for the masters' gown.

Full Dress Robes

Ph.D.: A royal blue panama robe of the Cambridge doctors' shape with facings and sleeve linings of gold silk embossed with the Phoenix.

Higher Doctors: As for the Ph.D. robe but with a blue cord and button on each sleeve and on the yoke.

Hoods

Ph.D.: A royal blue hood of the full shape, fully lined with gold embossed silk.

Higher Doctors: As for the Ph.D. hood with the addition of a border 1½" wide of the gold embossed silk round the cape and cowl.

Academical Caps

With black gowns a black cloth mortar board is worn.

Ph.D.: In full dress wear a royal blue cloth bonnet with gold cord and tassels.

Higher Doctors: Wear a royal blue velvet bonnet with gold cord and tassels.

Life Fellows: Wear an ultramarine blue gown with facings and cape collar in plain satinwood silk. The outside edge of facings and collar are trimmed with gold oakleaf. A royal blue cloth Tudor bonnet with gold cord and tassels is worn. No hoods are worn by Life Fellows.

Cranfield University, Bedfordshire
(1993)

Formerly the Cranfield Institute of Technology, this University is concerned mainly with military science and agriculture. The Chancellor is unique in that he has a red feather in his blue bonnet in place of the more usual gold cord and tassels!

Bachelors

Gowns
As for the basic bachelors' gown (fig. 3).

Hoods
An old gold grosgrain hood of the simple shape, lined throughout as follows:
Faculty of Agricultural Engineering, Food Production & Rural Land: Spectrum green.
Faculty of Military Science, Technology & Management: Guardsman red.

Masters

Gowns
A black Russell cord gown of the basic masters' shape, i.e. with square ending glove sleeves, but an inverted-T armhole, and an old gold cord and button on the yoke.

Hoods
A gold cord hood of the simple shape, lined with royal blue.

Doctors

Undress Gowns
As for the masters' gown.

Full Dress Robes
Ph.D.: As for the masters' gown faced with 4" of neyron rose silk.
D.Sc.: A neyron rose superfine cloth robe of the Cambridge doctors' shape with facings and sleeve linings of royal blue silk.

Hoods
Ph.D.: An old gold cord hood of the simple shape, lined with neyron rose.
D.Sc.: A neyron rose superfine cloth hood of the full shape, lined with royal blue silk.

Academical Caps
Bachelors, Masters, Doctors: In undress wear a black mortar board.
Doctors: In full dress wear a black velvet bonnet with gold cord and tassels.

De Montfort University, Leicester
(1993)

Undergraduates

No academical dress is worn.

Licentiates

Gowns
As for the bachelors' gown.

Sash
The sash is made in university gold, lined and bound with university red, and with the university emblem in red on each side. It also has three tassels of gold-red.

Bachelors

Gowns
As for the basic bachelors' gown (fig. 3).

Hoods
A university gold hood of the simple shape, lined with university red, and with the cowl bound inside and outside in the faculty colour. This is continued onto the top edge of the neckband.

Post-graduate Diplomas

Gowns
As for the bachelors' gown.

Hoods
A university gold hood of the simple shape, fully lined and with the cowl edged in university red, including the neckband.

Masters

Gowns
As of the basic masters' gown (fig. 4).

Hoods
M.Phil.: A university gold hood of the Cambridge full shape, fully lined with university red and with the cowl bound inside and out with the philosophy faculty colour.

Other Masters: As for the M.Phil. hood but the cowl is bound with the following faculty colour:

Faculty Colours
Art: Blue.
Science: Green.
Engineering: Grey.
Law: Blue.
Education: Brown.
M.B.A.: Lilac.
Philosophy: White.

Doctors

Full Dress Robes
Ph.D.: A black polyester robe of the same shape as for the masters, but with university gold facings, and university red on the outside of the facings. The yoke is also of university gold with a university red cord and button on the back.
Other Doctors: As for the Ph.D. shape but in university gold. The facings and yoke are of university red and there is a gold cord and button on the yoke.

Hoods
Ph.D.: A university gold hood of the Cambridge full shape, fully lined and the cape edged with university red. The cowl is bound with the philosophy faculty colour. The neckband is not edged. Doctors' hoods are larger than those of masters.
Higher Doctors: The same shape as for the Ph.D. hood, in university gold fully lined and the cape edged with university red. The neckband is bound inside and outside with the faculty colour. The neckband is not edged.

Academical Caps
All Licentiates, Diplomates, Graduates: Wear a black flexible mortar board.
Ph.D.: Wear a black cloth bonnet with red-gold cord and tassels.
Higher Doctors: Wear a black velvet bonnet with gold-red cord and tassels.

University of Derby
(1993)

Diplomas

Gowns
As for the bachelors' gown.

Hoods
A black hood of the C.N.A.A. shape, part lined in sky blue, and the front lined in scarlet.

Bachelors

Gowns
As for the basic bachelors' gown (fig. 3).

Hoods
A black hood of the full shape, lined with scarlet and bordered with 1½" of light blue.

Postgraduate

Gowns
As for the bachelors' gown.

Hoods
A blue hood of the full shape, lined with scarlet and bordered with 1½" of light blue.

Masters

Gowns
As for the basic masters' gown (fig. 4).
M.Phil.: As for the masters' gown but with scarlet facings.

Hoods
A black hood of the full shape, lined and edged with ¼" of scarlet and with a border inside of 2½" in light blue.

Doctors

Full Dress Robes
Ph.D.: A maroon robe of the London doctors' shape, with facings and sleeve linings of light blue. The facings have on the outer edge a 1" dark blue stripe, piped with scarlet.

Honorary and *Higher Doctors*: A scarlet robe as for the Ph.D. with facings and sleeves of dark blue piped with light blue. There is a light blue cord and button on the sleeves.

Hoods

Ph.D.: A maroon hood of the full shape, lined with light blue. There is a 1" border of dark blue piped with scarlet.

Honorary and *Higher Doctors:* A scarlet hood of the full shape, lined with light blue and with a 1" border of dark blue piped with scarlet.

Academical Caps

All Graduates: Wear a black cloth mortar board.

Ph.D.: In full dress wear a black cloth bonnet with maroon cord and tassels.

Higher Doctors: Wear a black velvet bonnet with scarlet cord and tassels.

University of Dundee
(1967)

The University was originally a component college (Queen's College) in the University of St Andrews, and became an independent body, awarding its own degrees in 1967.

The colour liturgical blue, or Stewart blue is used extensively in the official and graduate robes. This colour is traditionally associated with The Virgin Mary, the patron saint of the Royal Burgh of Dundee.

Undergraduates

A Union Jack red nap gown with cape sleeves, and with yoke, flap collar and square patch facings in serge or flannel of Stewart blue.

Bachelors

Gowns

As for the Cambridge M.A. gown, without strings, i.e. Tudor bag sleeves with the point facing forwards.

Hoods

All hoods at Dundee are of the Aberdeen style, but with an oblong (as opposed to pear-shaped) cape, with rounded corners.

Bachelors: A black silk hood lined with the faculty colour, the cowl being edged with white fur.

Other degrees have their own lining colour as follows:

M.B., Ch.B.: Cherry.
B.M.Sc.: Clover.
B.D.S.: Ruby.
B.Sc.: Buttercup.
B.Eng.: Powder blue.
LL.B.: Old gold.
B.Admin. & B.Acc.: Forget-me-not blue.
B.Ed.: Tuscan yellow.
B.A., fine art: Tartan green.
B.Des.: Reseda green.
B.Sc.Envir.Sc.: Gault grey.
B.Arch.: Heliotrope.

Masters

Gowns

As for the bachelors' gown.

SPECIFICATIONS: DUNDEE

Hoods

As for the Masters' hood in black silk, i.e. similar to the corresponding bachelors' hoods but without the fur and lined with the faculty colour:

Ch.M.: Imperial purple.
M.M.Ed.: Tuscan yellow.
M.M.Sc., M.S.Sc. & M.Sc. in medicine: Clover.
M.P.H.: Begonia.
M.D.S., M.D.Sc.: Ruby.
M.Sc.: Buttercup.
M.Sc.Eng.: Powder blue.
LL.M.: Old gold.
M.Acc.: Forget-me-not blue.
M.Phil.: Eggshell blue.
M.A.: Tartan green.
M.Ed.: Tuscan yellow.
M.S.W.: Jade green.
M.B.A.: Stone white.
M.Phil.: Verdigris.
M.Sc.Environ.St.: Gault grey.

Doctors

Undress Gowns

As for the bachelors' gown.

Full Dress Robes

Ph.D.: In full dress wear the masters' black gown with the Ph.D. hood.
Other Doctors: A Stewart blue ottoman robe of the Oxford doctors' shape. The yoke, cuffs and facings are of the same silk as the hood linings.

Hoods

These are of the basic Dundee shape in Stewart blue ottoman, and lined with the following faculty colours:

M.D.: Cherry.
D.D.S.: Ruby.
D.Sc.: Buttercup.
D.Sc.Eng.: Powder blue.
LL.D.: Old gold.
D.Litt.: Smalt blue.
D.Sc.Environ.St.: Gault grey.

Academical Caps

Undergraduates, Bachelors, Masters, Doctors: In undress wear a black cloth trencher (mortar board).
Ph.D.: In full dress wear a black velvet trencher with an egg shell blue tassel.
Other Doctors: Wear a black velvet Tudor bonnet with cord and tassels of the faculty colour.

University of Durham
(1832)

The university of Durham has an elaborate but by no means fully logical system of academical dress. Some of its hoods are exceptionally beautiful, and most of them incorporate palatinate purple, which is a special lilac shade. Until 1963, King's College, Newcastle upon Tyne was a constituent college of the university of Durham. It is now an independent body giving its own degrees. The Durham colleges have never awarded degrees in medicine, dentistry or architecture, these being available only at King's College. Hence the Durham university system of robes for these degrees has now been transferred to the university of Newcastle.

Undergraduates

Arts and Commerce: A black gown of the Oxford scholars' shape, but with the forearm seam left open as a vent (fig. 11).
Science: As for the Arts gown, but with the addition of a strip of black velvet from the top of the slit to the shoulder.
Scholars: As for the Arts gown, but without the vent.

Bachelors

Gowns
B.A., B.C.L., LL.B., B.Sc., B.Com & B.A.Econ.: A black gown of the Oxford B.A. shape, with the forearm seam left open for 6" to 8" from the wrist, and held together at the wrist with a loop and button. There is a cord and button on the yoke (fig. 41).
B.D.: As for the M.A. gown (fig. 49).
B.Mus.: As for the Oxford lay gown (frontispiece, i).

Hoods
A special full shaped hood, the cape being rounded at the corners, and the liripipe is narrow.
B.A.: A black stuff hood half lined with the cape edged in fur.
B.Sc.: A palatinate purple silk hood edged in fur and with ½" of scarlet silk ribbon next to the fur round the cape and cowl.
B.C.L.: A palatinate silk hood edged in fur.
LL.B.: A palatinate silk hood lined with maroon silk and edged in fur.
B.D.: A black corded silk hood lined with fine black silk, as of the doctors' shape.

SPECIFICATIONS: DURHAM

B.Mus.: A palatinate silk hood bound with 1" brocaded white satin.
B.Com., B.A.Econ.: A black silk hood lined with cerise and edged in fur.

Masters

Gowns
M.A., M.Sc., M.Litt., M.Ed., M.Com., M.A.Econ., M.B.A.: As for the Oxford M.A. gown with a cord and button on the yoke.
M.Mus.: As for the B.Mus. gown but with a single straight row of lace from below the armhole to the foot of the sleeve. There is no panel of gimp lace at the bottom of the sleeve.

Hoods
As for the Oxford plain shaped hood.

M.A.: Black silk lined palatinate.
M.Sc.: Black silk lined palatinate and bound with ½" of scarlet.
M.Litt.: Black corded silk lined with old gold satin.
M.Com., M.A.Econ.: Black silk lined with cerise.
M.Ed.: Black silk lined with white and bound 1" palatinate.
M.Mus.: Black silk lined white brocade and bound 1" palatinate.
M.B.A.: Black silk lined palatinate bound with ½" of red ribbon and with 3"of white inside the cowl.

Doctors

Undress Gowns
D.Sc., D.Litt., D.C.L.: As for the M.A gown.
D.D.: As for the M.A. gown with a black silk scarf.
D.Mus.: As for the B.Mus. gown but with a slit 13" at the back of the gown from the hem to the top of the gimp panel.
Ph.D.: As for the M.A. gown with a palatinate cord and button on the yoke.

Full Dress Robes
A scarlet cloth or cassimere robe of the Oxford doctors' shape with sleeves and facings as follows:

D.Sc.: Scarlet.
D.Litt.: Old gold satin.
D.C.L.: White silk.
D.D.: Palatinate.
Ph.D.: Scarlet, bound on the inner edge with 1" palatinate.
D.Mus.: A brocaded white satin robe with sleeves and facings of palatinate silk.

Hoods
A scarlet cassimere hood (except D.Sc. and D.Mus.) of the special full shape with linings as follows:

D.Litt.: Old gold satin.
D.C.L.: White silk.

D.D.: Palatinate.
Ph.D.: Scarlet, bound on all edges with 1" palatinate.
D.Sc.: Palatinate, lined with scarlet silk.
D.Mus.: Brocaded white satin, lined with palatinate.

Academical Caps
Bachelors, Masters, Doctors: In undress wear a black mortar board.
Doctors: In full dress wear a soft square black velvet cap i.e. 'John Knox' cap (fig. 90).
Undergraduates: Do not wear a cap.

Licentiates of Theology

Gowns
A black stuff gown of the London B.A. shape, the pleats at the elbow being held by a strip of black velvet 1" wide and with a black button at the top of the velvet.

Hoods
A black stuff hood of the same shape as for the bachelors, edged with black velvet 1" wide and bound a ¼" with palatinate.

University of East Anglia, Norwich
(1966)

The robes for this university were designed by a dressmaker—Mr. Cecil Beaton, and hence do not follow the traditional styles or patterns. Gowns and hoods are made in a dull indigo shade, the gowns being very plain indeed, not gathered at the yoke, but ruched, like a surplice, on a semi-circular collar. The hoods have the faculty silk in the form of folds on the *outside*, using considerably more silk than can ever be seen. For undergraduates and bachelors Mr. Beaton designed a black skullcap with brim, thus giving a 'Rev. Father Brown' effect. For masters, a tricorn hat, to convert them to highwaymen! Fortunately, these freakish hats have fallen into disuse, and their wearers have reverted to the more conventional mortar boards.

Undergraduates

A blue cloth cape-styled gown with black cloth facings, extended round the collar.

Bachelors

Gowns

A blue cloth gown with basic bachelors' shape sleeves. The yoke is not gathered in the usual way.

Hoods

All the hoods are of a special simple shape and made of blue (i.e. dull indigo) cloth. The faculty is indicated by a 6" fold of silk on the outside of the cowl.

B.A.: Blue faced with coral (BCC 93).
B.Ed.: Blue faced with blue (BCC 195).
B.Eng.: Blue faced with saffron (BCC 54).
LL.B.: Blue faced with magenta (BCC 198).
B.Phil.: Blue faced with blue (BCC 132).
B.Sc.: Blue faced with spectrum green (BCC 100).

Masters

Gowns

A blue cloth gown with surplice-type yoke and Cambridge M.A.-style sleeves.

Hoods

A special simple-shaped hood of blue grosgrain covered with 6" folds of the faculty colour.

M.A. & M.S.W.: Blue face with coral.
M.Ed.: Blue faced with blue (BCC 195).
LL.M.: Blue faced with magenta.
M.Mus.: Blue faced with Beaton pink.
M.Sc.: Blue faced with spectrum green.
M.Phil.: Blue faced with guardsman red (BCC 126).

Doctors

Undress Gowns
As for the masters' gown.

Full Dress Robes
Ph.D.: As for the masters' gown with facings of fine red grosgrain.
Higher Doctors: A blue grosgrain robe with wide coat-style sleeves.

Hoods
Ph.D.: As for the M.Phil. hood, i.e. blue faced with guardsman red (BCC 126).
D.C.L.: Blue faced with crocus.
LL.D.: Blue faced with magenta.
D.Litt.: Blue faced with coral.
D.Mus.: Blue faced with Beaton pink.
D.Sc.: Blue faced with spectrum green.

Academical Caps
The skull caps with brims for undergraduates and bachelors and the tricorn hats for masters designed by Mr. Beaton were found to be unacceptable by their wearers, and replaced by mortar boards.

All Doctors: In full dress wear a round black velvet bonnet with gold cord and tassels.

University of East London
(1993)

HNC/HND, College Awards

Gowns
A dark blue gown of the bachelors' shape.

Hoods
A dark blue C.N.A.A. shaped hood, lined with chile red plain silk.

Bachelors

Gowns
A dark blue gown of the basic bachelors' shape (fig. 3).

Hoods
A dark blue art silk hood of the full shape, partly lined with chile red embossed silk.

Masters

Gowns
A dark blue gown of the Open University shape, i.e. with glove sleeves and inverted-T armhole, the sleeves being longer than Open University.

Hoods
A dark blue hood of the full shape, fully lined and edged a ¼" all round with chile red embossed silk.

Doctors

Full Dress Robes
Ph.D.: A royal blue panama robe of the London doctors' shape with sleeves and facings of chile red embossed silk.
Higher Doctors: As for the Ph.D. robe but the facings are trimmed with silver oak leaf lace down the outer edge. There is a silver cord and button on the sleeves.

Hoods
Ph.D.: A royal blue panama hood of the full shape, lined and edged 1" with chile red embossed silk.

Higher Doctors: As for the Ph.D. hood but the cowl is trimmed with silver oak leaf lace.

Honorary Fellows

Gowns

A dark blue Queen's Counsel robe, with the facings and flap collar covered with chile red embossed silk.

Academical Caps

All Graduates: Wear a blue mortar board.

Doctors: In full dress wear a Royal blue panama Tudor bonnet with chile red cord and tassels.

Honorary Fellows: Wear a dark blue polyester Tudor bonnet with chile red cord and tassels.

University of Edinburgh
(1582)

At Edinburgh, a single black gown is used by all graduates, and a single scarlet robe is used by all doctors except the Ph.D. All the hoods except for Music are black, and this creates difficulties for a progressive bachelor-master-doctor system. Bachelors usually line their hoods with the faculty colour and edge it in fur. Doctors usually have the same hood without the fur, and where there is a corresponding masters degree the hood is usually lined with white and bordered with the faculty colour. Due to the proliferation of degrees in recent years the system has had to be augmented to accommodate the extra faculties.

Undergraduates

A scarlet Russell cord gown of the London undergraduate shape (fig. 10).

Bachelors

Gowns

A black stuff or silk gown of the Cambridge M.A. shape, but with an inverted-T armhole.

Hoods

A black silk hood (except for music) of the special simple shape (fig. 86), edged in white fur and lined as follows:

B.Sc., B.Sc.Engineering, B.Sc.Med.Sci., B.Sc.Ent.Sci., B.Sc.Vet.Sci.: Lined in green silk.
B.A.Relig.St.: Lined white and bordered with 3" of purple poplin.
B.Com.: Lined pale primrose yellow.
B.D.: Lined purple.
B.D.S.: Lined crimson and bordered with 3" of ivory. The neckband shows 3" of crimson on each side.
B.Eng.: Lined green and bordered with 3" of red.
B.Mus.: Scarlet gown lined white and edged in fur.
B.Sc.Soc.Sci.: Lined deep turquoise.
B.Sc.Nursing.: Lined deep turquoise with 2" of white ribbon border.
B.V.M.&S.: Lined maroon bound with 3" of golden yellow.
LL.B.: Lined with blue.
M.B., Ch.B.: Lined with crimson.

Masters

Gowns

As for the bachelors' gown.

Hoods

A black hood of the bachelors' shape.

Ch.M.: Black velvet lined with golden silk.
LL.M.: Black silk lined with blue silk.
M.A.: Black silk lined with white silk.
M.A.Rel.St.: Black silk lined with white silk and bordered with 3" of purple poplin.
M.Arch.: Black silk lined with orange-brown silk.
M.B.A.: Black silk lined with pale primrose yellow silk.
M.Ed.: Black silk lined with pale blue silk.
M.Eng.: Black silk lined with green silk and bordered with 3" of red poplin.
M.L.A.: Black silk lined white silk, bordered with 3" of green poplin and 1" of brown poplin.
M.Litt.: Black silk lined royal blue shot maize silk and bordered with 3" of ivory poplin with 3" of royal blue shot maize at the neckband.
M.Mus.: Scarlet silk lined white silk.
M.Phil.: Black silk lined silver silk bordered with 3" of blue shot brown silk.
M.Sc.: Black silk lined white silk and bordered with 3" of green silk and with 3" of green at the neckband.
M.S.W.: Black silk lined with mauve silk.
M.Theol.: Black silk lined with purple silk bordered with 3" of ivory and with 3" of purple at the neckband.

Doctors

Undress Gowns

As for the bachelors' gown.

Full Dress Robes

Ph.D.: No full dress robe is worn.
Other Doctors: A scarlet cloth robe of the Cambridge doctors' shape, except that the sleeves are much shorter and pointed. The facings and sleeve linings are of scarlet silk, and the yoke is also covered in scarlet silk. There is a scarlet cord piping round the yoke and four scarlet buttons.

Hoods

These are of the same shape as for the bachelors' hood.

D.D., LL.D., M.D.: Have in addition an appended cape which is faced and lined with the faculty colour.
D.D.: Black cloth lined with purple silk and with a purple appended cape.
D.D.S.: Black silk lined with crimson silk and bordered with 3" of white.
D.Litt.: Black cloth lined with royal blue shot maize silk.
D.Mus.: Rich scarlet cloth lined with rich white corded silk.

D.Psychol.: Black silk lined with grey silk.
D.Sc.: Black cloth lined with green silk.
D.Sc.Soc.Sc.: Black cloth lined with deep turquoise silk.
D.V.M.& Sc.: Black silk lined with maroon silk and bound with 3" of golden yellow.
LL.D.: Black cloth lined with blue silk and with an appended blue cape.
M.D.: Black silk lined with crimson silk and with an appended crimson cape.
Ph.D.: (pre-1991) Black cloth lined with blue shot brown silk. As from 1991, as above with the addition of 3" of red silk border.

Licentiates of Theology

L.Th.: Wear the graduate gown with an epitôge. This is of black silk, 28" long by 9½" wide at the back and 5½" wide at the front. There is an edging of purple silk, ½" wide all round and a purple button 1½" in diameter on the shoulder. The epitôge is worn on the left shoulder.

Academical Caps

Undergraduates, Bachelors, Masters, Doctors: In undress wear a black cloth mortarboard.
Doctors: In full dress wear a black silk velvet 'John Knox' cap (fig. 90).

University of Essex, Colchester
(1966)

A simple modern system of academical dress has been adopted at this university. No faculty colours are used; the gowns, hoods and robes simply indicate the degree level, i.e. bachelor, master or doctor.

Undergraduates

No academical dress is worn.

Bachelors

Gowns
As for the basic bachelors' gown (fig. 3).

Hoods
All Bachelors: A black hood of the Oxford simple shape, lined with red taffeta.

Masters

Gowns
All Masters: A black stuff gown as for the Oxford M.A. gown (fig. 48).

Hoods
Masters: A black hood of the Cambridge full shape, lined with red taffeta and edged with 1½" of white taffeta.

Doctors

Undress Gowns
As for the masters' gown.

Full Dress Robes
Ph.D.: A black stuff robe of the Oxford doctors' full dress shape, with sleeves faced in maroon taffeta.
Higher Doctors: A red stuff robe of the Oxford doctors' full dress shape, with 8" cuffs and facings of black silk, and with both edged 1" in white.
Honorary Doctors: As for the higher doctors' robe but with a 2" edge of white.

Hoods
Ph.D.: A red stuff hood of the Oxford doctors' shape lined with maroon taffeta.
Higher Doctors: A red silk hood of the Cambridge full shape, lined and edged with white and with a black ribbon 1" wide and ½" from the edge.
Honorary Doctors: As for higher doctors hood but with the black ribbon 2" wide.

Academical Caps
Bachelors, Masters, Doctors: In undress wear a black cloth mortar board.
Ph.D.: In full dress wear a black cloth Tudor bonnet with maroon cord and tassels.
Higher Doctors: Wear a black velvet bonnet with red cord and tassels.
Honorary Doctors: Wear a black velvet bonnet with white cord and tassels.

University of Exeter
(1955)

Exeter has adopted dove grey as its university colour, and incorporates this into all its hoods. The gowns have been copied without modification from Cambridge.

Undergraduates

As for the London undergraduates' gown, with a slit in the front of the sleeve seam from 3" at the top to 1½" from the bottom.

Bachelors and M.Eng.

Gowns
A black stuff gown of the Cambridge B.A. shape.

Hoods
A dove grey cloth hood of the full shape, unlined and bound with spectrum blue 2" each side round the cowl and cape.
B.Phil.: As above with the addition of white cord round all edges.

Masters

Gowns
Black stuff or silk gown of the Cambridge M.A. shape.

Hoods
A dove grey cloth hood of the full shape, lined with spectrum blue.
M.Eng.: As for the bachelors' hood with gold cord round all outside edges.

Doctors

Undress Gowns
Ph.D.: As for the masters' gown with Cambridge doctors' lace round the armhole.
Other Doctors: As for the masters' gown with Cambridge doctors' lace round the armhole and round the yoke.

Full Dress Robes
Ph.D.: A black gown the same shape as for the masters' gown, with silk facings of spectrum blue.
Other Doctors: A scarlet cloth robe of the Cambridge shape, with facings and sleeve linings of spectrum blue.

Hoods

Ph.D.: A dove grey cloth hood of the full shape, lined with scarlet cloth.
Other Doctors: A scarlet cloth hood of the full shape, lined with dove grey cloth and bound with spectrum blue.

Academical Caps

Undergraduates: Do not wear caps, but women students may wear a soft Oxford cap.
Bachelors, Masters, Doctors: In undress wear a black cloth mortar board.
Doctors: In full dress wear a round black velvet bonnet with cord and tassels of spectrum blue.

University of Glamorgan
(1993)

The distinctive feature seen in the hoods of this university is the use of a lining silk of gold embossed with the university logo—a capital G in blue and gold.

Undergraduates

No academical dress is worn.

Sub-Degree Awards—HNC/HND, Cert.H.Ed. etc.

Gowns
As for the bachelors' gown.

Hoods
A green hood of the simple shape, lined with white and with a red tip to the 'boot' of the cowl. This is the old polytechnic hood.

Bachelors (B.A., B.Sc., B.Eng., LL.B.)

Gowns
As for the basic bachelors' gown (fig. 3).

Hoods
A blue hood of the full shape, bordered with 3" of university gold embossed silk.

Post-graduate Certificates and Diplomas

Gowns
As for the basic masters' gown, i.e. glove sleeve with square cut sleeve ending.

Hoods
As for the bachelors' hood.

Masters (M.A., M.Sc., M.Eng., M.Phil.)

Gowns
As for the basic masters' gown.

Hoods
A blue hood of the full shape, fully lined with the gold embossed silk.

Doctors (D.Litt., D.Sc., D.Tech., LL.D., Ph.D.)

Undress Gowns
As for the masters' gown.

Full Dress Robes
Ph.D.: A dark blue panama robe of the same shape as for the masters' with facings and sleeve fronts of gold embossed silk.

Higher Doctors: A gold panama robe of the same shape as for the masters' but with facings and sleeve fronts of dark blue panama.

Hoods
Ph.D.: A dark blue panama hood of the full shape, fully lined and edged 1" all round with gold embossed silk.

Higher Doctors: A dark blue panama hood of the full shape, lined and edged 2" all round with gold embossed silk.

Honorary Doctors: As for the Ph.D. robe, hood and hat.

Academical Caps
With black gowns, a black cloth mortar board is worn.

Ph.D.: In full dress wear a black cloth Tudor bonnet with dark blue cord and tassels.

Higher Doctors: In full dress wear a black velvet bonnet with gold cord and tassels.

University of Glasgow
(1451)

There is a simple, logical system of academical dress at Glasgow. The shapes of the masters' gown and the doctors' undress gown are peculiar to this university.

Undergraduates

A scarlet cloth gown. The sleeves are wrist length, open at the front and sewn to the side seams of the gown at the back, giving a cape effect.

The faculty may be indicated by a narrow band of silk on the breast of each side of the faculty silk of the corresponding bachelors' hood.

Bachelors

Gowns
A black stuff gown of the Oxford B.A. shape (fig. 38).

Hoods
A black stuff hood of the full shape, with a square cut cape, but the liripipe is longer and narrower than that of the Cambridge hood. All the bachelors' hoods are lined with the faculty colour and piped with a scarlet cord on the outer edge of the cowl.

Faculty Colours
B.A. (*Dramatic Studies, Musical Studies*): Lined purple (bell heather).
B.Acc.: Lined slate grey.
B.Arch.: Lined lime green.
B.D.: Lined light cherry.
B.D.S.: Lined emerald green.
B.Ed.: Lined blue (bluebell of Scotland).
B.Eng.: Lined plum.
B.Eng. (*Product Design Engineering*): As for the B.Eng. hood.
B.L. (*Law*): Bordered inside with venetian red.
LL.B. (*Law*): Lined with venetian red.
B.Mus.: Lined azure blue.
B.N.: Lined cornflower blue.
B.Sc.: Lined gold (whin blossom).
B.Sc. (*Product Design Engineering*): As for the B.Sc. hood.
B.Tech.Ed. (*Bachelor of Technological Education*): Lined plum, bordered inside with blue (bluebell of Scotland).
B.V.M.S.: Lined terracotta.

M.B., Ch.B.: Lined scarlet.
B.A. (Fine Art, Design (Glasgow School of Art)): Lined on the right side with malachite green and on the left side with swiss white silk.

Masters

Gowns
A black stuff or silk gown of the Oxford M.A. shape, except that the boot of the sleeve faces backwards (fig. 53). There is a cord and button on the yoke.

Hoods
A black silk or stuff hood, lined and edged with the faculty colour.

Faculty Colours
M.A.: Lined and edged purple (bell heather).
M.A. (Social Sciences): As for the M.A. hood.
M.Acc.: Lined and edged slate grey.
M.App.Sci.: Lined and edged gold (whin blossom).
M.Arch.: Lined and edged lime green.
M.B.A.: Lined and edged orange (Slender St Johns Wort).
M.C.C. (Master of Community Care): Lined and edged sky blue.
Ch.M.: Lined and edged scarlet. Discontinued.
M.D.S.: Lined and edged emerald green.
M.Ed.: Lined and edged blue (bluebell of Scotland).
M.Eng.: Lined and edged plum.
M.Eng. (Product Design Engineering): As for the M.Eng. hood.
M.Litt., M.Phil.: Lined and edged white.
M.Mus.: Lined and edged azure blue.
LL.M.: Lined and edged venetian red.
M.N.: Lined and edged cornflower blue.
M.P.H. (Master of Public Health): As for the M.Sc. hood.
M.Sc.: Lined and edged gold (whin blossom).
M.Sc. (Science Education, Medical Science, Veterinary Science, Adult & Continuing Education, Economics): As for the M.Sc. hood.
M.S.W. (Master of Social Work): Lined and edged sky blue.
M.Univ.Admin.: Lined and edged orange (Slender St John's Wort). Discontinued.
M.V.M.: Lined and edged terracotta.
M.F.A., M.Des. (At the Glasgow School of Art): Lined and edged on the right side with malachite green and on the left side with swiss white.

Doctors

Undress Gowns
Black silk or stuff gown with bell shaped sleeves and with a flap collar over the yoke.

Full Dress Robes
Ph.D.: The undress robe with the addition of crimson silk facings.

Higher Doctors: A scarlet cloth robe with open pointed sleeves with facings and sleeve linings of the faculty colour. Cord and button on the yoke.

Hoods
A scarlet cloth hood (except the Ph.D.), lined and edged with the faculty colour.

Faculty Colours
D.Eng.: Lined and edged plum.
D.D.: Lined and edged white.
D.D.S.: Lined and edged emerald green.
D.D.Sc.: Lined emerald green and edged yellow. Discontinued.
D.Litt.: Lined and edged purple (bell heather).
LL.D.: Lined and eddged venetian red.
D.Mus.: Lined and edged azure blue.
M.D.: Lined and edged scarlet.
D.Sc.: Lined and edged gold (whin blossom).
D.V.M., D.V.S.: Lined and edged terracotta.
D.V.M.S.: As for the D.V.M. hood.
D.Univ.: Lined black and bordered in 1" of gold ribbon.
Ph.D.: Black silk, lined and edged with crimson silk.

Academical Caps
Ph.D., Undergraduates, Bachelors, Masters: Wear a black cloth trencher (mortar board) with black tassel.
Higher Doctors: Wear a square velvet 'John Knox' cap (fig. 90).

University of Greenwich, London
(1993)

HNC & HND
Certificate and Diploma in Higher Education/Certificate in Management

Gowns
As for the bachelors' gown.

Hoods
A black art silk hood of the simple shape, fully lined with blue damask and with 2" of plain scarlet silk inside the top edge.

Bachelors

Gowns
As for the basic bachelors' gown (fig. 3).

Hoods
A black art silk hood of the full shape, part lined with scarlet woven silk and the rest lined and edged 1" on the cape with blue damask.

Post-graduate Awards

Gowns
As for the bachelors' gown.

Hoods
A black art silk hood of the full shape, partly lined with scarlet silk and with the cape lined and edged with 1" gold damask.

Masters

Gowns
As for the basic masters' gown (fig. 4).
M.Phil.: As for the basic masters' gown with facings of university woven silk.

Hoods
All Masters: A blue damask hood of the full shape, fully lined and edged 1" outside with university red woven silk.

Doctors

Full Dress Robes
Ph.D.: A gold damask robe of the London doctors' style, with sleeves and facings in university red woven silk. There are blue cords and buttons on the sleeves and on the yoke.

Honorary and *Higher Doctors*: A gold damask robe. The yoke and sleeves are of blue damask and have gold cord and buttons.

Hoods
Ph.D.: A gold damask hood of the full shape, fully lined with university woven silk and with 1" of blue damask inside the top edge.

Honorary and *Higher Doctors*: A gold damask hood of the full shape, fully lined with university woven silk and with a binding 1" inside and outside of blue damask.

Academical Caps
All Graduates: Wear a black cloth mortar board.

Ph.D.: In full dress wear a gold damask Tudor bonnet with blue cord and tassels.

Honorary and *Higher Doctors*: Wear a gold damask Tudor bonnet with red cord and tassels.

Guildhall University, London
(1993)

Like many of the new universities, Guildhall has adopted a simple system of robes, which incorporates a distinctive scarlet silk embossed with the university logo.

Undergraduates

No academical dress is worn.

Bachelors

Gowns
A black gown of the Oxford B.A. shape but the sleeves reach to the mid-forearm only.

Hoods
A black stuff hood of the Oxford Burgon pattern, fully lined with scarlet embossed silk.

Masters (Except M.Phil.)

Gowns
A black stuff gown of the Oxford M.A. shape (fig. 49).

Hoods
A black stuff hood of the Oxford Burgon shape, fully lined with scarlet embossed silk and with 1" silver birch inside the cowl.

M.Phil.

Gowns
As for the masters' gown but with facings of scarlet embossed silk.

Hoods
A scarlet embossed silk hood of the Oxford Burgon shape, fully lined with black embossed silk.

Doctors

Undress Gowns
As for the masters' gown.

Full Dress Robes

Ph.D.: A black cloth robe of the Oxford doctors' shape (fig. 62), with facings and sleeve cuffs in scarlet embossed silk.

Higher Doctorates: A scarlet cloth robe of the Oxford doctors' shape, with facings and sleeve cuffs of black embossed silk.

Hoods

Ph.D.: A scarlet embossed silk hood of the Burgon shape, fully lined with black embossed silk and with 1" silver birch inside the cowl.

Higher Doctors: A scarlet cloth hood of the Oxford doctors' shape, lined with black embossed silk and with 1" silver birch inside the cowl.

Honorary Fellows

As for the M.Phil. gown without a hood or hat.

Academical Caps

Bachelors, Masters, Doctors: In undress wear a black cloth mortar board.
Ph.D.: In full dress wear a black cloth bonnet with scarlet cord and tassels.
Higher Doctors: Wear a black velvet bonnet with scarlet cord and tassels.

Hallam University, Sheffield
(1993)

Undergraduates

No academical dress is worn.

Undergraduate Certificates, Diplomas, BTEC, HNC & HND

Gowns
As for the bachelors' gown.

Hoods
A black hood of the simple shape, partly lined with maroon and with 1" light grey border inside the cowl.

Bachelors

Gowns
As for the basic bachelors' gown (fig. 3).

Hoods
A black hood of the full shape, but with a small liripipe, partly lined with maroon and with a 1" border of light grey inside the cowl. The neckband is black lined with maroon.

Post-graduate Certificates and Diplomas

Gowns
As for the masters' gown.

Hoods
A black hood of the same shape as for bachelors, lined with light grey and with a 1" border of maroon inside the cowl. The neckband is black, lined light grey.

Masters

Gowns
As for the basic masters' gown (fig. 4).

Hoods

A black full shaped hood, of the same shape as for the bachelors', lined with maroon silk and with a 1½" border of light grey inside the cowl. The neckband is black lined with maroon.

M.Phil.

Gowns

As for the masters' black gown with 2½" facings of maroon silk.

Hoods

As for the masters' hood.

Doctors

Undress Gowns

As for the masters' gown.

Full Dress Robes

Ph.D.: A maroon robe of the Cambridge doctors' shape, with facings and sleeve linings of light grey. There is ½" of black ribbon down the outer edge of the facings.

Higher Doctorates: A maroon robe of the Cambridge doctors' shape with facings and sleeve linings of black silk. The facings have ½" of silver oakleaf lace down the outer edge.

Hoods

Ph.D.: A maroon hood of the same shape as for the bachelors lined with light grey and with ½" of black ribbon border inside the cowl.

Higher Doctors: A maroon hood of the same shape as for the bachelors lined with black silk and with ½" of silver oakleaf lace border inside the cowl.

Academical Caps

With black gowns a black cloth mortar board is worn.

Ph.D.: In full dress wear a black cloth bonnet with maroon cord and tassels.

Higher Doctors: Wear a black velvet bonnet with maroon cord and tassels.

Heriot-Watt University, Edinburgh
(1966)

Undergraduates

No academical dress is worn.

Bachelors

Gowns
As for the Cambridge M.A. gown but with an inverted-T armhole.

Hoods
A black stuff hood of the full shape, lined with silk of the faculty colour and with the cowl edged ¾" inside with gold silk.

Masters

Gowns
As for the bachelors' gown.

Hoods
As for the bachelors' hood but without the gold edge.

Doctors

Undress Gowns
As for the bachelors' gown.

Full Dress Robes
As for the London B.A.-shape robe, i.e. open pointed sleeve looped up at the elbow with a cord and button. The robe is made of corded silk in the faculty colour, see below.

Hoods
A full shaped hood made of corded silk in the faculty colour, and lined with white corded silk.

Faculty Colours
Science: *B.Sc., M.Sc., D.Sc.*: Light blue.
Engineering: *B.Sc., B.Eng., M.Sc., M.Eng., D.Sc., D.Eng.*: Dark blue.

Economic & Social Studies: *B.A., M.Litt., M.B.A.*: Purple.
   M.Sc.: Purple, with ³/₈" white edge.
   (*M.Admin.*—awarded 1968-1976, now obsolete, as M.Sc.)
Environmental Studies: *B.Sc., B.Arch., B.A., M.Sc., M.Arch., M.U.R.P.*: Red.
Art & Design: *B.A., M.Des., M.F.A.*: Burgundy moire.
Textiles: *B.Sc., B.A., M.Sc., M.Litt., D.Sc., D.Litt.*: Silver grey.
Institute of Education: *B.A., B.Ed., M.A., M.Ed., M.Sc., D.Sc., D.Litt.*: Green.
Non-Faculty: *B.A., B.Sc.*: Black with gold edge.
   D.Univ.: A gold hood lined with white.
Philosophy: *M.Phil., Ph.D.*: Magenta.

Academical Caps
All Graduates: Wear a black cloth mortar board.

University of Hertfordshire, Hatfield
1993

The University of Hertfordshire has adopted the colours grey, white, purple and dark red for its hood colours. All hoods are of the same shape and size, made of grey cloth and Aberdeen-C.N.A.A. shaped. The hoods of higher doctors are very similar to those of bachelors, both being lined with white (the former with white rayon damask, the latter with white watered silk).

The academical dress of the University of Hertfordshire may be worn by former members of the Polytechnic who took degrees from C.N.A.A. or externally from London. Members of staff may also wear Hertfordshire robes in place of those of their own university.

Undergraduates

If academical dress is required at any time, an undergraduate may wear the bachelors' gown.

Bachelors' Diploma

Gowns

As for the bachelors' gown.

Hoods

A grey stuff hood lined with grey silk.

Bachelors (B.A., B.Ed., B.Eng., B.Sc., LL.B.)

Gowns

A black stuff gown with open pointed sleeves reaching to the hem of the gown. The forearm seam is gathered and held by a black cord and button., i.e. a slightly larger version of the London B.A. sleeve.

Hoods

A grey stuff hood lined with white watered silk.

Post-graduate Diplomas

Gowns

As for the bachelors' gown.

Hoods

A grey stuff hood lined with grey silk and the 'cowl' bordered with 1" of purple watered silk.

Masters (M.A., M.B.A., M.Ed., M.Sc., LL.M.)

Gowns
A black stuff gown with closed (glove) sleeves square cut at the base, i.e. the C.N.A.A. masters' gown.

Hoods
A grey stuff hood lined with purple watered silk.

Masters of Engineering (M.Eng.)

Gowns
As for the bachelors' gown.

Hoods
A grey stuff hood lined with white silk and the 'cowl' bordered with 1" of purple watered silk.

Masters of Philosophy (M.Phil.)

Gowns
As for the masters' gown.

Hoods
A grey stuff hood lined with dark red watered silk and the 'cowl' bordered with 1" of purple watered silk.

Doctors

Undress Gowns
As for the masters' gown.

Full Dress Robes
Ph.D.: A dark red cloth robe of the Oxford doctors' shape, with 5" facings and 5" sleeve cuffs of purple watered silk.
Higher Doctors: (D.Litt., D.Sc., LL.D.) A purple stuff robe with facings and sleeve cuffs of white rayon damask.

Hoods
Ph.D.: As for the M.Phil. hood, i.e. grey stuff, lined dark red watered silk and bordered with 1" of purple watered silk.
Higher Doctors: Grey stuff hood lined white rayon damask.

Academical Caps
Undergraduates, Bachelors, Masters, Doctors, All Diplomates: In undress wear a black cloth mortar board.
Ph.D.: In full dress wear a black cloth Tudor bonnet with grey cord and tassels.
Higher Doctors: In full dress wear a black velvet bonnet with grey cord and tassels.

University of Huddersfield
(1993)

Associates, GRAD.DIP. and A.T.I.

Gowns
As for the bachelors' gown.

Hoods
A cyan blue hood of the simple shape, fully lined with turquoise.

Diplomas

Gowns
As for the bachelors' gown.

Hoods
A cyan blue hood of the simple shape, partly lined with navy blue.

Bachelors

Gowns
As for the basic bachelors' gown (fig. 3).

Hoods
A cyan blue hood of the simple shape, fully lined with navy blue and bordered with 1" of the faculty colour.

Post-graduates

Gowns
As for the bachelors' gown.

Hoods
A cyan blue hood of the simple shape (but 4" larger than bachelors), fully lined with the cape edged in navy blue.

Masters

Gowns
As for the basic masters' gown (fig. 4).

Hoods

A cyan blue hood of the simple shape (as for the post-graduate), lined navy blue and the cowl bordered with 2" of the faculty colour.

Faculty Colours

Arts: White.
Education: Grey.
Law: Lilac.
Engineering: Red.
Science: Yellow.
Music: Pink.
M.B.A.: Orange.
Philosophy: Maroon.

M.Phil.: A cyan blue hood of a larger simple shape, lined with navy blue, and bordered with 4" of maroon.

Doctors

Full Dress Robes

As for the masters' gown made in cardinal red, with cyan blue facings. The yoke is also cyan blue with a cardinal red cord and button.

Hoods

Ph.D.: A cyan blue hood of a larger simple shape, lined with navy blue and bordered with 3" of maroon (i.e. the M.Phil. hood).
D.Litt., D.Sc., Honorary Doctors: A cyan blue hood of a larger simple shape, lined with navy blue and bordered with 3" of old gold satin.

Academical Caps

All Graduates: In undress wear a black flexible mortar board.
Ph.D: In full dress wear a black cloth bonnet with a cyan blue tassel.
Higher Doctors: In full dress wear a cardinal red bonnet with an old gold tassel.

University of Hull
(1954)

Hull has adopted turquoise blue as its university colour, and this silk is used to line all the hoods, and for the facings and sleeve cuffs of doctors' robes. Gowns and robes for B.D., all masters and all doctors are equipped with corded silk strings, as for Cambridge. These are black for gowns and scarlet or claret for full dress robes.

In the original scheme of dress, faculties were indicated by coloured cords and buttons on the yoke and forearm gathers. These were: Arts (silver), Science (rich gold), Law (blue), Theology (scarlet), Music (cream), Economic Science (grey), Education (white). Faculty colours have now been abolished and replaced by black cords and buttons.

Undergraduates

A black gown in Russell cord or ribbed rayon of the London undergraduate pattern (fig. 10).

Bachelors

Gowns

B.D., B.Phil., B.A.(Ed.): A black gown in Russell cord, ribbed rayon, poplin or corded ottoman silk of the Oxford M.A. pattern.

Other Bachelors: A black gown of the London B.A. shape, the sleeves reaching to the hem of the gown (fig. 42).

Hoods

B.D., B.Phil., B.A.(Ed.): A black superfine cloth hood of the Oxford doctors' shape, lined with the university silk.

Other Bachelors: A black hood of ribbed rayon, poplin or corded ottoman silk of the Oxford Burgon pattern lined with the university silk.

Masters

Gowns

M.Th.: A ribbed rayon, poplin or corded ottoman silk, Oxford M.A. gown.

M.Mus.: A black ribbed rayon, poplin or corded ottoman silk gown of the Oxford lay pattern, the flap collar trimmed with a row of gimp, the inverted-T armholes have a single row of gimp; one panel of gimp on each sleeve and one panel of gimp astride the central seam at the back.

Other Masters: A ribbed rayon, poplin or corded ottoman silk as for the Oxford M.A. gown.

Hoods

M.Th.: As for the B.D. hood.
M.Mus.: A cream silk brocade hood of the Oxford Burgon pattern, lined with university silk.
Other Masters: A black ribbed rayon, poplin or corded ottoman silk hood of the London full shape, fully lined with the university silk and the cape edged 3/8" with the same silk.

Doctors

Undress Gowns

Ph.D.: As for the masters' gown with a single row of Cambridge miniature lace round the armhole.
D.Mus.: As for the M.Mus. gown.
Other Doctors: As for the masters' gown with two rows of Cambridge miniature lace round the armhole.

Full Dress Robes

Ph.D.: A claret cloth robe in the Oxford doctors' shape with facings and sleeve cuffs of the university silk.
D.Mus.: A figured cream silk brocade, or damask robe of the Oxford doctors' shape with facings and sleeve cuffs of the university silk.
Other Doctors: A scarlet superfine cloth robe of the Oxford doctors' shape with facings and sleeve cuffs of the university silk.

Hoods

Ph.D.: A claret cloth hood of the Oxford doctors' shape lined with university silk.
D.Mus.: A cream silk brocade hood of the Oxford doctors' shape lined with the university silk.
Other Doctors: A scarlet superfine cloth hood of the Oxford doctors' shape lined with the university silk.

Academical Caps

Undergraduates, Bachelors, Masters, Doctors: In undress wear a black cloth mortar board.
Ph.D.: In full dress wear a black cloth Tudor bonnet with claret cord and tassels.
D.D.: In full dress wear a soft square velvet cap without tuft or tassel (Cranmer cap), fully lined with scarlet silk.
Other Doctors: In full dress wear a black velvet Tudor bonnet with scarlet cord and tassels.

Humberside University, Hull
(1993)

Undergraduates

No academical dress is worn.

Diplomas

Gowns
As for the bachelors' gown.

Hoods
A black polyester hood of the simple shape, partly lined in blue and with the cowl bound with yellow. The neckband is not edged.

Bachelors

Gowns
As for the basic bachelors' gown (fig. 3).

Hoods
A black art silk hood of the simple shape, fully lined with blue and the cowl bound ½" inside and outside with yellow. The neckband is not edged.

Post-graduate Diplomas

Gowns
As for the bachelors' gown.

Hoods
A black art silk hood of the simple shape, fully lined in blue and with the cowl bound 1" with yellow inside and outside. The neckband is also edged on both edges with ½" of yellow.

Masters

Gowns
A black gown of the basic masters' shape (fig. 4).

Hoods
Taught Masters: A blue art silk hood of the simple shape, fully lined with blue, and with the cowl partly lined with yellow. The neckband is bound, top and bottom with yellow.

M.Phil.: A claret hood of the full shape, fully lined with blue and with the cape and cowl edged in blue. The neckband is also edged top and bottom with blue.

Honorary Masters (M.Univ.): A blue art silk hood of the simple shape, fully lined in yellow. The cowl is bound 2" inside and ½" outside in blue. The bottom of the neckband is also blue.

Doctors

Full Dress Robes

Ph.D.: A claret coloured panama robe of the Cambridge doctors' shape, but with pointed sleeves. The sleeve linings and facings are of blue. There are claret cords and blue buttons on the sleeves and yoke.

Honorary Doctors (D.Univ.): A scarlet panama robe of the same shape as for the Ph.D. The sleeves and facings are of blue. There are scarlet cords and blue buttons on the sleeves and yoke.

Hoods

Ph.D.: A claret panama hood of the full shape, fully lined and the cape and cowl edged in blue. The neckband is edged top and bottom in blue.

Honorary Doctors: A scarlet panama hood of the full shape, fully lined and edged with blue. The neckband is edged top and bottom with blue.

Academical Caps

Diplomates, Bachelors, Masters, Doctors: In undress wear a black flexible mortar board.

Ph.D.: Wear a black cloth bonnet with blue cord and tassels.

Honorary Doctors: Wear a black velvet bonnet with blue cord and tassels.

Ushers

Wear a mid-blue polyester gown of the same shape as for London B.A. (fig. 42). This has yellow cords and buttons on the sleeves and yoke. No hood or hat is worn.

John Moores University, Liverpool
(1993)

Like many of the new universities, John Moores has adopted a special silk—in this case grey—embossed with the university coat of arms. This makes the hoods and robes unique and specific to this institution.

Undergraduates

No academical dress is worn.

HNC, HND and College Awards

Gowns
A dark blue gown of the Oxford B.A. shape.

Hoods
A dark blue hood of the simple shape, fully lined with the grey embossed silk.

Bachelors

Gowns
A dark blue gown of the Oxford B.A. shape.

Hoods
A dark blue hood of the full shape, partly lined with the grey embossed silk.

Masters

Gowns
A dark blue, C.N.A.A. patterned gown with glove sleeves (fig. 4).

M.Phil.: Wear the masters' gown with the addition of the grey embossed silk facings.

Hoods
All Masters (including *M.Phil.*): Wear a dark blue hood of the full shape, fully lined with grey embossed silk.

Doctors

Undress Robes
As for the masters' gown.

Full Dress Robes
Ph.D.: A scarlet cloth robe of the Cambridge doctors' style, the facings and sleeve linings are of blue embossed silk.
Higher Doctors: Have not been decided yet.

Academical Caps
With the dark blue gown, a dark blue mortar board is worn.

Ph.D.: In full dress wear a blue velvet bonnet with scarlet cord and tassels.

Members of Council

A dark blue robe of the same shape as for the Ph.D. but with the facings and sleeve linings of the grey embossed silk. With this robe, a blue cloth bonnet with silver cord and tassels is worn.

University of Keele
(1962)

The main innovation of this university has been to dispense with the traditional scarlet full dress robe of doctors, in favour of a purple cloth one. Following the Cambridge system, the Ph.D. has only coloured facings (in this case gold cloth) to distinguish it from the masters.

Undergraduates

A black gown of the London undergraduates pattern (fig. 10).

Bachelors

Gowns
A black stuff gown of the Oxford B.A. pattern, except that the forearm seam is shorter and there are no buttons and loops at the wrist.

Hoods
B.A., B.Soc.Sc., B.Sc.: A black stuff hood of the full shape, bordered inside with 5" of gold, and piped on the top edge of the neckband and cowl with the university red cord.
B.Ed.: A black stuff hood of the full shape, bordered with 5" of silver, and piped on the neckband and cowl in university red.

Masters

Gowns
As for the Oxford M.A. gown with a gimp lace frog above each armhole.

Hoods
All Masters: A black silk hood of the full shape, lined with university red silk. The cowl and neckband piped with gold cord.

Doctors

Undress Gowns
As for the masters' gown.

Full Dress Robes
Ph.D.: As for the masters' robe but with facings of gold cloth.
Higher Doctors: A purple cloth robe of the Cambridge doctors' shape with plain facings piped with gold cord. The sleeves are lined with a lighter shade of purple, and they are held with a gold cord and button.

Academical Caps
Bachelors, Masters, Doctors: In undress wear a black cloth mortar board.
Ph.D.: In full dress wear a black velvet bonnet with university red cord and tassels.
Higher Doctors: Wear a black velvet bonnet with gold cord and tassels.

University of Kent, Canterbury
(1966)

The 'Hoods' were designed by a dressmaker—Hardie Amies—and hence do not conform to the standard pattern. They cannot correctly be called hoods, since they have no cowl. Each consists of a heart-shaped cape with no cowl. A V-shaped panel of velvet in the centre denotes the faculty. There is no neckband, but the two sides are held together by a cord with a button at each end, these being also of the faculty colour, except for the M.Phil.

Undergraduates

As for the bachelors' gown.

Gowns
B.A., B.Sc., LL.B., B.Eng.: A black stuff gown of the Cambridge B.A. shape but without the forearm open seam, i.e. the basic bachelors' gown (fig. 3).

Hoods/Capes
These are of the shape described in the introduction, and are of silver. The V-shaped velvet panel in the centre shows the faculty colour.

Faculty Colours
Natural Science (*B.Sc.*): Purple.
Social Sciences: (*B.A., LL.B.*): Grey.
Humanities (*B.A.*): Green.
Information Technology (*B.A., B.Sc., B.Eng.*): Royal blue.
Education (*B.Ed.*): Red.
Degrees from Accredited Colleges: Blue.

Masters

Gowns
A black stuff gown with Tudor bag sleeves, the bottom of the sleeve cut square (fig. 4).

Hoods/Capes
The same shape as for the bachelors but in gold cloth, and with the V-shaped panel of velvet in the faculty colour:

Faculty Colours
Natural Science (*M.Sc., M.Phil., M.Biotech.* [Biotechnology]): Purple.

Social Sciences (*M.A., M.B.A., M.E.B.A.* [European Business Admin.], *M.B.S.* [Business Studies], *M.Phil., LL.M., M.Sc.*): Grey.
Humanities (*M.A., M.Phil.*): Green.
Information Technology (*M.A., M.Sc., M.Phil.*): Royal blue.

Note: For M.Phil., the buttons and cord are wine coloured.

Doctors

Undress Gowns
As for the masters' gown.

Full Dress Robes
Ph.D.: A black stuff gown of the masters' pattern but with facings of scarlet velvet, 2½" wide.
Higher Doctors (D.D., D.Litt., D.Sc., LL.D.): A scarlet cloth robe of the Oxford doctors' pattern with scarlet velvet facings 5" wide and with two bands of scarlet velvet on the sleeves.
D.C.L.: As for other higher doctorates but with purple velvet in place of the scarlet velvet.

Hoods/Capes
Ph.D.: A cardinal red cloth hood the same shape as for the bachelors. The V-shaped panel and the cord and buttons are in the faculty colour.
Higher Doctors (D.D., D.Litt., D.Sc., LL.D.): As for the Ph.D. hood but the outer part is in scarlet cloth.
D.C.L.: A black velvet panel.
D.Mus.: A green velvet panel (as for Humanities).

Academical Caps
Bachelors, Masters, Doctors: In undress wear a black cloth mortar board with black tassel.
Ph.D.: In full dress wear a black cloth Tudor bonnet and maroon cord and tassels.
Higher Doctors: A black velvet bonnet with maroon cord and tassels.
D.C.L.: A black velvet bonnet with gold silk cord and tassels.
D.Mus.: A black velvet bonnet with maroon cord and tassels.

Note: D.C.L. and D.Mus. are conferred as Honorary Degrees only.

Kingston University

(1993)

This university has decided to use the style of gown worn by continental universities. This does not apply to the hats and hoods, which are still of British design!

Sub-degrees

Gowns
The style is similar to that worn by the University of Dusseldorf, i.e. plain black with sleeves like those of a coat, and facings which are continued round the neck to form a collar.

Hoods
A grey panama hood of the full shape, fully lined in mid-blue. The neckband is grey on both sides.

Bachelors

Gowns
A Dusseldorf shaped gown, i.e. with coat-style sleeves and facings which continue round the neck as a collar. The facings are 2½" and are made of mid-blue art silk.

Hoods
A grey panama hood of the full shape, fully lined in mid-blue. The neckband is grey both sides.

Post-graduates

Gowns
Dusseldorf shaped, i.e. with coat-style sleeves in black polyester. There are 4" facings in mid-blue which continue round the yoke.

Hoods
A grey panama hood of the full shape, fully lined in blue. The neckband is grey on both sides.

Masters

Gowns
The shape is that of the Cologne style, in black polyester, with facings of 5½" at the top to 7½" at the bottom, of which the outer edge has four mid-blue pleats (2"

at the top to 4" at the bottom) the inner edge of polyester. The sleeve cuffs are mid-blue.

Hoods
A grey panama hood of the full shape and fully lined in mid-blue. The neckband is grey both sides.

Honorary Masters

Gowns
The shape is similar to that of Cologne. It is of mid-blue panama with facings of 5½" at the top becoming 7½" at the bottom, of which the outer edge has four black pleats (2" at the top to 4" at the bottom) the inner edge is in mid-blue. The sleeve cuffs are black.

Hoods
A grey panama hood of the full shape, fully lined in mid-blue. The outer cape has a 1" tape on it, 1" from the edge. The neckband is grey both sides.

Doctors

Full Dress Robes
Ph.D.: The shape is similar to that of the Cologne Faculty of Law. It is of grey panama, with facings of 5½" at the top to 5½" at the bottom, of which the outer edge has four mid-blue pleats (2" at the top to 4" at the bottom), the inner edge is grey panama. The cuffs are mid-blue.
Honorary and *Higher Doctors*: The shape is that of the Cologne Faculty of Law. It is of mid-blue panama, with facings of 5½" at the top to 7½" at the bottom, of which the outer edge has four grey pleats (2" at the top, 4" at the bottom). The inner edge is mid-blue. The cuffs are mid-blue.

Hoods
Ph.D.: Wear a full shaped hood in grey panama and fully lined in mid-blue. The neckband is grey on both sides.
Honorary and *Higher Doctors*: Wear a full shaped hood in grey panama and fully lined in mid-blue. The outer cape has a 1" tape placed 1" from the edge.

Academical Caps
All Graduates: Wear a black cloth mortar board.
Ph.D.: In full dress, wear a grey panama cloth bonnet with mid-blue tassels and cord.
Honorary and *Higher Doctors*: Wear a blue panama bonnet with grey tassels and cord.

Lancaster University
(1966)

The University's official colours are Lancaster red (pillar box red) and Quaker grey (very pale grey). These are to be found also in the academical dress.

Undergraduates
No academical dress is worn.

Bachelors and M.Eng.
Gowns
As for the Cambridge B.A. gown without the forearm slit.

Hoods
B.A.: A black ribbed rayon hood of an improved Burgon pattern, fully lined in grey taffeta. The cowl is bordered inside with ½" of Lancaster red taffeta.
LL.B.: As for the B.A. hood with the addition of ½" dark blue band inside the cowl, ½" from the red band.
B.Mus.: As for the B.A. hood with the addition of ½" light blue band inside the cowl, ½" from the red band.
B.Ed.: As for the B.A. hood with the addition of ½" white band, ½" from the red band.
B.Sc.: As for the B.A. hood with the addition of ½" gold band, ½" from the red band.
B.Eng.: As for the B.A. hood with the addition of ½" tangerine band, ½" from the red band.
B.Phil.: As for the B.A. hood with the addition of ½" green band, ½" from the red band.
B.B.A.: As for the B.A. hood with the addition of 1" royal blue band, ½" from the red band.

Masters
Gowns
M.A., LL.M., M.Sc., M.Phil., M.B.A. M.Mus.: Black stuff or silk with Tudor bag sleeves, the bottom of the sleeve is cut at an angle of 45 degrees from a semi-circular cut-out portion to the back (frontispiece, c).
M.Litt.: As for the M.A. with the addition of two rows of 1" velvet sewn vertically above each armhole, 1½" long, mitred at the top, and ½" between each row.

Hoods
M.A.: A black rayon or silk hood of the Cambridge full shape, lined with Lancaster red, and with a binding 1½" wide inside and outside the cowl only of grey.

LL.M.: As for the M.A. hood with purple binding instead of grey.
M.Sc.: As for the M.A. hood with gold binding instead of grey.
M.Phil.: As for the M.A. hood with Lancaster red binding instead of grey.
M.Litt.: As for the M.A. hood with blue binding instead of grey.
M.B.A.: As for the M.A. hood with dark blue binding instead of grey.
M.Mus.: As for the M.A. hood with light blue binding instead of grey.
M.Eng.: As for the B.A. hood with a 2" band of tangerine silk ½" from the red band.

Doctors

Undress Gowns

Ph.D.: As for the M.A. gown with one row of 1" braid round the armhole and round the yoke.
Higher Doctors: As for the M.A. gown with two rows of 1" braid round the armholes and round the yoke.

Full Dress Robes

Ph.D.: A grey cloth robe of the full shaped Cambridge doctors' style with sleeve linings and facings in Lancaster red cloth, the sleeve turnbacks held by grey cords and buttons. There is a red cord and button on the yoke.
LL.D.: As for the Cambridge doctors' robe in Lancaster red cloth, the sleeve linings and facings in grey taffeta. The cords and buttons are red.
D.Litt.: As for LL.D. robe but the sleeve linings and facings are in blue.
D.Sc.: As for LL.D. robe but the sleeve linings and facings are in gold.
D.Mus.: As for LL.D. robe but with sleeve linings and facings in cream damask.

Hoods

Ph.D.: A Lancaster red cloth hood of the Cambridge full shape, lined with Lancaster red taffeta.
LL.D.: As for the Ph.D. hood but lined in grey taffeta.
D.Litt.: As for the Ph.D. hood but lined in blue taffeta.
D.Sc.: As for the Ph.D. hood but lined in gold taffeta.
D.Mus.: As the for Ph.D. hood but lined in cream damask.

Academical Caps

Male *Graduates:* Wear a black cloth mortar board.
Female *Graduates:* Wear a soft black Oxford square cap, or a mortar board.
Ph.D.: In full dress, wear a black cloth bonnet with red cord and tassels.
Higher Doctors: Wear a black velvet bonnet with red cord and tassels.

Post-graduate Diploma

Gowns

As for the bachelors' gown.

Hoods

A black ribbed rayon hood of the C.N.A.A. shape lined grey with the cowl bound in Lancaster red.

University of Leeds

(1904)

All Leeds hoods incorporate one or more of the three shades, dark, mid- or light green, and the Ph.D. is unique among British graduates in having a green full dress robe.

Undergraduates

As for the Oxford scholars' gown (fig. 8).

Bachelors

Gowns

As for the basic bachelors' gown (fig. 3), with the addition of a vertical strip of Cambridge miniature lace over the forearm seam from wrist to shoulder and round the yoke. This gown is also worn by M.Eng.

Hoods

A green silk hood of the simple shape.

B.A.: Dark green, lined dark green.

B.A. (Collegiate): Dark green, lined dark green with a 1" edge of mid-green on the outside. No longer awarded.

B.Mus.: Dark green, lined dark green with a 1" edge of white on the outside. No longer awarded.

B.D.: Dark green, lined white with a 1" edge of scarlet on the outside. No longer awarded.

B.Comm.: Light green, lined dark green. No longer awarded.

B.Ed.: Dark green, lined dark green with a 1" edge of light green outside.

LL.B.: Light green, lined light green.

B.Health Sc.: Middle green, lined middle green with a 1" edge of light green outside.

B.Sc.: Middle green, lined middle green.

B.Sc.: (Collegiate) Middle green, lined middle green with a 1" edge of dark green outside. No longer awarded.

B.Eng.: Middle green, lined dark green.

M.B., Ch.B.: Dark green, lined light green.

B.Ch.D.: Dark green, lined middle green.

Masters

Gowns

As for the Oxford M.A. but with the crescent cut on both sides of the sleeve bottom (fig. 54). There is a strip of Cambridge miniature lace round the yoke.

Hoods

These are the same shape and materials as for the bachelors' hood.

M.A.: Dark green, lined white.
M.Mus.: Dark green, lined white with a 1" white edge on the outside.
M.Ed.: Dark green, lined white with a 1" band of middle green on the white.
M.B.A.: Light green, lined white and edged in dark green.
M.Comm.: As for the M.B.A hood. No longer awarded.
LL.M.: Light green, lined white.
M.Sc.: Middle green, lined white.
M.Sc.Eng.: Middle green, lined white with a 1" border of dark green on the white.
M.Pub.Health: Dark green, lined light green with a 1" band of dark green on the light green.
M.Psychotherapy: Dark green, lined light green with a 1" band of white on the light green.
M.Med.Sc.: Dark green, lined white with 1" light green on the white.
M.Ch.: Dark green, lined white and edged in light green.
M.D.Ch.: Dark green, lined white and edged in middle green.
M.Dent.Sc.: Dark green, lined and edged white with 1" dark green on the white.
M.Eng.: Middle green, lined dark green with a 1" edge of dark green outside.
M.Phil.: A black stuff or silk hood of the full shape, lined middle green and piped with scarlet round the cowl.

Doctors

Undress Gowns

As for the masters' gown.

Full Dress Robes

Ph.D.: A mid-green robe of the Cambridge doctors' shape with sleeve linings and facings of mid-green. The facings have a narrow piping of scarlet down the centre.
Other Doctors: A scarlet robe of the Cambridge doctors' shape with sleeve linings and facings as follows:

D.D.: Sleeve linings are dark green and the facings, white.
D.Mus.: Sleeve linings and facings are dark green with 1" white watered silk on the green, 1" from the outside edge.
D.Litt.: Sleeve linings and facings are dark green.
LL.D.: Sleeve linings and facings are light green.
D.Sc.: Sleeve linings and facings are mid-green.
D.Eng.: Sleeve linings and facings are middle green with a 1" edge of dark green.
M.D.: Sleeve linings and facings are dark green, edged with light green.
D.D.Sc.: Sleeve linings are dark green and facings are middle green.

Hoods

These are of the full shape.

Ph.D.: Middle green, lined with middle green and piped with scarlet.

D.D: Scarlet, lined dark green bound white.
D.Mus.: Scarlet, lined dark green with 1" white watered silk on the green 1" from the edge.
D.Litt.: Scarlet, lined dark green.
D.Sc.: Scarlet, lined middle green.
LL.D.: Scarlet, lined light green.
D.Eng.: Scarlet, lined middle green with 1" dark green, 1" from the edge.
M.D.: Scarlet, lined dark green edged light green.
D.D.S.: Scarlet, lined dark green bound mid-green.

Academical Caps

Bachelors, Masters, Doctors: In undress, wear a black cloth mortar board.
Ph.D.: In full dress, wear a black velvet bonnet.
Other Doctors: In full dress, wear a black velvet bonnet with gold cord and tassels, and with a lining of green in the shade of the faculty.

Leeds Metropolitan University
(1993)

Diplomas

Gowns
A black gown of the bachelors' shape.

Hoods
A gold art silk hood of the simple shape, the cowl partly lined with blue. There is no edging.

Bachelors

Gowns
As for the basic bachelors' gown (fig. 3).

Hoods
A gold art silk hood of the simple shape, fully lined and edged with blue.

Masters

Gowns
A plain black gown of the basic masters' shape (fig. 4).

Hoods
A gold art silk hood of the simple shape (although 4" larger), fully lined and edged with 2" of blue.

Post-graduates

Gowns
A plain black gown of the bachelors' style.

Hoods
A gold art silk hood of the simple shape, fully lined and edged with 1" of blue. The cape has a gold tape 1" on the inside.

Honorary Masters

Gowns
A plain black gown of the style as for the masters with gold art silk facings, and with a gold cord and button on the yoke.

Hoods
A gold art silk hood of the simple shape (but 4" larger), fully lined and with the cowl edged with 2" of blue. This hood is identical with the taught masters.

M.Phil.

Gowns
A plain black gown of the masters' style.

Hoods
A gold art silk hood of the full shape, fully lined with blue. The neckband is not edged.

Ph.D.

Full Dress Robes
A London shaped robe with the body of the robe in claret panama, with blue facings, and the sleeves lined with gold art silk.

There is a blue cord and button on the yoke. (This gown is also worn by the D.Univ.)

Hoods
A gold art silk hood of the full shape, fully lined with the cape edged in blue. The neckband is not edged. (This hood is identical to the M.Phil. hood.)

Academical Caps
All Graduates: In undress, wear a black mortar board.
Ph.D.: Wear a black cloth bonnet with a dark blue tassel and cord.

Leicester University

(1957)

Leicester has adopted a deep cherry shade which it calls university red, and incorporates it into all its hoods. The same shade is used for doctors' full dress robes, in place of the more usual scarlet. Masters and doctors wear a very small, full shaped hood—a modified Aberdeen shape—without a liripipe, doctors wearing the corresponding masters' hood inside out.

Undergraduates

A black gaberdine gown of the Oxford scholars' shape, with the forearm seam left open. The sleeves and back are ruched but not pleated in the usual way.

Bachelors

Gowns

A black stuff gown of the Oxford B.A. shape except that the forearm seam is shorter, i.e. reaches to the elbow only and not to the wrist.

Hoods

A university red silk hood of a small simple shape, lined with the following degree colours:

B.A., M.A., M.Phil., D.Litt.: Silver grey.
B.Sc., M.Sc., D.Sc.: Royal blue.
LL.B., LL.M., LL.D.: Black.
M.B., Ch.B., M.D.: Turquoise blue.
B.Ed., M.Ed., M.Ed.Studies: Tartan green.
B.Phil.(Ed.): Silver grey, bordered and edged tartan green.
B.Med.Sci.: Turquoise blue bordered and edged royal blue.
B.Mus., M.Mus., D.Mus.: Cream brocade.
B.Eng.: Purple.
M.B.A.: Gold.
M.B.A.(Education): Gold bordered and edge tartan green.

Masters

Gowns

A black stuff gown of the Oxford M.A. shape, except that there is a crescent-shaped cut on both sides at the bottom of the sleeve, and an inverted-T armhole (fig. 55).

SPECIFICATIONS: LEICESTER 147

Hoods
A university red silk hood of a special full shape (figs. 80 and 81), lined with the degree colour (see above under bachelors' hoods).

Doctors

Undress Gowns
Ph.D.: As for the masters' gown with a row of black Birmingham doctors' braid down the facings and round the yoke (frontispiece, d).
Higher Doctors: As for the Ph.D. gown with the addition of a flap collar trimmed with braid round the edge.

Full Dress Robes
Ph.D.: As for the black undress gown with red braid in place of the black braid.
Other Doctors: A lightweight university red cloth robe of the Oxford doctors' shape. The facings and sleeve cuffs are of the degree colour.

Hoods
Ph.D.: The same shade and shape as for the masters' hood, but lined with a lighter shade of university red watered taffeta.
Other Doctors: The same shape as for the masters' hood, made in the degree colour and lined with university red watered taffeta.

Academical Caps
Undergraduates, Bachelors, Masters, Ph.D., Other Doctors: In undress, wear a black-cloth mortar board.
Higher Doctors: In full dress wear a black velvet modified biretta.

See also Nene College.

University of Liverpool
(1903)

Only a single black gown is used at Liverpool for all graduates and undergraduates alike, this being the Cambridge M.A. gown. The system of hoods is logical—the masters wearing the bachelors' hoods without the fur; thus the splendour of the hood is reduced for the higher degree.

Undergraduates

Not normally used by undergraduates, but if necessary the graduate gown is worn.

Bachelors

Gowns

As for the Cambridge M.A. gown with a cord and button on the yoke.

Hoods

All hoods of the University of Liverpool are of the same simple shape. Bachelors' hoods are of black cloth, lined with the faculty colour (below) and edged with fur.

B.A. (*Arts, Social and Environmental studies, Law*): Lined with apple-blossom and edged in white fur.
B.Phil. (*Arts, Education and Affiliated Institutions*): Lined with yellow.
B.Sc. (*Science, Medicine, Affiliated Institutions*): Lined with slate blue.
M.B., Ch.B.: Lined with lavender.
B.D.S.: Lined with dark red and edged with white fur.
LL.B.: Lined with bronze silk and edged with white fur.
B.Clin.Sc., B.Nurs., B.Sc.Med.: Lined with lavender (no fur).
B.Comm. (with Brighton University): Lined citron. No longer awarded.
B.Eng.: Lined with orange.
B.V.Sc.: Lined with grey.
B.Arch.: Lined with white and with two narrow lines of black velvet on the white.
B.Des.: Lined with silver grey.
B.Ed.: Lined green.

Masters

Gowns

As for the bachelors' gown.

Hoods

A black cloth or corded silk hood of the simple shape, lined with the following faculty colour.

M.A., M.Phil.: Apple-blossom.
M.Mus.: Blue.

M.Ar.Ad.: Yellow, with two narrow lines of black velvet.
M.Sc.: Slate blue.
M.Sc.(Med.): Lavender silk.
Ch.M., M.Ch.Orth., M.Ch.Otol., M.Clin.Psychol., M.Comm.H., M.Obstet.Gynaec., M.Psy.Med., M.Rad., M.Trop.Med., M.D.S., M.Dent.Sci.: Dark red.
LL.M.: Bronze.
M.Eng.: Orange, with one broad line of white.
M.Sc. (Eng.): Orange.
M.V.Sc.: Grey.
M.Anim.Sc.: Terracotta silk.
M.A. (Social & Enviromental Studies): Yellow.
M.Arch.: White, with two lines of black velvet.
M.A. (Education): Yellow.
M.Ed.: Green.
M.T.D.: White, with one line orange velvet.
M.C.D.: White, with one broad line of black velvet.
M.B.A.: Gold, with one broad line of white ribbon.
M.P.A.: White, edged with one broad line of scarlet ribbon.
M.Comm.: Citron.
M.Des.: Silver grey.

Doctors

Undress Gowns

As for other graduates, i.e. the Cambridge M.A. gown with cord and button on the yoke.

Full Dress Robes

Ph.D.: A scarlet cloth robe of the Cambridge doctors' shape with facings and sleeve linings of black silk and with a narrow band of scarlet velvet ⅝" wide on the black, ½" from each edge.
Higher Doctors: A scarlet cloth robe of the Cambridge doctors' shape with sleeve linings and facings of the faculty colour.

Hoods

Ph.D.: Scarlet cloth lined with black silk and bound with scarlet velvet.
D.Mus.: Scarlet cloth lined with blue silk.
Litt.D.: Scarlet cloth lined with apple-blossom silk.
D.Sc.: Scarlet cloth lined with slate blue silk.
M.D.: Scarlet cloth lined with lavender silk.
LL.D.: Scarlet cloth lined with bronze silk.
D.Eng.: Scarlet cloth lined with orange silk.
D.V.Sc.: Scarlet cloth lined with grey silk.

Academical Caps

Bachelors, Masters, Doctors: In undress wear a black cloth mortar board.
Higher Doctors: In full dress wear a black velvet mortar board.

University of London

(1836)

At London University, great importance is attached to membership of convocation, and distinctions are made between the academical dress of members and non-members of convocation. Bachelors who are not members of convocation have only a 3" border of colour inside a black hood, whereas members have a full lining of white silk in addition to the faculty colour. Doctors' full dress robes are worn only by members of convocation, non-members being restricted to a black gown and hood.

Undergraduates

Any matriculated internal or external student is entitled to wear the undergraduate gown. It is of the standard type with open pointed sleeves, the point of the sleeve not to come below the knee (fig. 10).

Bachelors

Gowns

B.A., B.Sc., B.Comm.*, B.Ed., B.H.*, B.Eng.: A black stuff gown of the Cambridge B.A. shape, except that there is no armhole, and the forearm seam is gathered at the elbow and held by a black cord and button (fig. 42).

B.D.: As for the B.A. gown with the addition of a black cord and sarum red button on the yoke.

B.Mus.: A black-flap collar gown with Tudor bag sleeves, the bottom of the sleeve being hollowed out to a double ogee curve. If a member of convocation, the B.Mus. may wear this gown in light blue corded silk.

LL.B.: As for the B.Mus. gown but with the bottom of the sleeve cut square, and a slit behind as in the Q.C. gown.

M.B., B.S., B.D.S., B.Pharm., B.Vet.Med.: As for the B.Mus. gown but in black only (fig.47).

Hoods

As for the full shape Cambridge hood but with the corners of the cape rounded off. Bachelors (except B.Mus.) have a black stuff or silk hood bordered 3" inside and edged ⅜" outside the cowl with the faculty colour. Bachelors who are members of convocation may also have the hood fully lined with white silk in addition to the faculty colour.

SPECIFICATIONS: LONDON

Faculty Colours
B.A.: Russet brown.
B.D.: Sarum red.
LL.B.: Blue.
M.B., B.S.: Violet.
B.D.S.: Olive green.
B.Pharm.: Old gold.
B.Vet.Med.: Lilac.
B.Sc.: Gold.
B.Eng: Turquoise.
B.Comm.*: Deep orange.
B.Ed.: Eau-de-Nile green.
B.H.: Pale pink (Humanities).
B.Mus.: Light blue corded silk bordered and edged with white watered silk.

Masters

Gowns
M.A., M.Sc., M.Eng., M.B.A., M.Ed., M.Comm.*: As for the Cambridge M.A. gown with the bottom point of the sleeve rounded off to form a double ogee curve.
M.Th.: As for the M.A. gown but with a black cord and sarum red button on the yoke.
LL.M.: As for the LL.B. gown.
M.Mus., M.S., M.D.S., M.Pharm., M.Vet.Med.: As for the M.B. gown.
M.Phil.: The same shape as for the masters in the same faculty.

Note: The following, if members of convocation, may wear a coloured gown:
M.S.: Violet corded silk.
M.D.S.: Olive green corded silk.
M.Mus.: Light blue corded silk.
M.Phil.: A claret coloured ribbon 1" wide down the outside edge of the gown facings.

Hoods
All Masters: (except M.Mus. and M.Phil.) Wear a black corded silk hood fully lined and edged with the faculty colour. Masters who are members of convocation may add a border 1½" wide, of white silk, inside the cowl.

Faculty Colours
M.A.: Russet brown.
M.B.A.: Fawn.
M.Comm.*: Deep orange.
M.D.S.: Olive green.
M.Ed.: Eau-de-nil green.
M.Eng.: Turquoise.
LL.M.: Blue.

M.Pharm.*: Old gold.
M.S.: Violet.
M.Sc.: Gold.
M.Th.: Sarum red.
M.Vet.Med.*: Lilac.
M.Mus.: Medium blue corded silk, lined with white watered silk.
M.Phil.: Black, lined with claret silk and all edges bound ½" with the faculty colour.

Doctors

Undress Gowns

D.D.: As for the M.Th. gown.
D.Lit., D.Sc.: As for the M.A. gown.
LL.D.: As for the LL.B. gown.
M.D., D.Vet.Med., D.Mus.: As for the M.B. gown.

Full Dress Robes

(Only for doctors who are members of convocation)

Ph.D.: A claret cloth robe of the Cambridge doctors' shape, except that the sleeve ending is pointed and not rounded off. The facings and sleeve linings are of a lighter shade of claret and there is a 1" wide band of the faculty colour down the facings.

Higher Doctors: A scarlet cloth robe of the same shape as for the Ph.D., the sleeve linings and facings of the faculty silk.

Hoods

Ph.D.: Claret cloth, lined with a lighter claret silk. All edges are bound ½" with the faculty colour.
D.D.: Scarlet, lined sarum red.
D.Lit.: Scarlet, lined russet brown.
LL.D.: Scarlet, lined blue.
D.Mus.: Scarlet, lined white watered silk.
M.D.: Scarlet, lined violet.
D.Vet.Med.: Scarlet, lined lilac.
D.Sc.: Scarlet, lined gold.

Academical Caps

Undergraduates, Bachelors, Masters, Doctors: In undress wear a black cloth mortar board. Women may wear a soft black cloth cap of the Oxford pattern.
Ph.D.: In full dress wear a black cloth bonnet with claret cord and tassels.
Higher Doctors: In full dress wear a black velvet bonnet with cord and tassels of the faculty colour.

Note: * These degrees are no longer awarded.

University of Loughborough

(1966)

Undergraduates

A black stuff gown of the Oxford scholars' shape.

Bachelors

Gowns

A black stuff gown of the London B.A. shape (fig. 42).

Hoods

A purple stuff hood of the full shape, lined with the following degree colour.

B.A.: Dark green taffeta.
B.Ed.: Green-grey taffeta.
B.Sc.: Grey taffeta.
B.Sc.Engineering: As for the B.Sc. hood with 1" purple ribbon on lining 1½" from the edge.
B.Tech.: Yellow taffeta.
B.Tech.Engineering.: As for the B.Tech. hood with 1" purple ribbon on lining 1½" from the edge.

Masters

Gowns

A black stuff gown of the London M.A. shape (fig. 56).

Hoods

As for the bachelors' hood with the addition of ½" of edging in the degree colour all round the hood.

M.A.: Purple, lined and edged with dark green.
M.B.A.: Purple, lined and edged with peach.
M.Ed.: Purple, lined and edged with grey-green.
M.Eng. (first degree): Purple, lined and edged with lilac.
M.Library Studies.: Purple, lined and edged with dark red.
M.Phil.: Purple, lined white and edged all round with 1" purple.
M.Sc.: Purple, lined and edged with grey.
M.Tech.: Purple, lined and edged with yellow.

Doctors

Undress Gowns

As for the masters' gown.

Full Dress Robes

Ph.D.: As for the masters' gown in purple stuff.
Higher Doctors: A scarlet cloth robe of the Oxford doctors' shape with sleeves and facings of university purple silk and with a 1" stripe of the degree colour down the inner edge of the facings and round the cuff of the sleeve.

Hoods

Ph.D.: a purple stuff hood of the full shape, lined and edged 1" all round with maroon taffeta.
Higher Doctors: A full shaped hood in the degree colour, lined and edged 1" all round with scarlet taffeta.
D.Litt.: Dark green, lined and edged scarlet.
D.Sc.: Grey, lined and edged scarlet.
D.Tech.: Yellow, lined and edged scarlet.

Academical Caps

Undergraduates, Bachelors, Masters, Doctors: For men in undress, a black cloth mortar board. For women either a mortar board or a soft black cloth square hat.

* For 'Luton University' see p. 243

University of Manchester
(1903)

There is a complete system of faculty colours at Manchester, where bachelors' hoods are lined with fur and edged with the faculty colour—a reversal of the usual arrangement. This breaks down with some bachelors' degrees—such as M.B. and LL.B.—where no fur is used, but a wide border of the faculty silk.

There is only one full dress robe and one hood which is used by all doctors, no faculty colours being indicated. The robe has glove sleeves of the same shape as for masters—a most unusual shape for doctors.

Undergraduates

No academical dress is worn.

Bachelors

Gowns

B.Arch., B.D., B.Landscape Design, B.Linguistics, M.B., B.D.S., B.Planning, B.Town and Country Planning: As for the masters' gown.
Other Bachelors: As for the Cambridge B.A. gown.

Hoods

A black woollen cord or silk hood of the Burgon shape (except for B.Mus.).

B.Arch., B.L.D., B.Ling., B.Pl., B.T.C.Pl.: Bordered with 2" of pale blue silk.
B.A.: With 8" white fur and bordered with 2" of pale blue.
B.A. in Accounting and Law: With 2" fur and bordered with violet.
B.A. in Economics and Politics, Commerce, Administration, Economic and Social Studies, B.Soc.Sc., B.A. Finance: With 2" fur and bordered with orange silk.
B.A. in Music, Town and Country Planning: With 2" fur and bordered with pale blue.
B.A. in Education: Double edged in pale blue and bluish-green with fur in between.
B.A. in Theology, B.A. in Religious Studies: With 2" fur and bordered with heliotrope.
B.A. or B.Sc. (Board of Part Time Education): With 2" fur and bordered with silver silk.
B.D.S.: With 2" fur and bordered with fawn silk.
B.D.: With 2" fur and bordered with heliotrope.
B.Ed.: With 2" fur and bordered with bluish-green silk.
LL.B.: With a 2" border of violet silk.

M.B.: With a 2" border of red silk.
B.Nurs.: With fur and with a 2" border of red silk.
B.Sc. in Education: With a double edging of salmon silk and bluish-green silk with fur in between.
B.Sc.: With 2" fur and bordered with salmon silk.
B.Tech.Sc., B.Sc.Tech.: With 2" fur and bordered with terracotta.
B.Mus.: A dark blue silk hood, bound by 2" inside and outside the cowl with light blue silk.

Masters

Gowns

As for the Oxford M.A. gown with the lower point removed to form a right angle and the upper point forming an acute angle (fig. 57).

Hoods

A black silk hood the same shape as for the bachelors and lined and edged with the faculty colour.

Faculty Colours

M.A., M.Sc. (Board of Part Time Studies): Silver silk.
M.A., M.A. in Landscape Design, Urban Design, M. Town and Country Planning, M.Linguistics, M.Phil. in Arts: Pale blue.
M.A. in Economics and Politics, Commerce, Administration, Economic & Social Studies, European Community Studies: Orange.
M.Mus.: Dark blue silk.
M.Mus. (Performance): Dark blue with a narrow border of gold inside the cowl.
M.A. in Theology, M.Phil. in Theology: Heliotrope.
M.B.A., M.B.Sc., M.Phil. in Business Admin.: Gold.
M.Dent.S.: Fawn.
M.Ed., M.Phil. in Education: Bluish-green silk.
M.A. in Ed.: Bluish-green, edged 2" pale blue.
LL.M., M.Juris., M.Phil. in Law: Violet silk.
M.Sc. in Education: Bluish-green with a 2" border of salmon.
M.Sc. in Medicine: Red with a 2" border of salmon silk.
M.S.: Red silk.
M.Sc.: Salmon silk.
M.Tech.Sc., M.Sc.Tech.: Terracotta silk.
M.Eng.: With a 2" border of terracotta.
M.Eng in Science: A 2" border of salmon
M.Eng in Tech and M.Phys.: A 2" border of terracotta.

Doctors

Undress Gowns

As for the masters' gown.

Full Dress Robes
All Doctors: A scarlet cloth robe of the same shape as for masters, i.e. a glove sleeve. The facings of the robe and the fronts of the glove sleeves below the armhole are of pale gold silk.

Hoods
All Doctors (that is D.Dent.Surg., D.D., LL.D., D.Litt., M.D., D.Mus., Ph.D., D.Sc.): A gold hood of satin serge or velvet lined with a lighter shade of gold silk.

Academical Caps
Bachelors, Masters, Doctors: In undress wear a black cloth mortar board.
Doctors: In full dress wear a black velvet bonnet with a black ribbon and a bow.

U.M.I.S.T.

University of Manchester Institute of Science and Technology

1955

The degrees awarded by this Institute are those of the parent body, i.e. the University of Manchester. However U.M.I.S.T. has its own Chancellor and Vice-Chancellor and awards its own honorary degrees.

Honorary Graduates

Robes
M.Sc.: A black robe of the London doctors' style, i.e. with pointed sleeves, with collar and facings of terracotta silk.
D.Sc.: A navy blue russell cord robe of the London doctors' style, with sleeve linings of cream silk, the sleeves held with a cream button and cord.
D.Eng.: As for D.Sc. but the facings and sleeve linings of blue silk.

Hoods
These are of the full shape, but with the cape being pointed instead of the usual square cut.
M.Sc.: Black russell cord lined with terracotta silk.
D.Sc.: Navy blue lined with cream silk.
D.Eng.: Navy blue lined with mid-blue silk.

Academical Caps
M.Sc.: A black mortar board.
D.Sc.: A navy blue bonnet with cream cord and tassels.
D.Eng.: A navy blue bonnet with mid-blue cord and tassels.

Manchester Metropolitan University
(1993)

A very simple system of gowns and hoods is used by this university. Hoods are of blue with an edge or lining of red silk embossed with the university logo.

Undergraduates

No academical dress is worn.

Holders of Certificates or Diplomas

Gowns
As for the bachelors' gown.

Hoods
A blue silk hood of the simple shape, bordered with plain red silk and lined with blue satin.

Bachelors and M.Eng.

Gowns
As for the basic bachelors' gown (fig. 3). This gown is also worn by holders of Certificates, Diplomas and the M.Eng. degree. The gown is worn 12" off the ground.

Hoods
A blue silk hood of the full shape, without the liripipe, partly lined with the university red crested silk.
Also worn by M.Eng.

Masters
(Except M.Eng.)

Gowns
As for the basic masters' gown, i.e. a glove sleeve with square cut end (fig. 4). It is worn 8" off the ground.

Hoods
A blue silk hood of the full shape, fully lined with university red crested silk.

SPECIFICATIONS: MANCHESTER METROPOLITAN

Doctors

Undress Gowns

As for the masters' gown.

Full Dress Robes

Ph.D., Higher and *Honorary Doctors, Honorary Fellows of the University*: Wear a blue panana robe of the Cambridge doctors' shape with facings and sleeve linings of university red crested silk.

Hoods

Ph.D.: A blue panama hood of the full shape, fully lined and edged 1" all round the outside with university red crested silk.
Higher Doctors: As for the Ph.D. but edged with 2" of university red crested silk.
Honorary Fellows: No hood is worn.

Academical Caps

Diplomas, Certificates, Bachelors, Masters' Degrees, Doctors: In undress wear a black cloth mortar board. Women holders may opt for the Oxford soft cap.
Ph.D.: In full dress wear a black cloth bonnet with cord and tassels of red-blue.
Higher and Honorary Doctors: In full dress wear a black velvet bonnet with cord and tassels as for the Ph.D. cap.
Honorary Fellows: Wear a black mortar board.

Queen Margaret College, Edinburgh

(1994)

Diplomas

Gowns
As for the bachelors' gown.

Hoods
A green hood of the simple shape, lined in dark blue.

SCOTVEC

Gowns
As for the bachelors' gown.

Hoods
A blue hood of the simple shape, lined with white and edged in red SCOTVEC Jacquarded silk.

Bachelors

Gowns
As for the basic bachelors' gown (fig. 3).

Hoods
A dark blue hood of the simple shape, lined with green and bound in white.

Post-graduates

Gowns
As for the masters' gown.

Hoods
A green hood of the simple shape, lined with dark blue and bound in white.

Masters

Gowns
As for the basic masters' gown (fig. 4).

Hoods

A green hood of the simple shape, lined with white and bound with dark blue.

Doctors

Ph.D.: Not yet decided.
Higher Doctors (*Arts & Business*): A blue panama robe of the Cambridge style with facings and sleeve linings in white.
Higher Doctors (*Science*): A green panama robe of the Cambridge style with facings and sleeve linings in white.

Hoods

Ph.D.: Not yet decided.
Higher Doctors (*Arts & Business*): A blue panama hood of the simple shape, lined with white and bound in blue.
Higher Doctors (*Science*): A green panama hood of the simple shape, lined with white and bound in green

Academical Caps

All Graduates: Wear a black cloth mortar board.
Higher Doctors (*Arts and Business*): Wear a dark blue velvet bonnet with white cord and tassels.
Higher Doctors (*Science*): Wear a dark green velvet bonnet with white cord and tassels.

Middlesex University
(1993)
Undergraduates
No academical dress is worn.

Diplomas, Certificates, B.TEC (HND/HNC)

Gowns

As for the London undergraduate gown in black polyester.

Hoods

Diplomas, Certificates: No hood is worn.
B.TEC (HND/HNC): A scarlet hood of the simple shape, lined with dark blue.

Bachelors

Gowns

B.A., B.Ed., B.Eng., LL.B., B.Sc.: As for the London B.A. gown (fig. 42).
B.Phil.: As for the London B.A. gown in black polyester with 1" of red ribbon down the front facings.

Hoods

A black silk hood of the full shape, partly lined with the university red silk, and the cowl edged with the faculty colour.

Faculty Colours

B.A.: White.
B.Sc.: Dark blue.
B.Ed.: Green.
LL.B.: Light blue.
B.Eng.: Purple.
B.Phil.: No faculty binding is used.

Post-graduate Courses

Gowns

As for the masters' gown in royal blue stuff.

Hoods

As for the bachelors' hood nearest to the course, e.g. PGCE wears B.Ed. and P.G. in Computer Technology wears B.Sc.

SPECIFICATIONS: MIDDLESEX

Masters

Gowns
Taught Masters: As for the basic masters' gown (fig. 4) in royal blue polyester.
M.Phil.: As for the masters' gown (see above) with university red facings.
M.Univ.: As for the masters' gown but in grey worsted.

Hoods
A black silk hood of the full shape, fully lined with university red silk and bound all round with the following faculty colour.

Faculty Colours
M.A.: White.
M.Sc.: Dark blue.
M.Ed.: Green.
LL.M.: Light blue.
M.Eng.: Purple.
M.B.A.: Yellow.
M.Phil.: Royal blue, lined red with no faculty colour.
M.Univ.: Grey worsted, lined with university red.

Doctors

Undress Gowns
As for the masters' gown.

Full Dress Robes
Ph.D.: A scarlet robe of the London doctors' shape, i.e. pointed sleeves, the facings and sleeve linings of university red.
Higher Doctors: A grey panama robe of the London doctors' shape, the facings and sleeve linings of university red and with a stripe of the faculty colour down the outer edge of the facings.
Honorary Doctors: A grey panama robe of the London doctors' shape with facings and sleeve linings of university red. No faculty colours.

Hoods
Ph.D.: A grey panama hood of the full shape, lined and edged ¼" all round with university red silk.
Higher Doctors: A grey panama hood of the full shape, lined in university red and bound all round with the faculty colour.
Honorary Doctors: A grey panama hood, lined and edged with university red.

Academical Caps
Diplomas, Certificates, Bachelors, Post-graduates, Taught Masters, M.Phil., Doctors: In undress wear a black cloth mortar board.
M.Univ.: Wear a grey cloth mortar board.
Ph.D., Honorary Doctors: Wear a black cloth Tudor bonnet with Middlesex red silk cord and tassels.
Higher Doctors: Wear a black velvet bonnet with Middlesex red cord and tassels.

Napier University, Edinburgh

(1993)

Undergraduates

No academical dress is worn.

HNC/HND

Gowns

As for the basic bachelors' gown with Napier tartan piping down the outer edge of the facings. There is also a black, blue and white twisted cord on the yoke with a black button.

Hoods

A black cloth hood of the simple shaped, fully lined with claret silk with the top edge bound with 1½" of white silk.

Bachelors

Gowns

As for the HNC/HND gown.

Hoods

B.A.: A black cloth hood of the full shape, fully lined and bound on the cape with 1½" of Alice blue silk.
B.Sc.: A black cloth hood of the full shape, fully lined and bound on the cape with 1½" of imperial purple silk.
B.Ed.: A black cloth hood of the full shape, fully lined and bound on the cape with 1½" of forest green silk.
B.Eng.: A black cloth hood of the full shape, fully lined and bound on the cape with 1½" of yellow silk.

Post-graduate Certificates and Diplomas

Gowns

As for the HNC/HND gown.

Hoods

Arts: A black cloth hood of the full shape, fully lined and bound on the cape edge with ½" of Alice blue.

Science: A black cloth hood of the full shape, fully lined and bound on the cape edge with ½" of Imperial purple.
Education: A black cloth hood of the full shape, fully lined and bound on the cape edge with ½" of forest green.
Engineering: A black cloth hood of the full shape, fully lined and bound on the cape edge with yellow.
Business: A black cloth hood of the full shape, fully lined and bound on the cape edge with ½" of rust silk.

Masters

Gowns

M.A., M.Sc., M.B.A.: As for the basic masters' gown with facings covered in Napier vertical striped silk and the outer edge of facings piped yellow cord. There is a twisted cord of black, blue and white on the yoke, with a black button.
M.Phil.: As for the basic masters' gown with facings covered in Napier red silk and the outer edge of facings piped in Napier tartan.

Hoods

M.A.: A black cloth hood of the full shape, fully lined and bound 1½" on cape edge with Alice blue silk.
MSc.: A black cloth hood of the full shape, fully lined and bound 1½" on cape edge with imperial purple silk.
M.B.A.: A black cloth hood of the full shape, fully lined and bound 1½" on cape edge with rust silk.
M.Phil.Arts: As for the M.A. hood.
M.Phil.Science: As for the M.Sc. hood.
M.Phil.Education: A black cloth hood of the full shape, fully lined and bound 1½" on cowl edge with forest green silk.
M.Phil.Engineering: A black cloth hood of the full shape, fully lined and bound 1½" on cape edge with yellow silk.
M.Phil.Business: As for the M.B.A. hood.

Full Dress Robes

A black robe of the Cambridge shape, the facings and sleeve linings are of Napier red silk with the outer edges piped with Napier tartan. There is a twisted cord of black, blue and white on the yoke together with a black button.

Hoods

Ph.D.Arts: As for the M.A. hood.
Ph.D.Science: As for the M.Sc. hood.

No academical caps are prescribed, nor any academical dress for higher doctors.

Nene College, Northampton

Diplomas

Gowns
As for the basic bachelors' gown (fig. 3).

Hoods
A mid-blue hood in a modified Aberdeen shape, fully lined with college green silk.

All other awards are validated by Leicester University and wear the academical dress of that university.

University of Newcastle
(1963)

Originally founded as the Newcastle upon Tyne School of Medicine, it eventually became one division of the federal University of Durham. In 1963 the Universities of Durham and Newcastle upon Tyne Act dissolved the federal organisation, each part becoming a separate university and each awarding its own degrees. Since degrees in medicine, dentistry and architecture were awarded only to Newcastle students, the academical dress for these faculties have been retained from the Durham system. The black gowns of graduates are exactly the same as for Durham, but new hoods have been designed for faculties which exist in both Universities.

Undergraduates

A black rayon or cord gown of the Oxford scholar's shape with an open forearm seam.

Bachelors

B.A., B.Arch., B.Sc., LLB., B.Eng., B.Med.Sci.: A black gown of the Oxford B.A. shape with the forearm seam left open for 6" to 8" from the wrist and held together with a loop of tape and a button (fig. 41).

M.B., B.S., B.D.S.: A black gown with long closed sleeves. These are decorated with four rows of gimp from the shoulder to elbow, and the sleeve also has two consecutive squares of gimp at the foot (fig. 46).

Hoods
B.A.: Black stuff trimmed with fur and edged with old gold.
M.B., B.S.: Scarlet silk lined palatinate purple bound with fur.
B.Arch.: As for the B.A hood.
B.Sc.: Black stuff trimmed with fur and edged with royal blue.
LL.B.: Maroon silk lined palatinate purple and edged with fur.
B.D.S.: Rose silk lined ivory white silk and edged with fur.
B.Med.Sci.: As for the B.Sc. hood.
B.Eng.: Black stuff lined royal blue edged with fur.
B.Phil.: Black stuff lined with old gold.

Masters

Gowns

M.A., M.B.A., M.Ed., M.Eng., M.F.A., M.Int.Hsng.Sc., M.Litt., M.L.D., M.Med.Sc., M.Mus., M.Phil., M.Sc., M.T.P., LL.M.: A black gown with glove sleeves, i.e. like the Oxford M.A., and with a cord and button on the yoke.

Hoods

M.A.: Black stuff lined with old gold.
M.Litt.: As for the M.A. hood.
M.Phil.: Black stuff lined with scarlet silk.
M.Mus.: As for the M.A. hood.
M.Sc.: Black stuff lined with royal blue.
M.Ed.: As for the M.A. hood.
LL.M.: Maroon Silk lined with palatinate purple silk.
M.F.A.: As for the M.A. hood.
M.B.A.: As for the M.Sc. hood.
M.Eng.: As for the M.Sc. hood.
M.Int.Hsg.Sc.: As for the M.A. hood.
M.Med.Sc.: As for the M.Sc. hood.
M.T.P.: As for the M.A. hood.
M.L.D.: As for the M.A. hood.
M.Sc.(Int.Grad.Development Sc.): Black stuff lined with grey, faced with maroon.

Doctors

Undress Gowns

Doctors: In undress, wear the masters' gown.

Full Dress Robes

Ph.D.: As for the M.A. gown but with facings of white silk and with a border of scarlet silk.
D.Eng.: A scarlet cassimere robe of the Oxford shape (fig. 62) with sleeves and facings of royal blue.
D.D. (Honorary only): Scarlet cassimere with sleeves and facings of palatinate purple. A white scarf is worn with this robe.
D.Mus. (Honorary only): Scarlet cassimere with sleeves and facings of old gold.
LL.D.: Scarlet cassimere with sleeves and facings of maroon.
D.D.S.: Scarlet cassimere with sleeves and facings of rose silk, the facings having an edge of ivory together with a border across the bottom of the sleeve.
D.D.Sc. (Honorary only): As for the D.D.S. robe.
D.Litt.: Scarlet cassimere faced with old gold silk.
D.Ch. (Honorary only): Scarlet cassimere with sleeves and facings of rose silk. The facings have an edge of palatinate purple down the outer side and across the bottom of the sleeve.
M.D.: Scarlet cassimere with sleeves and facings of scarlet silk. There is a border down the outside of the facings and across the bottom of the sleeve of palatinate purple.

D.Sc.: Scarlet cassimere with sleeves and facings of scarlet silk.
D.C.L. (Honorary only): Scarlet cassimere with the sleeves and facings of white silk.

Hoods
Ph.D.: Scarlet cassimere lined with scarlet silk.
D.Eng.: Scarlet cassimere lined with royal blue.
D.D.: Scarlet cassimere lined with palatinate purple.
*D.Mu*s.: Scarlet cassimere lined with brocaded white silk.
LL.D.: Scarlet cassimere lined with maroon silk.
D.D.S.: Scarlet cassimere lined rose silk and edged with ivory.
D.D.Sc.: As above.
D.Litt.: Scarlet cassimere lined white and edged with old gold.
D.Ch.: Scarlet cassimere lined with rose silk and faced, palatinate.
M.D.: Scarlet cassimere lined scarlet, faced, palatinate.
D.Sc.: Scarlet cassimere lined with white and edged in royal blue silk.
D.C.L. (Honorary only): Scarlet cassimere lined with white silk.

Academical Caps
All Graduates: In undress, wear a black mortar board.
D.C.L., D.D.: In full dress, wear a soft square black velvet cap with a white tuft.
All Other Doctors: In full dress, wear a soft square velvet cap with a black tuft.

University of Northumbria, Newcastle
(1993)

HNC/HND & Certificates in Education

Gowns
A black gown of the London B.A. style (fig. 42) as for the bachelors.

Hoods
A black hood, amended from the Aberdeen shape and lined in university red.

Bachelors

Gowns
A black gown of the London B.A. style (fig. 42).

Hoods
A black hood, amended from the Aberdeen shape, partly lined with university red and bound 1" with gold.

Post-graduates

Gowns
The basic masters' gown with the facings trimmed with gold.

Hoods
A black hood of the full shape, partly lined with university red, and bound with gold silk.

Masters

Gowns
The basic masters' gown with the facings trimmed with gold moire.

Hoods
A black hood of the full shape, lined with university red and bound with gold moire.

Honorary Masters

Full Dress Robes
A light blue cloth robe of the doctors' style with facings of gold moire silk.

Hoods
A light blue hood of the full shape, lined with university red and bound with gold moire silk.

Masters of Philosophy

Full Dress Robes
A bright blue robe in the doctors' style with fronts trimmed with gold silk.

Hoods
A bright blue hood of the full shape, lined in university red and bound with gold silk.

Doctors of Philosophy

Full Dress Robes
As for the M.Phil. robe.

Hoods
As for the M.Phil. hood but with both cowl and cape bound with gold silk.

Higher Doctors

Full Dress Robes
A light blue cloth robe of the Cambridge doctors' style with facings and sleeve linings of gold moire silk.

Hoods
A light blue cloth hood of the full shape, lined with university red and with cape and cowl bound with gold moire silk.

Academical Caps
All Graduates: Wear a black cloth mortar board.
Ph.D.: In full dress, wear a bright blue cloth bonnet with gold tassels.
Higher Doctors: Wear a light blue cloth bonnet with gold tassels.

The University of North London

(1993)

HNC/HND

Gowns
As for the bachelors' gown.

Hoods
As for the B.TEC hood (scarlet lined blue).

University Awards

Gowns
As for the bachelors' gown.

Hoods
A blue hood of the full shape, bordered with narrow strip of university red satin.

Bachelors

Gowns
As for the basic bachelors' gown (fig. 3).

Hoods
A blue hood of the full shape, partly lined with university red satin.

Post-graduate Awards

Gowns
As for the bachelors' gown.

Hoods
A blue hood of the full shape, fully lined with university red satin.

Masters

Gowns
As for the basic masters' gown (fig. 4).

SPECIFICATIONS: NORTH LONDON 173

Hoods
As for the post-graduates' hood.

Honorary Masters

Gowns
As for the basic masters' gown with facings of university red satin.

Hoods
As for the masters' hood.

Doctors of Philosophy

Full Dress Robes
A university blue robe of the Cambridge shape with facings and sleeve linings of university red satin.

Hoods
A university blue hood of the full shape, lined and edged with university red satin.

Higher Doctors

A university red robe of the Cambridge shape with facings and sleeve linings of university blue satin.

Academical Caps
All Graduates: Wear a black cloth mortar board.
Ph.D.: In full dress wear a blue cloth bonnet with red cord and tassels.
Higher Doctors: Wear a red velvet bonnet with blue cord and tassels.

Fellows of the University

As for the masters' gown in university red with facings and a cape collar trimmed with university blue.

The University of Nottingham
(1948)

The University of Nottingham has a completely straightforward system of academical dress, using a set of faculty colours and a university colour. Unfortunately bachelors are allowed a hood only partly lined with the faculty and university colours. The black gowns of all graduates are copied directly from Cambridge without any modification.

Undergraduates

A black stuff gown of the Cambridge shape (fig. 37).

Bachelors

Gowns
B.D: A stuff or silk gown of the Cambridge M.A. style (fig. 48).
Other Bachelors: As for the Cambridge B.A. gown (fig. 37).

Hoods
A black stuff hood of the full shape.
B.D.: Lined with university blue silk and bound 1" inside and ½" outside with the faculty colour, purple.
Other Bachelors: Bordered with 3" of university blue silk and bound 1" inside and ½" outside with the following faculty colour.

Faculty Colours
Arts: Cherry red.
Divinity: Purple.
Laws: Maroon.
Music: Pink.
Education: Lilac.
Pharmacy: Dove grey.
Science: Royal blue.
Agriculture & Horticulture: Green.
Engineering: Light navy blue.
Architecture: Orange.
Medicine: Gold.

Masters

Gowns

A black stuff or silk gown of the Cambridge M.A. pattern (fig. 48).

Hoods

A black stuff or silk hood of the full shape, lined with university blue silk and bound 1" inside and ½" outside with the faculty colour.

Doctors

Undress Gowns

Ph.D.: As for the Cambridge M.A. gown with 4" of Birmingham doctors' lace over the armhole.

Higher Doctors: As for the Cambridge M.A. gown with a row of lace along the full length of the armhole.

Full Dress Robes

Ph.D.: A claret cloth robe of the Cambridge doctors' shape with facings 3" wide in the university blue silk.

Higher Doctors: A scarlet cloth robe of the Cambridge doctors' shape with facings in university blue silk.

Hoods

Ph.D.: A claret silk or cloth hood lined with the university blue silk and bound 1" inside and ½" outside with the faculty colour.

Higher Doctors: A scarlet silk or cloth hood lined with the university blue silk and bound 1" inside and ½" outside with the faculty colour.

Academical Caps

Undergraduates, Bachelors, Masters, Doctors: In undress wear a black cloth mortarboard. Women may wear a soft Oxford cap.

Ph.D.: In full dress wear a round black cloth bonnet.

Other Doctors: In full dress wear a round black velvet bonnet.

The Open University

(1969)

The system of academical dress worn by graduates of the Open University is based on the two colours of blue and gold. No academical dress is worn by undergraduates.

Bachelors

Gowns

B.A., B.Phil.: A dark blue gown with special sleeves which are unique to the Open University. They are miniature glove sleeves with an inverted-T armhole and a square-cut end to the sleeve.

Hoods

B.A.: A light blue Russell cord hood of the simple shape, faced gold inside the cowl.
B.Phil.: A royal blue Russell cord hood of the simple shape, faced inside the cowl with gold.

Masters

Gowns

As for the bachelors' shape but made of light blue Russell cord.

Hoods

M.A., M.Sc.: A dark blue panama hood of the full shape, fully lined and edged gold.
M.Phil.: A light blue Russell cord hood of the full shape, fully lined and edged gold.
M.Univ.: A gold panama hood of the full shape, fully lined and edged royal blue.

Doctors

Ph.D., D.Sc., D.Litt.: A royal blue panama robe, with facings of gold silk.
Doctors of the University (*Honorary*): A robe made entirely of gold cloth.

Hoods

Ph.D.: A royal blue panama hood of the full shape, fully lined and edged gold.
D.Sc.: A gold panama hood of the full shape, fully lined and edged light blue.
D.Litt.: A gold panama hood of the full shape, fully lined with royal blue.
D.Univ.: A royal blue hood of the full shape, fully lined with light blue.

Academical Caps

Academical caps, a mortar board for bachelors, and a bonnet for doctors, are officially part of the dress of graduates, but are not worn or carried on these occasions.

University of Paisley
(1993)

Undergraduates

No academical dress is worn.

Bachelors

Gowns

As for the basic bachelors' gown (fig. 3).

Hoods

A black cloth hood of the full shape with the cowl bordered inside with red Paisley brocade.

Masters

Gowns

As for the basic masters' gown (fig. 4).

Hoods

A black cloth hood of the full shape, fully lined with red Paisley brocade.

Doctors

Full Dress Robes

Ph.D.: A black cloth robe of the Cambridge doctors' shape with facings and sleeve linings of red Paisley brocade.

Higher Doctors: A red Paisley brocade robe with facings and sleeve linings of the same material.

Hoods

Ph.D.: black cloth hood of the full shape, fully lined and edged on the cape and cowl with red Paisley brocade.

Higher Doctors: As for the Ph.D hood.

Honorary Fellows

Gowns

A black cloth gown with facings and a flap collar of red Paisley brocade.

Honorary Masters

Gowns

As for the masters' gown in silver grey, with facings of red Paisley brocade.

Hoods

The silver grey cloth hood of the full shaped, fully lined with red Paisley brocade.

Honorary Doctors

Full Dress Robes

A red Paisley brocade robe of the Cambridge shape.

Hoods

A black cloth hood of the full shape, fully lined and bound round the cape and cowl with red Paisley brocade.

University of Plymouth
(1993)

HNC, Certificates and Diplomas

Gowns
The black traditional Oxford B.A. shape, with pointed sleeves.

Hoods
A blue hood of the simple shape, partly lined with black and terracotta.

Bachelors and M.Eng.

Gowns
As for the Oxford B.A. gown.

Hoods
A blue hood of the full shape, partly lined with terracotta.

Masters

Gowns
M.Phil.: A black traditional gown of the Cambridge M.A. style with facings of terracotta silk.
Other Masters' Degrees: A black gown of the Cambridge M.A. style.

Hoods
M.Eng., M.Math.: A blue hood partly lined with terracotta silk. The cowl is edged with ½" of black ribbon.
Other Masters: A blue hood of the full shape, fully lined and edged ¼" round the cowl and cape with terracotta silk.
Post-graduate Certificates: As for the bachelors' hood with 1" silver ribbon above the terracotta.

Doctors

Full Dress Robes
Ph.D.: A terracotta panama robe of the Cambridge doctors' style with facings and sleeves trimmed with university blue silk.

Higher Doctorates: A terracotta panama robe of the Cambridge style with facings and sleeves covered with university blue silk and ½" of silver oakleaf down the facings.

Hoods

Ph.D.: A terracotta silk hood of the full shape, fully lined and edged with blue panama.

Higher Doctorates: A terracotta silk hood of the full shape, fully lined and edged 1½" all round with blue panama, and the cowl trimmed with ½" of silver oakleaf lace.

Academical Caps

Certificates, Diplomas, Bachelors, Masters: Wear a black cloth mortar board.

Ph.D.: Wear a black cloth tudor bonnet with a terracotta cord and tassels.

Higher Doctors: Wear a black velvet bonnet with terracotta and silver cord and tassels.

University of Portsmouth

(1993)

Certificates in Education and Higher Education

Gowns
As for the B.A. gown. No hood is prescribed.

Diplomas in Higher Education

Gowns
As for the B.A. gown.

Hoods
A black cloth hood of the Burgon shape, lined in blue-purple taffeta. The strap, cowl and cape are edged ³/₈" with blue-purple.

University Diplomas

Gowns
As for the B.A. gown.

Hoods
A black cloth hood of the Burgon shape, lined with white taffeta. The strap, cowl and cape are edged ³/₈" with white.

Post-graduate Certificates in Education

Gowns
As for the B.A. gown.

Hoods
A black cloth hood of the full shape lined in blue-purple taffeta. The cowl is edged with 1" of mid-cherry ribbon. The strap is lined and edged ³/₈" top and bottom with blue-purple.

Post-graduate Certificates

Gowns
As for the B.A. gown.

Hoods

A black cloth hood of the full shape lined in blue-purple taffeta. The cowl is edged on the outside with 1" of grey ribbon.

Bachelors

Gowns

All Bachelors (except B.Arch.): Wear the Oxford B.A. gown.

B.Arch.: As for the M.A. gown i.e. a glove sleeve gown with a square cut sleeve end.

Hoods

B.Arch.: A black imitation silk hood of the full shape. The hood is lined in lilac taffeta with the cape edged 1" in lilac. The cape is edged with silver Benet lace 1" next to the lilac.

B.A.: A black cloth hood of the full shape, but smaller than those used by doctors and masters. It is lined and the cape is edged with blue-purple taffeta and 1" of white ribbon next to the blue-purple.

B.Eng.: As for the B.A. hood but with 1" of maroon ribbon in place of the white.

LL.B.: As for the B.A. hood but with 1" of light cherry ribbon in place of the white.

B.Mus.: As for the B.A. hood but with 1" of cream ribbon in place of the white.

B.Nurs.: As for the B.A. hood but with 1" of mid-blue ribbon in place of the white.

B.Sc.: As for the B.A. hood but with 1" of scarlet ribbon in place of the white.

B.Sc.Econ.: As for the B.A. hood but with 1" of old gold ribbon in place of the white.

B.Ed.: As for the B.A. hood but with 1" of shot pink ribbon in place of the white.

Masters

Gowns

M.A., M.A.(Educ.), M.B.A., M.Mus., M.Sc., M.Eng.: A black gown of the basic masters' shape (fig. 4).

M.Phil.: A black cloth gown of the basic masters' shape, the facings are edged each side with ½" of silver Benet braid. The armhole is similarly edged.

M.Arch.: A black gown as for the M.A. but with silver Benet lace on the outside of the facings only.

LL.M.: A black cloth gown as used by Queen's Counsel, with flap collar and inverted-T armhole.

Hoods

M.Phil.: A blue-purple imitation silk hood of the full shape, lined with dove grey taffeta. The cape is also edged with 1" dove grey. The strap is lined dove grey and edged ³⁄₈" top and bottom.

M.Arch.: As for the M.Phil. hood but the lining is of lilac taffeta.

M.A.: As for the M.Phil. hood but the lining is of white taffeta.

M.A.(Educ.): As for the M.Phil. hood except that the lining is of mid-cherry.

M.B.A.: As for the M.Phil. hood except that the lining is of old gold.
LL.M.: As for the M.Phil. hood except that the lining is of light cherry taffeta.
M.Mus.: As for the M.Phil. hood except that the lining is of cream damask.
M.Sc.: As for the M.Phil. hood except that the lining is of scarlet taffeta.
M.Eng.: As for the M.Phil. hood except that the lining is of maroon taffeta.

Doctors

Full Dress Robes

Ph.D.: A scarlet polyester robe with glove sleeves cut in the Cambridge style, i.e. with a single pointed boot. The robe is faced with blue-purple, and has silver Benet braid down each side of the facings. The fronts of the sleeves are covered with blue-purple taffeta below the horizontal armhole.

D.Univ.: A blue-purple robe of the Cambridge doctors' style. The facings, which are edged on both sides with ½" of Benet braid, and the sleeves are of grey taffeta. There is a silver button and cord holding the sleeves in place.

D.D.: A blue-purple robe of the same style as D.Univ., except that the facings and sleeves are of red-purple. The sleeves are held by a red-purple cord and button and the facings are edged on both sides with ½" of purple and gold Benet braid.

D.Mus.: A cream damask robe of the Cambridge shape, the facings and sleeves being in blue-purple. The facings are edged both sides with ½" of purple and gold Benet braid. The sleeves are held with a blue-purple cord and button.

D.Sc.: A blue-purple robe of the Cambridge style with sleeves and facings of scarlet taffeta. The facings have silver Benet braid on both sides, and the sleeves are held by a scarlet cord and button.

LL.D.: A blue-purple robe of the Cambridge style with sleeves and facings of light cherry taffeta. The facings are edged with ½" of silver Benet lace, and the sleeves are held in place by a light cherry cord and button.

D.Litt.: A blue-purple robe in the Cambridge style with facings and sleeve linings of white taffeta. The facings are edged on both sides with ½" of silver Benet lace and the sleeves are held with a white cord and button.

Hoods

Ph.D.: A scarlet polyester worsted hood of the full shape, lined in blue-purple taffetta. The hood is edged with 1" blue-purple taffeta and there is 1" silver Benet braid next to the blue-purple. The strap is lined with blue-purple and edged ³/₈" both top and bottom.

D.Univ.: A blue-purple russell cord hood of the full shape, with square corners, fully lined and edged with grey shot silk. An edge of 1" silver Benet braid is added to the cape, next to the turned out shot grey. The strap is lined and edged ³/₈" with shot grey.

D.D.: A blue-purple robe of the full shape, lined and edged with red-purple damask with 1" purple and gold Benet braid next to the turned out red-purple.

D.Mus.: A cream damask hood of the full shape, fully lined blue-purple taffetta. The cape is edged with blue-purple and there is 1" purple and gold Benet braid next to the blue-purple.

D.Sc.: A blue-purple hood of the full shape, fully lined with scarlet taffeta. The cape is edged with scarlet and there is silver Benet braid 1" wide next to the scarlet.

LL.D.: A blue-purple hood of the full shape, fully lined with light cherry taffeta. The cape is edged with light cherry and there is silver Benet braid 1" wide next to the light cherry.

D.Litt.: A blue-purple hood of the full shape, fully lined with white. The cape is edged with white and there is silver Benet braid 1" wide next to the white.

Honorary Fellows

Gowns

A blue-purple imitation silk gown in the style of Queen's Counsel, i.e. sleeves long, gloved and with an inverted-T slit. There is a flap collar and a slit at the rear. The T slit and shoulders are edged with silver Benet lace as are the sleeve ends. In the centre of the flap collar is an embroidered rose and crescent.

Honorary Associates

Gowns

As for Honorary Fellows, made in scarlet imitation silk. The facings and flap collar are in grey taffeta with silver Benet braid edging each side of the facing. In the centre of the flap collar there is a an embroidered rose and crescent.

Academical Caps

All members of the university except Doctors and Honorary Fellows wear a black mortar board with a blue-purple button and tassel.

Ph.D.: Wear a black cloth bonnet with a blue-purple cord and tassels.

Higher Doctors: Wear a black velvet bonnet with a blue-purple cord and tassels.

University of Reading

(1926)

The University of Reading has no faculty colours, being the first university to adopt a system in which all bachelors wear the same robes as do all masters and all doctors (except the Ph.D.). Cream silk is the university colour, used in a dark blue hood for bachelors and masters, and in crimson or scarlet for doctors.

Undergraduates

A black stuff gown of the Oxford scholars' shape, with blue facings.

Bachelors

Gowns
As for the Cambridge B.A. gown but with the ends of the sleeves rounded off, and there are no strings (fig. 43).

Hoods
As for the Oxford pattern of dark blue silk with a 3" cream silk stripe.

Masters

Gowns
As for the Cambridge M.A. gown (fig. 48).

Hoods
As for the Cambridge pattern of dark blue silk lined with cream silk.

Note: *Masters of Philosophy* in the joint Reading/Birmingham degree Breeding and Crop Improvement wear a hood as follows: A blue art silk hood of the full shape, fully lined and edged 1" all round with grey moire silk.

Doctors

Undress Gowns
A black stuff gown of the Cambridge pattern with a row of braid (of the type in frontispiece, d) over the armhole.

Full Dress Robes

Ph.D.: A crimson cloth robe of the Cambridge doctors' shape with facings and sleeve linings of cream silk.

Higher Doctors: A scarlet cloth robe of the Cambridge shape with facings and sleeve linings of cream silk.

Hoods

Ph.D.: A crimson cloth hood of the full shape lined with cream silk.

Higher Doctors: A scarlet cloth hood of the full shape lined with silk.

Academical Caps

Undergraduates, Bachelors, Masters, Doctors: In undress wear a black cloth mortar board.

Ph.D.: In full dress wear a black cloth bonnet without cords and tassels.

Higher Doctors: Wear a black velvet bonnet with gold cord and tassels. Women may wear a soft Oxford hat.

Robert Gordon University, Aberdeen

(1993)

Undergraduates

No academical dress is worn.

Bachelors and Diplomas

Gowns

A black gown with long closed sleeves i.e. glove sleeves with a straight cut at the foot. As for the basic masters' gown (fig. 4).

Hoods

Note: The white lining and facings are of a special white material which has the four elements of the university woven in at regular intervals. The hoods are full shaped.

B.A., B.Sc., B.Eng.: A black hood partly lined with the special white material.
Diplomas: A black hood partly lined with white.
Post-graduates: A black hood fully lined with white.

Masters

Gowns

As for the basic masters' gown with facings 2½" wide in the special white material.

Hoods

M.A., M.Sc., M.Phil.: A black hood, fully lined with the special white material.

Doctors

Full Dress Robes

As for other graduates, in black with facings 5" wide in the special white material.

Fellows of the University: Wear a black wool gown with white facings and a white collar.
Honorary Doctors: Wear a scarlet wool robe with 5" facings of the white material.
Honorary Fellows: Wear a scarlet wool robe with 1" wide facings of white.

Hoods

A black hood, fully lined with white and edged 2" with white.

University of Salford

(1967)

Undergraduates

Undergraduates wear a black stuff gown of the Oxford style with rounded sleeves.

Bachelors

Gowns

As for the standard bachelors' gown with plain pointed sleeves (fig 3).

Hoods

A light university blue corded silk hood of the Aberdeen shape, lined with gold satin and faced with 3" of the faculty colour.

Advanced Certificates

Gowns

As for the bachelors' gown.

Hoods

A light university blue corded silk hood of the Aberdeen shape, lined with gold satin faced with 2" of light green.

Diplomas in Advanced Studies

Gowns

As for the masters' gown, i.e. similar to the University of London M.A.

Hoods

A light university blue corded silk hood of the Aberdeen shape, lined with gold and faced with 3" of dark green.

Diplomas in Engineering

Gowns

A black stuff or silk gown of the London M.A. pattern.

Hoods

A light university blue corded silk hood of the Aberdeen shape, lined with gold and edged with 3" of light grey and 1" of light blue.

SPECIFICATIONS: SALFORD

Masters

Gowns

As for the London M.A. gown in black stuff or silk (fig. 56).

Hoods

A light university blue hood of the Aberdeen shape, the cape lined and edged with gold and with 3" of the faculty colour.

Doctors

Full Dress Robes

Ph.D.: A black gown of the same shape as for masters, i.e. the London M.A. gown, the facings covered with 3" of university blue silk.

Higher Doctors: A scarlet cloth robe of the Cambridge shape, the sleeves and facings of gold satin.

Hoods

Ph.D.: A light blue hood of the Aberdeen shape, lined and edged with scarlet satin.

Higher Doctors: A dark blue hood of the Aberdeen shape, lined and edged all round with gold satin.

Academical Caps

Diplomates, Graduates: Wear a black cloth mortar board.

Ph.D.: Wear a bonnet of black cloth with scarlet cord and tassels.

Higher Doctors: Wear a black velvet bonnet with gold cord and tassels.

University of Sheffield
(1905)

The system of academical dress used at Sheffield University is a very simple one, with no anomalies at all. Bachelors and masters wear a dark green hood, doctors wear a red one. These are edged or lined with the faculty colour.

Undergraduates
A black stuff gown of the Oxford scholars' shape (fig. 8).

Undergraduate Certificates
Gowns
A black stuff gown of the B.A. shape. The yoke and facings are edged in narrow corded ribbon of the colour distinctive to the faculty. No hood is worn.

Undergraduate Diplomates
Gowns
As for the Certificates, but the facings and yoke are edged with a broad corded ribbon in the faculty colour. No hood is worn.

Bachelors
Gowns
As for the Oxford B.A. shaped gown (fig. 38).

Hoods
A dark green cloth hood of the Cambridge shape, half lined with fur, and edged round the cape with a border of the faculty colour.

Post-graduate Diplomates
Gowns
As for the bachelors' gown.

Hoods
A dark green silk hood of the Cambridge shape, edged with silk distinctive to the faculty in which it is conferred.

SPECIFICATIONS: SHEFFIELD

Masters

Gowns
A stuff or silk gown similar to the Oxford M.A. gown (fig. 49).

Hoods
A dark green silk hood of the Cambridge shape, lined throughout with the faculty colour. The hood of a master within the Joint Awards Scheme of the University and Sheffield Hallam University is of blue cloth and the Cambridge shape, lined throughout with dark blue silk.

Doctors

Undress Robes
A black silk robe similar to the Oxford doctors' undress gown.

Full Dress Robes
Ph.D.: A scarlet cloth robe with bell-shaped sleeves (as of the Oxford doctors' robe), and with facings of dark green.

Higher Doctors: A scarlet cloth robe of the Cambridge shape. The facings are dark green silk, and the sleeves lined with scarlet silk and looped with a green button and cord.

Hoods
A red ottoman silk hood of the Cambridge doctors' shape, lined throughout with the faculty colour.

Faculty Colours
Arts: Crushed strawberry.
Science: Apricot.
Music: Cream brocade.
Medicine & Surgery: Red.
Dental Surgery: Pale rose pink.
Law: Pale green.
B.A.(Law) & M.A.: Olive green.
Engineering: Purple.
Metallurgy: Steel grey.
Technical Science: Lilac.
Social Science: Lemon yellow.
Architectural Studies: Old gold.
Education: Pearl.
Board of Collegiate Studies: Saxon blue.
Philosophy (Ph.D. & M.Phil.): Dark green.

Academical Caps
All Graduates and Undergraduates: Wear a cloth mortar board.
Doctors: Wear a velvet mortar board.

South Bank University, London

(1993)

B.TEC, HNC/HND

Gowns
As for the bachelors' gown.

Hoods
As for the BTEC hood, i.e. scarlet of the simple shape, lined blue.

Diplomas/Certificates and University Awards

Gowns
As for the bachelors' gown.

Hoods
A black hood of the Aberdeen shape lined with the university blue-black satin.

Bachelors

Gowns
As for the basic bachelors' gown (fig. 3).

Hoods
A black hood of the full shape, bordered with the university blue-black satin.

Post-graduate Diplomas and Certificates

Gowns
As for the masters' gown.

Hoods
A black hood of the full shape, bordered with blue-black satin and trimmed with silver.

Postgraduate Certificates in Education

Gowns
As for the masters' gown.

Hoods

A black hood of the full shape, bordered with blue-black satin and trimmed with silver at the middle of the satin lining.

Masters

Gowns

As for the basic masters' gown (fig. 4).

Hoods

A black hood of the full shape, fully lined with the university blue-black satin.

Masters of Philosophy

Gowns

As for the basic masters' gown with facings of blue-black satin.

Hoods

A black hood of the full shape, fully lined with blue-black satin and bound round the cowl and cape with silver.

Doctors

Full Dress Robes

Ph.D.: A bright blue robe of the Cambridge shape with facings and sleeve linings of blue-black satin.

Higher Doctors: As for the Ph.D. robe with the addition of a blue cord and button on the sleeve.

Hoods

Ph.D.: A bright blue hood of the full shape, fully lined with the university blue-black satin.

Higher Doctors: A bright blue hood of the full shape, lined and bound with the university blue-black satin.

Academical Caps

All Graduates: Wear a black cloth mortar board.

Ph.D.: In full dress wear a black cloth bonnet with blue cord and tassels.

Higher Doctors: Wear a black velvet bonnet with blue cord and tassels.

University of Southampton

(1952)

The University of Southampton uses a blue cord and button on the gowns of all graduates, and the same blue is used to line all hoods. Formerly the University used different colours of cords and buttons to indicate the faculty, but these are now confined to degrees in philosophy (M.Phil. and Ph.D.) and to doctors' full dress robes.

Undergraduates

As for the London undergraduate gown.

Bachelors

Gowns
A black Russell cord, poplin, or ribbed rayon gown of the London B.A. shape (fig. 42). There is a cord and button at the elbow and on the yoke in university blue. This gown is also used by M.Eng., M.Soc.Work, M.Chem., M.Math., M.Phys.

Hoods
A black Russell cord, poplin or ribbed rayon hood of the Burgon shape (figs. 70 and 71), lined with university blue silk. The cowl is bound ³/₈" inside and outside with the degree colour.

Masters

Gowns
Masters (except as above): Wear a black Russell cord, poplin, ribbed rayon or corded ottoman silk gown, of the Oxford M.A. pattern (fig. 49) with a cord and button on the yoke in university blue.

Hoods
Masters (except M.Ch., M.Eng., M.Soc.Work, M.Chem., M.Math., M.Phys.): Wear a black poplin, ribbed rayon or corded ottoman silk hood of the full shape with rounded corners to the cape. This is lined with university blue silk and edged ³/₈" round the cape and cowl with the degree colour. The neckband is cut on a curve and not edged.

Masters of Surgery: Wear a black superfine cloth hood of the Oxford doctors' shape, fully lined with the university blue silk. The cowl is edged ³/₈" inside and outside with crimson, and the cape is edged ³/₈" with university blue.

M.Eng., M.Soc.Work, M.Chem., M.Math., M.Phys.: Wear a black poplin hood of the Burgon shape lined with university blue silk. The cowl is bound 1" inside and outside with the degree colour.

Doctors

Undress Gowns

Ph.D.: In undress wear the masters' gown with a single row of Southampton braid round the armhole.

Higher Doctors: Wear the same gown as for the Ph.D. but with two rows of Southampton braid. There is a cord and button in the degree colour on the yoke.

Full Dress Robes

Ph.D.: Wear a claret coloured robe of the Oxford doctors' pattern, the sleeves and facings are of university blue, and there is a claret coloured button and cord on the yoke.

Higher Doctors: Wear a scarlet robe of the Oxford doctors' pattern, the sleeves and facings being of university blue, and there is a cord and button in the degree colour on the yoke.

Degree Colours

Arts & Letters: Mid-cerise.
Music: Ivory.
Theology: Purple.
Science, Chemistry, Mathematics and Physics: Rich gold.
Education: White.
Laws: Blue.
Social Science and Social Work: Light green.
Medicine & Surgery: Crimson.
Nursing and Nursing Science: Powder blue.
Business Administration: Petrol blue.
Philosophy: Claret.
Engineering: Primrose yellow.

Hoods

Ph.D.: A claret cloth hood of the Oxford doctors' shape, lined with university blue.
Higher Doctors: A scarlet cloth hood of the Oxford doctors' shape, lined with university blue silk.

Academical Caps

Bachelors, Masters, Doctors: In undress wear a black cloth mortar board.
Ph.D.: In full dress, wear a black cloth bonnet with claret cord and tassels.
Higher Doctors: Wear a black velvet bonnet with cord and tassels in the above degree colour.

St Andrews University
(1411)

There is an unusual system of hoods in use at St Andrews University. Most bachelors' hoods are made of the faculty colour, unlined but edged with fur. Doctors' full dress robes are also made of cloth using the faculty colour throughout. In undress, doctors wear a black gown with cassock front, as worn by graduates of French universities.

Undergraduates

Undergraduates (except divinity): Wear a scarlet cloth gown, with a yoke of burgundy velveteen. The sleeves are of wrist length, but are open down the front seam, so giving a cape effect.

Divinity students (if not a graduate): Wear a black stuff gown with short open sleeves and with a violet Cross of St Andrew on the left facing.

Bachelors

Gowns

A black stuff gown of the Oxford shape, except that the points of the crescent-cut face backwards. There is a black cord and button on the yoke (fig. 53).

Hoods

As for the Cambridge shaped hood.

B.Litt.: Saffron yellow silk bordered with fur.
B.D.: Violet silk or cloth bordered with fur.
B.Sc.: Purple lilac silk or cloth bordered with fur.
B.Phil.: Gold silk bordered with fur.

Masters

Gowns

As for the bachelors' gown.

Hoods

A black silk hood as of the Cambridge shape.

M.A.: Lined with cherry silk.
M.Litt.: Lined with saffron yellow silk or cloth.

M.Theol.: Lined with violet silk or cloth.
M.Sc.: Lined with purple-lilac silk or cloth.
M.Phil.: Lined with gold silk or cloth.

Doctors

Undress Gowns
Honorary Doctors: In undress wear a black silk cassock with buttons of the faculty colour, and with full sleeves.
Other Doctors: Wear the bachelors' gown.

Full Dress Robes
A robe of a special Oxford shape made throughout in the faculty colour. The facings and cuffs are of silk.
Ph.D.: Is of Nanking blue.
Other Doctors: They may also wear a black silk cassock with buttons and cincture of the faculty colour.

Hoods
These are of the faculty colour and lined with white satin.

Academical Caps
Undergraduates: Wear a black cloth mortar board with a tassel appropriate to the year of study, namely:
 Bejant—blue.
 Semi—crimson.
 Tertian—yellow.
 Magistrand—black.

Bachelors, Masters, Doctors: In undress wear a back cloth mortar board.
Doctors: In full dress wear a black velvet 'John Knox' cap—a square soft cap without tassels (fig. 90).

University of Stafford

(1993)

Certificates and Higher Certificates

Gowns
A black gown of the London B.A. shape.

Hoods
A black hood of the Oxford Burgon shape, fully lined and edged ³/₈" with white and the strap also white.

Diplomas and Higher Diplomas

Gowns
As for the London B.A. gown.

Hoods
A black hood of the Burgon shape, fully lined and edged with grey.

Bachelors

Gowns
As for the London B.A. gown (fig. 42).

Hoods
A grey cotton viscose hood of the Burgon shape, fully lined and edged ³/₈" in red.

Post-graduate Certificates

Gowns
As for the London B.A. gown.

Hoods
A black hood of the Burgon shape, lined and edged with blue.

Masters

Gowns
A grey cotton viscose gown of the Cambridge doctors' style (fig. 60).

Hoods
A grey hood of the full shape, fully lined and edged with blue. Strap edged blue.

Doctors

Full Dress Robes
Ph.D.: A scarlet robe of the Cambridge doctors' shape with no trim to the sleeves or facings.

Higher and *Honorary Doctors*: As for the Ph.D. robe, but the sleeves and facings are in red taffeta.

Hoods
Ph.D.: A scarlet hood of the full shape, lined with blue. The cowl and cape are edged ³⁄₈" with blue.

Higher and *Honorary Doctors*: A gold cotton viscose hood of the full shape, lined and edged ³⁄₈" with white. There is a white strap.

Academic Caps
Certificates, Diplomas, Bachelors, Post-graduate Certificates: Wear a black mortar board.

Masters: In all faculties wear a grey mortar board with grey tassel.

Ph.D.: Wear a scarlet velvet bonnet with a blue cord and tassels.

Higher Doctors: Wear a scarlet velvet bonnet with a gold cord and tassels.

University of Stirling

(1967)

The University of Stirling is a law unto itself going against all rules and regulations for academical dress, in that they add fur to the masters' hoods!

Bachelors

Gowns
All graduates wear a black glove sleeved gown.

Hoods
A black hood of the Edinburgh shape, lined as follows:

B.A.: Dove grey.
B.Acc.: Calamine blue.
B.Sc.: Dove grey and edged with malachite green.
B.Ed.: Bunting azure blue.
B.Educ. Studies: Saphire blue.

Masters

Gowns
As for the graduate gown.

Hoods
M.A. (Honorary degree): A black hood of the full shape, lined medici crimson.
M.Sc.: A black hood of the Edinburgh shape, lined malachite green and bordered with fur.
M.Litt.: As for the M.Sc. hood, lined malachite green bordered with fur.
M.Ed.: As for the M.Sc. hood, lined bunting azure blue and bordered with fur.
M.Phil.: As for the M.Sc. hood, lined with stone white edged with malachite green and bordered with fur.
M.B.A.: As for the M.Sc, hood, lined with maroon and bordered with fur.

Doctors

Full Dress Robes
Ph.D.: As for the masters' gown with dove grey facings.
D.Sc.: A dove grey robe of the masters' style with crocus facings.
D.Litt.: A dove grey robe of the masters' style with violet facings.

D.Univ. (Honorary degree): A dove grey robe with square flap collar and glove sleeves. The facings and edging of the collar are of powder blue.

Hoods

Ph.D.: A dove grey hood of the Edinburgh shape, lined with malachite green.
D.Sc.: A dove grey hood of the full shape, lined with crocus.
D.Litt.: A dove grey hood of the full shape, lined with violet.
D.Univ.: A malachite green hood of the full shape and lined with powder blue.

Academical Caps

No caps are worn.

University of Strathclyde
(1964)

Strathclyde is unusual in having fur on only two of its hoods—one of these being a master's hood! Also the doctors' hoods are identical with the bachelors' hoods, whereas the masters' hoods are edged in addition to the lining.

Undergraduates

A black stuff gown of the Oxford scholars' shape. The facings, which are 4½" wide at the bottom, taper away to a point 12" from the top. There is a blue cord and button on the yoke, and the gathers are separated from the yoke by a blue cord, with a blue button at each end.

Bachelors

Gowns

As for the basic bachelors' gown with a cord and button on the yoke (fig. 3).

Hoods

A saltire blue hood of the full shape, lined as follows:

B.A.: White.
B.Ed.: White piped gold cord.
B.Sc.: Gold.
B.Eng.: Gold edged with fur.
B.Arch.: Gold piped with scarlet cord.
B.Com.: White piped green cord.
LL.B.: White piped with scarlet cord.
B.Tech.: Gold piped white cord.

Masters

Gowns

Black stuff with cord and button on the yoke and glove sleeves of the Oxford style, save that the crescent cut faces backwards (fig. 53).

Hoods

M.A., M.Sc., M.Arch., LL.M., M.Com.: A saltire blue hood lined and edged as the corresponding bachelors' hood.

M.Eng.: Lined and edged with gold and partly trimmed with fur.
M.B.A.: Lined and edged with white and piped with black cord.
M.Litt.: Lined and edged with white and piped with blue cord.
M.T.M.: Lined and edged with gold and piped with white cord.
M.Phil.: Lined with gold, edged with white.

Doctors

Undress Gowns
A black gown with full sleeves half the length of the gown. There is a flap collar, concave at the base, covering the yoke.

Full Dress Robes
Ph.D., D.B.A.: A blue silk robe with sleeves half the length of the robe.
D.Sc., LL.D., D.Litt., D.Univ.: A scarlet cloth robe of the London shape with facings of blue, and with three cords and buttons on the yoke.

Hoods
These are of saltire blue, full shaped and lined with the corresponding bachelors' lining.

Ph.D.:
   Arts: White.
   Science: Gold.
   Architecture: Gold piped scarlet cord.
   Law: White piped with scarlet cord.
   D.B.A.: Lined and edged with white piped with black cord.

Higher Doctors (*D.Litt., D.Sc., LL.D., D.Sc. in Architecture*): As for the corresponding bachelors' hood.
D.Univ.: A saltire blue hood lined with saltire blue.

Fellows of the University

A blue silk robe with open sleeves half the length of the robe, and with facings of scarlet silk.

Academical Caps
All Graduates (except higher doctors): Wear a black cloth mortar board.
Higher Doctors: Wear a black velvet modified John Knox cap (fig. 90).
Fellows: Wear a black velvet bonnet.

University of Sunderland
(1993)

Undergraduates
No academical dress is worn.

Diplomas and Certificates

Gowns
As for the bachelors' gown.

Hoods
A dark blue silk hood of the modified Aberdeen shape lined with mauve and edged with nasturtium.

Bachelors

Gowns
As for the basic bachelors' gown (fig. 3).

Hoods
A dark blue hood lined with nasturtium.

Masters

Gowns
As for the basic masters' gown (fig. 4).

Hoods
A dark blue hood lined with gold satin and edged with nasturtium.

Masters of Philosophy

Gowns
As for the masters' gown.

Hoods
A dark blue hood lined with wedgwood satin and edged with nasturtium.

Doctors

Full Dress Robes

Ph.D.: A dark blue panama robe with facings of blue silk.

Higher and *Honorary Doctors*: A nasturtium robe of the London shape, with facings and sleeve linings of dark blue damask.

Honorary Fellows

Full Dress Robes

A dark blue silk robe with facings of nasturtium, trimmed with gold lace.

Hoods

Ph.D.: A dark blue silk hood lined with jade satin and edged with nasturtium.

Higher and *Honorary Doctors*: A nasturtium panama hood lined with jade satin and edged with blue damask.

Honorary Fellows: A dark blue silk hood lined with nasturtium.

Academical Caps

All Graduates (except doctors and honorary fellows): Wear a black cloth mortar board.

Ph.D.: A dark blue panama bonnet with gold cord and tassels.

Higher and *Honorary Doctors*: A nasturtium panama bonnet with cord and tassels of blue.

Honorary Fellows: A blue silk bonnet with cord and tassels of gold.

University of Surrey

(1963)

The university uses a special blue brocade to line all its hoods.

Undergraduates

No academical dress is worn.

Bachelors

Gowns
As for the London B.A. gown. This gown is also worn by M.Eng (fig. 42).

Hoods
A simple shaped hood lined with blue brocade.
B.A.: Trimmed with a 1" band of red ribbon.
B.Ed.: Trimmed with a 1" band of green ribbon.
B.Eng.: Trimmed with a 1" band of grey ribbon.
B.Mus.: Trimmed with a 1" band of white brocade.
B.Sc.: Fully lined with blue brocade but no trimming.
M.Eng.: Trimmed with a 2½" band of grey ribbon.
B.Univ. (Honorary): Fully lined with blue brocade and with a band of gold satin edging the hood.

Masters

Gowns
As for the basic masters' gown (fig. 4).

Hoods
A modified Aberdeen shape hood, fully lined with blue brocade.
M.A.: Trimmed with a 2½" band of red ribbon.
M.B.A.: Trimmed with a 2½" band of gold ribbon.
M.Ed.: Trimmed with a 2½" band of green ribbon.
M.Mus.: Trimmed with a 2½" band of white brocade.
M.Sc.: Fully lined with blue brocade but no trimming.
M.Phil.: The blue brocade lines and edges the hood with 1½".
M.Univ. (Honorary): Fully lined with blue brocade and with a 2½" edging of gold satin.

Doctors

Full Dress Robes

Ph.D.: As for the masters' gown with 2½" of blue brocade facings.
D.Sc., D.Litt., D.Univ.: A cardinal red wool robe of the same shape as for the masters, with the lower part of the sleeves and the facings in blue brocade.

Academical Caps

All Graduates: In undress wear a black cloth mortar board.
Ph.D.: In full dress wear a black cloth bonnet with red cord and tassels.
D.Sc., D Litt.: Wear a black cloth bonnet with gold cord and bonnet.
D.Univ.: Wear a black velvet bonnet with gold cord and tassels.

University of Sussex, Falmer

(1961)

The University of Sussex has decided not to follow too closely the pattern of academical dress used by the older universities. But rather than showing some future trends in this field, the garments which have been approved show a reversion to styles which were in use in medieval universities. There is a distinctly continental style about them.

Undergraduates

Undergraduates are not required to wear academical dress on any occasion.

Bachelors

Gowns

B.A., B.Sc., B.Eng., B.Ed., LL.B.: A black cloth gown of the London undergraduate style, but sewn up in front from the point to the elbow. There is a vertical opening at the elbow to free the arms (fig. 44).

Hoods

A black cloth hood of the simple shape, with a small fold of stuff sewn on as a liripipe. The hood is lined with grey nylon fur in the form of 4" squares.

Masters

Gowns

M.A., M.B.A., LL.M., M.Sc., M.S.W., M.Ed.Psych.: A black cloth gown with glove sleeves and square ends. There is a tight vertical slit for the armhole. The back of the gown is gathered in the usual way but the lower border of the yoke, which normally has a concave outline, is here in the form of a double bracket. The facings are of black grosgrain. When any of these degrees are awarded *honoris causa*, the doctors' robe is in gamboge, but with no shoulder ribbon (fig. 64).

M.Univ.: As for the Ph.D. gown but with a double line of black braid on each shoulder. For Full Dress occasions, a robe of black is worn, with a red collar and facings, but with no shoulder ribbon.

Hoods

M.A., M.B.A., M.Sc., LL.M., M.S.W., M.Ed.Psych., M.Univ.: A black alpaca hood of the same shape as for the bachelors' hood, lined with dove grey.

M.Univ.: A black stuff hood of the full shape, lined with red silk.

M.Phil.: A black alpaca hood of the full shape, lined with dove grey and with a band of scarlet 1" wide and ¼" from the edge of the hood.

Joint Masters Degree (with Brighton University): A black alpaca hood lined grey.
   M.A.: As for Joint Masters and edged gold and blue.
   M.Sc.: As for Joint Masters and edged gold and red.

Doctors

Undress Gowns

Ph.D: A black cloth gown as for the masters, except that the bottom of the sleeve is scalloped and each shoulder has a single line of braid.

Higher Doctors, D.Univ: As for the Ph.D. but each shoulder has two rows of braid.

Full Dress Robes

Ph.D.: A deep royal blue robe of the same shape as the Ph.D. undress gown except that it has a high upstanding collar. On the right shoulder a wide band of scarlet ribbon is fastened by a scarlet button, the ends hanging down at the back and front.

Higher Doctors: As for the Ph.D. robe but in gamboge.

The colours of the shoulder ribbons are as follows:
   LL.D.: Red.
   D.Litt.: Blue.
   D.Mus.: Oyster white.
   D.Sc.: Green.

D.Univ.: As for the higher doctors but of red material with a blue silk collar and facings and no shoulder ribbons.

Hoods

Ph.D.: A deep royal blue hood of the Cambridge shape, lined with scarlet.

Higher Doctors: A gamboge hood of the Cambridge shape, lined as follows:
   LL.D.: Red.
   D.Litt.: Blue.
   D.Mus.: Oyster white.
   D.Sc.: Green.

D.Univ.: A red material hood of the Cambridge shape, lined with blue silk.

Academical Caps

All Graduates: In undress wear a black cloth mortar board.

M.Univ., D.Univ.: In full dress wear a doctors' bonnet in black velvet with gold cord and tassels.

Ph.D.: Wear a black velvet pileus (fig. 92) with a royal blue button.

Higher Doctors: Wear the same with a gamboge coloured button.

University of Teesside
(1993)

Certificates

Gowns
A grey gown of the bachelors' shape. No hood is worn.

BTEC Certificates and Diplomas

Gowns
A grey gown of the bachelors' shape.

Hoods
A black hood of the Aberdeen shape, lined and edged university red with the addition of a narrow grey strip inside the hood. This is known as the 'University Hood'.

Bachelors

Gowns
As for the basic bachelors' gown in black (fig. 3).

Hoods
As for the 'University Hood'.

Masters

Gowns
A university red gown in the Aberdeen style (fig. 50).

Hoods
As for the 'University Hood'.

Doctors

Full Dress Robes
Ph.D.: A university red gown of the Cambridge style with facings and sleeve linings of grey silk trimmed with black.
Higher and *Honorary Doctors*: As for the Ph.D. robe.

Hoods

Ph.D.: As for the 'University Hood'.
Higher and *Honorary Doctors*: A black hood of the Aberdeen shape lined with university red and trimmed all round with silver lace.

Academic Caps

Undergraduate Certificates (etc.): Wear a grey cloth mortar board.
Bachelors: Wear a black cloth mortar board.
Masters: Wear a black cloth mortar board with a red tassel.
Ph.D.: Wear a black cloth bonnet with a red cord and tassels.
Higher Doctors: Wear a black velvet bonnet with red cord and tassels.

Thames Valley University, London
(1993)

Undergraduates
No academical dress is worn.

HNC, HND, College Awards
Gowns
As for the bachelors' gown.

Hoods
A purple silk hood of the full shape, partly lined with university gold silk.

Bachelors
Gowns
As for the basic bachelors' gown (fig. 3).

Hoods
A purple silk hood of the full shape, part lined with university gold silk.

Masters
Gowns
As for the basic masters' gown (fig. 4).
M.Phil.: As for the masters' gown but with gold facings.

Hoods
A purple silk hood of the full shape, fully lined with university gold silk.

Doctors
Undress Gowns
As for the masters' gown.

Full Dress Robes
Ph.D.: A purple panama robe of the London shape, the facings and sleeve linings of gold.

Higher and *Honorary Doctors*: As for the Ph.D. robe but with a cord and button on each sleeve and on the yoke.

Hoods
Ph.D.: A purple hood of the full shape, fully lined with gold.
Higher and *Honorary Doctors*: As for the Ph.D. hood but lined and edged 1½" with gold.

Academical Caps
All Graduates: In undress wear a black cloth mortar board.
Ph.D.: In full dress wear a black cloth Tudor bonnet with purple tassels.
Higher and *Honorary Doctors*: Wear a black velvet bonnet with gold cord and tassels.

Honorary Professors
A purple panama robe of the Queen's Counsel shape, with gold silk facings and flap collar and on the sleeve wings.

Nottingham Trent University

(1993)

HNC/HND

Gowns
As for the bachelors' gown.

Hoods
A blue hood of an amended Aberdeen shape, lined with green.

Bachelors

Gowns
As for the basic bachelors' gown (fig. 3).

Hoods
A blue hood of the full shape, lined with green and faced with 1" of the faculty colour:

Faculty Colours
Arts: Yellow.
Science: Orange.
Engineering: Blue.
Philosophy: Silver.
Laws: Rust.
Education: Pink.
Business: Ruby.

Masters

Gowns
As for the basic masters' gown (fig. 4).

Hoods
As for the bachelors' hood but lined with green and trimmed all round with 2" of the faculty colour (see above).

Masters of Philosophy

Gowns

As for the masters' gown with silver braid trim.

Hoods

As for the bachelors' hood but trimmed with 2" of silver braid.

Doctors

Full Dress Robes

Ph.D.: A maroon robe of the Cambridge doctors' style with facings and sleeve linings of green with silver lace round the edge.

Higher Doctors: A scarlet robe of the same shape as for the Ph.D. gown with green facings and sleeve linings and silver lace decoration.

Hoods

Ph.D.: A maroon hood of the full shape, lined with green and trimmed with silver.

Higher Doctors: A scarlet hood of the full shape, lined with green and trimmed with silver.

Academical Caps

All Graduates: Wear a black cloth mortar board.

Ph.D.: In full dress wear a black cloth bonnet with green cord and tassels.

Higher Doctors: Wear a black velvet bonnet with green cord and tassels.

University of Ulster at Coleraine
(1984)

Certificates, Diplomas, Post-graduate Certificates and Diplomas

Gowns
As for the bachelors' gown.

Hoods
A black hood of the full shape, lined with university green and bound ⅝" each side with apple green.

Bachelors and M.Eng.

Gowns
An open sleeved gown of the Oxford B.A. pattern but much shorter sleeves (fig. 3).

Hoods
A black stuff, Russell cord or rayon hood lined with university green and the cape and cowl bound ⅝" inside and outside with the faculty colour.

Faculty Colours
B.Sc.: Shannon green.
B.A.: Royal blue.
B.Phil.: Gold.
B.Eng.: Rose Tyrien.
B.Litt.: Pale blue.
B.Ed.: Cobalt blue.
B.Mus.: White.
B.Tech.: Chestnut.
M.Eng.: Scarlet.

Masters

Gowns
As for the Oxford M.A. gown (fig. 49).

Hoods
A bordeaux hood of the full shape, lined with university green with cape and cowl bound ⅝" each side with the faculty colour.

Faculty Colours
M.Sc.: Shannon green.
M.A.: Royal blue.
M.Phil.: Gold.
M.B.A.: Spectrum yellow.

Doctors

Undress Gowns
As for the masters' gown.

Full Dress Robes
A scarlet superfine robe of the Oxford doctors' shape with scarlet silk facings (fig. 62).

Hoods
A scarlet hood lined with university green and with the cape and cowl bound ⅝" each side with the faculty colour.

D.Phil.: Gold:
D.Sc.: Shannon green:
D.Litt.: Royal blue.

Academical Caps
Bachelors, Masters, Doctors: In undress, wear a black mortar board.
Doctors: In full dress, wear a black velvet bonnet with gold cord and tassels.

University of Wales

(1893)

The University of Wales is composed of constituent colleges at Aberystwyth, Bangor, Cardiff, Swansea, St David's University College, Lampeter, and the Welsh National School of Medicine at Cardiff.

The faculty colours are shot silks which give a very beautiful effect inside a black or scarlet hood.

Undergraduates

As for the Oxford scholars' shape gown (fig. 8).

Bachelors

Gowns

A black stuff or silk gown of the Oxford B.A. shape, except that the forearm seam is divided for about 4" and turned back, leaving a right angle between the two points. There is a vertical strip of ½" of ribbon about 4" long in the midline. The two turned back flaps and the ribbon are each held in place by a button (fig. 45).

Hoods

These are of black stuff or silk of the simple shape (fig. 83) with the distal end of the cowl being rounded off. The hood is bordered 3" to 4" with the faculty colour. The neckband is cut on a curve and faced with faculty silk.

Faculty Colours

<u>Arts or Letters</u>

B.A., M.A., D.Litt.: Mazarin blue shot with green.
B.Lib., M.Lib.: Mazarin blue shot with green, edged with white.

<u>Science</u>

B.Sc., M.Sc., D.Sc.: Bronze colour (yellow shot with black).
B.Sc.(Tech.): Bronze colour, edged with white.
B.Eng., M.Eng.: Red shot with green.
B.Pharm., M.Pharm.: Shot silk of saxe blue.

SPECIFICATIONS: WALES

Music

B.Mus., M.Mus., D.Mus.: The B.Mus. and M.Mus. hoods are dark blue lined pearl silk (a shot silk of three hues).

Law

LL.B., LL.M., LL.D.: Red shot with purple.

Theology or Divinity

B.D., M.Th., D.D.: Mazarin blue shot red.
B.Th.: Mazarin blue shot with red, edged with white.

Medicine

M.B., B.Ch., M.Ch., M.D.: Green shot with black edged white.
B.Med.Sc.: Bronze edged with green shot black.
B.D.S., M.Sc.D., D.Ch.D.: Shot silk of saxe blue, edged with purple.
B.N., M.N.: Green shot with white, edged with red.
M.P.H.: Green shot with black, edged with emerald green.

Architecture

B.Arch.: Shot silk of scarlet red.
Economic/Social Studies, B.Sc.Econ., M.Sc.Econ., D.Sc.Econ.: Red shot with yellow.
M.B.A.: Red shot with yellow, edged with pale blue.

Education

B.Ed., M.Ed.: Green shot with white.

Masters

Gowns

A stuff or silk gown as of the Oxford M.A. shape, with the upper sleeve point retained and the lower one removed to form a right angle. The armhole is of the inverted-T shape (fig. 59).

Hoods

A black corded silk hood of the full shape (fig. 75), fully lined with the faculty colour. The neckband is cut on the curve and faced with the faculty colour.
M.Mus.: Dark blue lined pearl.

Doctors

Undress Gowns

As for the masters' gown.

Full Dress Robes

Ph.D.: A crimson cloth robe of the London shape (fig. 63) with facings and sleeve linings in the faculty colour.

Other Doctors: A scarlet robe of the Ph.D. shape with facings and sleeve linings in the faculty colour.

Hoods
Ph.D.: A crimson cloth hood of the full shape, lined in the faculty colour.
Other Doctors: A scarlet cloth hood, as for the Ph.D. shape, lined with the faculty colour.

Academical Caps
Undergraduates, Bachelors, Masters, Doctors: In undress, wear a black cloth mortar board.
Doctors: In full dress, wear a black velvet mortar board.

University of Warwick

(1964)

Undergraduates

No academical dress is worn.

Bachelors

Gowns

As for the Oxford B.A. gown (fig. 38).

Hoods

These are simple shaped in black stuff fully lined and bound on the cowl and neckband with taffeta in the faculty colour as follows:

B.A.: Red.
B.Sc.: Blue.
B.Ed.: Green.
B.Phil.(Ed.): Light green.
LL.B.: Purple.
B.Eng.: Light blue.

Masters

Gowns

A black stuff or silk gown with closed sleeves, the bottom of the sleeves having small cut-out portions at the front and back. The armhole is of the inverted-T shape.

Hoods

A black corded silk hood of the C.N.A.A./Aberdeen shape, fully lined and bound with the faculty colour as follows:

M.A.: Red.
M.B.A.: Gold.
M.Hist.: Red.
M.Sc.: Blue.
M.Ed.: Green.
M.Eng.: Navy blue.
LL.M.: Purple.

M.Phil.: Red shot green.
M.S.: Red.
M.Med.Sci.: Blue

Doctors

Undress Gowns
All Doctors: In undress wear the masters' gown.

Full Dress Robes
Ph.D.: As for the masters' gown with red shot green facings.
Eng.D.: As for the masters' gown with blue silk facings.
M.D.: As for the masters' gown with red silk facings.
D.Litt, D.Sc., LL.D.: A crimson robe of the Oxford doctors' shape with facings 4" wide and sleeve cuffs 5" wide in the faculty colour.

Hoods
A crimson cloth hood of a large C.N.A.A./Aberdeen shape lined and bound as follows:

Ph.D.: Red shot green.
Eng.D.: Navy blue.
M.D.: Deep red.
D.Litt.: Red
D.Sc.: Blue.
LL.D.: Purple.

Academical Caps
Bachelors, Masters, Doctors: In undress wear a black cloth mortar board for men and either a mortar board or a soft Oxford cap for women.
Ph.D.: Wear a black cloth bonnet with red and green mixed cord and tassels.
Higher Doctors: Wear a black velvet bonnet with cord and tassels in the faculty colour.

University of the West of England, Bristol
(1993)

Undergraduates

No academical dress is worn.

Certificates and Diplomas

Gowns
As for the London B.A. gown, i.e. an open sleeved gown gathered at the elbow and held with a cord and button (fig. 42).

Hoods
A black C.N.N.A.-type hood, part lined with plain red.

Bachelors

Gowns
As for the London B.A. gown.

Hoods
A black stuff C.N.A.A.-type hood, fully lined with red brocade.

Post-graduate Certificates and Diplomas

Gowns
As for the London B.A. gown.

Hoods
A black C.N.A.A.-type hood, fully lined with red brocade and with red brocade ribbon on the top edge.

Masters

Gowns
As for the basic masters' gown but with the facings trimmed in red brocade (fig. 4).

Hoods
A plain red C.N.A.A.-type hood, fully lined with red brocade.

Doctors

Undress Gowns
As for the masters' gown.

Full Dress Robes
Ph.D.: A red panama cloth robe of the London doctors' shape with the facings and sleeve linings in grey silk.
Higher Doctors: As for the Ph.D. robe but with grey facings and sleeve linings in red brocade.

Hoods
Ph.D.: A plain red, C.N.A.A.-type hood, lined in grey silk.
Higher Doctors: A grey panama, C.N.A.A.-type hood, fully lined in red brocade.

Academical Caps
All Graduates: Wear a black mortar board for men or for women a soft Oxford cap.
Ph.D.: In full dress, wear a black Tudor bonnet with red cord and tassels.
Higher Doctors: Wear a black velvet bonnet with grey cord and tassels.

University of Westminster
(1993)

Undergraduates

No academical dress is worn.

Bachelors

Gowns

As for the basic bachelors' gown (fig. 3).

Hoods

A black hood of the Burgon shape and lined as follows:

B.A.: Claret:
B.Sc.: Silver grey:
LL.B.: Claret and edged with 2" of purple:
B.Eng.: Silver grey and edged with 2" of dark blue.

Neckbands are the same colour as the linings.

Masters

Gowns

As for the basic masters' gown (fig. 4).

Hoods

These are Burgon shaped.

M.A.: Claret and lined claret.
M.Sc.: Dark silver-grey and lined lighter silver-grey.
LL.M.: Claret and lined purple.
M.Eng.: Dark silver-grey and lined dark blue.
M.Phil.: Claret and lined silver-grey.
M.B.A.: Dark blue and lined claret.

Doctors

Undress Gowns

Ph.D.: As for the masters' gown with a 1" band of black velvet above the armhole.
D.Sc., D.Litt., D.Tech., LL.D.: Two bands of black velvet each 1" wide above the armhole.

Full Dress Robes
As for the Oxford doctors' shape.

Ph.D.: A red panama robe with facings and the lower half of the sleeves of grey silk.

D.Litt.: A scarlet robe with facings and sleeves in claret.

D.Sc., D.Tech.: A scarlet robe with facings and sleeves in silver-grey.

LL.D.: A scarlet robe with facings and sleeves in purple.

Hoods
As for the Oxford doctors' shape, and using the same colours as the robes, i.e.:

Ph.D.: Claret lined silver-grey.

D.Litt.: Scarlet lined claret.

D.Sc., D.Tech.: Scarlet lined silver-grey.

LL.D.: Scarlet lined purple.

Academical Caps
All Graduates: Wear a black cloth mortar board.

Doctors: In full dress, wear a velvet bonnet of claret colour with silver cord and tassels.

University of Wolverhampton
(1993)

Undergraduates

No academical dress is worn.

Postgraduate Diplomas, Certificates and Diplomas

Gowns
A black gown of the B.A. Oxford shape.

Hoods
A black hood of the Aberdeen shape, lined in red taffeta and with the cowl edged in gold.

Bachelors

Gowns
As for the Oxford B.A. gown (fig. 38).

Hoods
A black hood of the Aberdeen shape, lined in red damask and bordered inside the cowl with 1" of gold damask.

Masters

Gowns
As for the basic masters' gown with an inverted-T armhole (fig. 4).

Hoods
A black hood of the Aberdeen shape, lined with gold damask and bordered inside the cowl with 1" of red damask.

Doctors

Undress Gowns
As for the masters' gown.

Full Dress Robes
Ph.D.: A crimson Russell cord robe of the Oxford doctors' shape, with 4" facings and narrow sleeve endings of gold damask.

Honorary and *Higher Doctors*: A scarlet Russell cord robe with 4" facings and narrow sleeve endings of gold damask.

Hoods
Ph.D.: A crimson hood lined with gold damask.
Honorary and *Higher Doctors*: A scarlet hood lined with gold damask.

Academical Caps
All Graduates: Wear a black cloth mortar board.
Ph.D.: In full dress, wear a black cloth bonnet with gold cord and tassels.
Higher Doctors: Wear a black velvet bonnet with gold cord and tassels.

Honorary Fellowships
A black masters' shaped gown with red damask facings.
A full shaped hood in black silk lined in red taffeta with the cowl bordered inside with 2" of gold taffeta and the cape edged 2" with gold taffeta.
With this outfit a black mortar board is worn.

University of York
(1963)

Undergraduates

No academical dress is worn.

Bachelors

Gowns
As for the basic bachelors' gown in grey stuff (fig. 3).

Hoods
A grey cloth hood of the Aberdeen shape with the cowl edged in the faculty colour.

Faculty Colours
B.A.: White.
B.Sc.: Pale blue.
B.Eng.: Dark blue.
Eng.Dip.: A red hood with a dark blue edging.

Masters

Gowns
As for the bachelors' gown, except for M.Univ., who wear the doctors' full dress robe (fig. 3).

Hoods
A grey hood, lined as follows:

M.A.: Red.
M.Sc.: Pale blue.
M.Eng.: Dark blue.
M.S.W.: White.
M.Phil.: A red hood with a grey edging.
M.Univ.: A grey hood with a red edging.

Doctors

Undress Gowns
As for the bachelors' gown.

Full Dress Robes
Ph.D.: As for the bachelors' gown.
D.Sc., D.Litt., D.Mus.: A grey gown with closed sleeves and inverted-T armhole. The facings and the fronts of the sleeves below the armhole are covered in red silk.

Hoods
D.Phil.: A red hood with grey lining.
D.Sc.: A red hood lined and edged with blue.
D.Litt.: A red hood lined and edged with grey.
D.Mus.: A red hood lined and edged with white.
D.Univ.: A red hood lined with grey.

Academical Caps
All Graduates: In undress wear a grey mortar board.
All Doctors: In full dress, wear a grey bonnet.

IRISH UNIVERSITIES

University of Dublin

(1591)

(TRINITY COLLEGE)

There is a simple system of gowns and hoods at Dublin. The hoods are distinctive, having a 1" wide edging to the cape and cowl.

Undergraduates

A black stuff gown similar to the Oxford Advanced Students' gown, i.e. sleeveless and with a flap collar. Over the armholes there are broad flaps about 12" long, decorated with three rows of tassels. There are three rows of tassels towards the bottom of each side, ½" below the armholes. There is a 9" slit in the mid-line at the back of the gown, from the hem (fig. 9). Foundation scholars wear the bachelors' gown.

Bachelors

Gowns

A black Irish Russell cord gown of the Oxford B.A. shape, except that the sleeves are considerably shorter, like the London undergraduate gown (fig. 40).

Hoods

All hoods of Trinity College Dublin are of a special full shape (figs. 79 & 80).

B.A.: Black and lined with white fur.
B.D.: Black and lined fine black silk.
LL.B.: Black and lined white.
M.B.: Black and lined crimson.
B.Ch.: Black, lined white and edged blue.
B.A.O.: Black and lined olive.
B.Dent.Sc.: Myrtle green, lined with black watered silk and edged in crimson.
B.A.I.: Black and lined green.
Agr.B.: Black and lined brown.
Agr.(Forest)B.: Black, lined brown and edged in green.
M.V.B.: Black, lined maroon and edged in olive green.
B.B.S. (*Business Studies*): Black and lined gold (either in silk or poplin).
B.B.S. (*Social Studies*): Black, lined gold (silk or poplin) and edged in white.
Mus.B.: Pale blue and lined with white fur.
B.Sc.: Dark green and lined black.
B.Ed.: Blue and lined blue.
B.Arch.Sc.: Dark green and lined with white fur.
B.Mus.Ed., B.Mus.(*Performance*): Pale blue and lined rose.
B.Th.: Black, lined black and edged in purple.

Masters

Gowns

A black cloth, silk or poplin gown of the Oxford M.A. shape, the crescent-shaped cut at the base of the sleeve being higher up than in any other university, so giving a deep blunt point. There is a cord and button on the yoke (fig. 52).

Hoods

M.A.: Black and lined white.
M.Sc.: White and lined myrtle green.
M.Litt.: White and lined blue.
M.Ch.: Crimson, lined white and edged in blue.
M.A.O.: Black and lined purple.
M.A.I.: White and lined green.
M.Dent.Sc.: Myrtle green, lined pale blue and edged in crimson.
Agr.M.: White and lined brown.
M.V.M.: White and lined maroon.
Agr.(Forest)M.: White, lined brown and edged in green.
M.B.A.: White and lined gold.
M.Ed.: White, lined blue and edged in white.
M.Sc.(Econ.), M.Sc.(Mgmt.): Gold and lined white.
M.Phil.: White and lined yellow.

Doctors

Undress Gowns

As for the masters' gown.

Full Dress Robes

A scarlet robe of the Oxford doctors' shape (fig. 62). (Except D.Mus. which is white flowered damask.) There is a cord and button on the yoke. The sleeves and facings are as follows:

Litt.D.: Blue.
LL.D.: Pink.
Sc.D.: Myrtle green.
M.D.: Crimson black velvet.
Mus.D.: Rose satin.
Ph.D.: Yellow.

Hoods

A scarlet cloth hood, lined and edged 1" round the cape and cowl with the same silk as the facings of the full dress robe.

Academical Caps

Undergraduates, Bachelors, Masters, Doctors: In undress wear a black cloth mortar board.
Doctors: In full dress wear a round black velvet bonnet.

National University of Ireland

(1908)

A wide range of degrees is offered by the N.U.I. including some, such as Public Health and Celtic Studies, which are peculiar to this university. No silks are used for hoods, but only Irish poplins throughout. All the hoods are dark green.

Undergraduates

A black gown of the Oxford scholars' shape.

Bachelors

Gowns

LL.B.: As for the masters' gown.
Other Bachelors: A black Irish Russell cord gown of the Oxford B.A. shape (fig. 38).

Hoods

A dark green Irish poplin hood of the simple shape and lined as follows:

B.A.: White.
B.A.F.S.: Strawberry, bordered 1½" white.
B.Mus.: Coral pink.
B.Sc.: St Patrick's blue.
M.B.: Scarlet.
B.Med.Sc.: Scarlet bordered 1" St Patrick's blue and 1" white.
B.Agr.Sc.: Light green.
B.Eng.: Terracotta.
B.Arch.: Gold.
B.Comm.: Strawberry.
B.F.S./B.B.S.: Strawberry bordered 1" white.
B.F.S.T.(*Food Sc. and Tech.*): Orange.
M.V.B.: Celtic blue.
B.D.S.: Silver grey and bordered by 1" of scarlet.
B.Sc.Arch.Sc.:Gold bordered 1" St Patrick's blue.
B.Sc.Pharm.: St Patrick's blue and bordered by 1" of crimson.
B.Soc.Sc.: White and bordered by 1" of maroon.
B.S.W.: White bordered 1½" maroon.
B.Ed.: White and bordered by 1" of maroon, 1" of white and 1" of maroon.
B.C.S. (*Celtic studies*): White and bordered by 1" of strawberry.
B.P.A.: Strawberry and bordered by 1" of white, 1" of strawberry and 1" of white.

B.Tech.: White and bordered terracotta.
B.Nursing Studies: White and bordered scarlet.
B.Physio.: Scarlet and bordered by 1" of white.
B.Sc.Public Health: Lilac.
B.Radiog.: St Patrick's blue and bordered by 1" of scarlet.
B.F.S.: Strawberry and bordered by 1" of white.
B.B.L.S.: Strawberry and bordered by 1" of prune.
LL.B.: As for the masters' hood, lined white and bordered by 1½" of prune, 1½"of white and a further 1½" of prune.
B.C.L.: Green lined prune.

Masters

Gowns

Masters: In undress wear a black Irish Russell cord gown of the Oxford M.A. shape (fig. 49). In full dress, the same in black Irish poplin.

Hoods

A dark green Irish poplin hood of the full shape, lined in white and trimmed as follows:

M.A.: Bordered by 3" of blue.
M.Acc.: Bordered by 1" of strawberry, 1" of St Patrick's blue and 1" of strawberry.
M.Acc.St.: Bordered 1" strawberry, 1" St Patrick's blue, 1" strawberry.
M.A.O.: Bordered by 3" of gold and 1" of scarlet.
M.Agr.Sc.: Bordered green.
M.Animal Sc.: Bordered 1½ celtic blue and 1½ St Patrick's blue.
M.Appl.Sc.: Bordered by 1½" of blue, 1½" of white and 1½" of blue.
M.Arch.Sc.: Bordered by 1½" of gold and 1½" of St Patrick's blue.
M.Arch.: Bordered 3" gold.
M.B.A.: Bordered by 1½" of maroon, 1½" of white and 1½" of strawberry.
M.B.S.: Bordered by 1½" of strawberry, 1½" of white and 3" of strawberry.
M.Ch.: Bordered 3" red.
M.Coun.: Bordered by 1" of maroon, 1" of blue and 1" of maroon.
M.Comm.: Bordered 3" strawberry.
M.D.S.: Bordered by 3" of grey and 1" of scarlet.
M.Develop. Studies.: Bordered 1" green, 1" white and 1" strawberry.
M.E.D.: Bordered by 1½" of terracotta, 3" of white and 1½" of terracotta.
M.Econ.Sc.: Bordered by 1½" of strawberry, 1½" of white and 1½" of strawberry.
M.Ed.: Bordered by 1½" of maroon, 1½" of white and 1½" of blue.
M.Eng.: Bordered 3" terracotta.
M.Eng.Design: Bordered 1½" terracotta, 3" white and 1½" terracotta.
M.Eng.Sc.: Bordered by 1½" of terracotta and 1½" of St Patrick's blue.
M.Eq.S.: Bordered by 1½" of light green and 1½" of celtic blue.
M.Equal.S.: Bordered by 1" of maroon, 1" of white and 1" of prune.
M.G.C.: Bordered by 1" of blue, 1" of white and 1" of maroon.
M.I.E.: Bordered by 1½" of terracotta, 1½" of white and 1½" of terracotta.
M.I.T.: Bordered by 1" of terracotta, 1" of blue and 1" of strawberry.
LL.M.: Bordered by 3" of prune.

M.L.Arch.: Bordered by 1½" of light green and 1½" of gold.
M.L.I.S.: Bordered by 1½" of white, 1½" of maroon and 1½" of blue.
M.Mangt.Sc.: Bordered by 2" of strawberry, 3" of white and 1½" of strawberry.
M.Med.Sc.: Bordered by 1½" of scarlet, 1½" of St Patrick's blue and 1½" of scarlet.
M.Mus.: Bordered by 3" of coral pink.
M.P.A.: Bordered by 2" of strawberry, 2" of white and 2" of strawberry.
M.P.H.: Bordered by 3" of lilac.
M.Phil.: Bordered by 3" of maroon.
M.Psych.Sc.: Bordered by 1½" of blue and 1½" of maroon.
M.R.U.P.: Bordered by 1½" of gold, 1½" of white and 1½" of terracotta.
M.Rural development: Bordered by 2" of strawberry, 2" of white and 2" of maroon.
M.S.W.: Bordered by 1" of maroon, 1" of white and 1" of maroon.
M.Sc.: Bordered by 3" of St Patrick's blue.
M.Sc.Agr.: Bordered by 1½" of light green and 1½" of St Patrick's blue.
M.Soc.Sc.: Bordered by 1½" of maroon, 1½" of white and 1½" of maroon.
M.U.B.C.: Bordered by 1" of gold, 2" of white and 1" of terracotta.
M.V.M.: Bordered 3" celtic blue.
M.Sc.Vet.Med.: Bordered 1" celtic blue, 1" white and 1" St Patrick's blue.

Doctors

A black Irish Russell cord gown with bell-shaped sleeves like those of the Oxford doctors' full dress robe (fig. 62). There are no facings.

Full Dress Robes
Ph.D.: An Irish scarlet cloth robe of the same shape as for the masters.
D.Econ.Sc.: A scarlet Oxford doctors' shaped robe with facings and sleeve cuffs of white, with 1½" of strawberry, 1½" from the edge of facings and 3" of strawberry 1½" from the bottom of the cuffs.
Other Doctors: An Irish scarlet cloth robe of the Oxford doctors' shape with sleeve cuffs and facings in the faculty colours.

Faculty Colours
Agricultural Science: Light green.
Arts: White.
Architecture: Gold.
Celtic studies: Saffron.
Commerce: Strawberry.
Dentistry: Silver grey.
Engineering: Terracotta.
Food science & Tech.: Orange.
Law: Prune.
Medicine: Scarlet.
Music: Coral pink.
Pharmacy: Crimson (No longer awarded).
Philosophy: Maroon.
Science: St Patrick's blue.
Veterinary Medicine: Celtic blue.

Hoods

Ph.D.: A dark green hood of the full shape, lined with maroon and bordered in 2" of faculty colour.

D.Econ.Sc.: A dark green hood of the full shape, lined white and with 1½" of strawberry, 1½" from the edge.

Other Doctors: A dark green hood of the full shape, lined throughout with the faculty colour.

Academical Caps

Bachelors, Masters, Doctors: In undress wear a black cloth mortar board.

Ph.D.: In full dress, wear a black velvet mortar board with a tassel in the faculty colour.

Other Doctors: Wear a black velvet bonnet with cord and tassels in the faculty colour.

Dublin City University

(1989)

(The former National Institute for Higher Education in Dublin)

This university follows the American Intercollegiate system for the shapes of gowns and hoods, differentiating between bachelors, masters and doctors by the size of the hood, i.e. bachelors 36" long, masters 42" long and doctors 48" in length.

Bachelors

Gowns
As for the basic gown (fig. 3).

Hoods
A hood in the USA Intercollegiate shape, 36" in length, in university blue cloth, lined and edged in 1½" of the faculty colour. The cape and cowl are bound with ⅜" of antique gold.

Masters

Gowns
A black cloth, glove sleeved gown.

Hoods
These are identical with the corresponding bachelors' hood except that the overall length is 42" and the edging is 2½" wide.

Doctors

Full Dress Robes
Ph.D.: A red cloth robe of the Oxford doctors' shape with university blue facings and cuffs. The facings are edged with ⅞" of antique gold braid.

Hoods
As for the bachelors' hood except that the overall length is 48" and the edging is 4" wide in the faculty colour.

Faculty Colours
Science: Green.
Engineering: Orange.
Education: Light blue.
Computing/Maths: Grey.
Communications/Human Studies: White.
Distance Education: Russet.
Dublin Business School: Drab.

Dublin Institute of Technology
(1992)

Certificates

One Year: Green epitôge with a 1" stripe of the faculty colour.
Two Year: Green epitôge with two 1" stripes of the faculty colour.

Bachelors

Gowns
As for the basic bachelors' gown.

Hoods
A black cloth hood of the simple shape and following the American Intercollegiate pattern, lined with black and with an edging of the faculty colour.

Faculty Colours
Arts: White.
Science: Gold.
Engineering: Orange.
Business: Drab.
Technology: Silver grey.
Philosophy: Maroon.
Medicine: Red.

NOTE

THE INSTITUTE IS CURRENTLY REVISING ITS ENTIRE SYSTEM OF ACADEMICAL DRESS.

University of Limerick
(1989)

Bachelors

Gowns

As for the basic bachelors' gown.

Hoods

A black cloth of a simple style, fully lined with the faculty colour. The cowl is bound with corporate gold braid.

Faculty Colours

Arts: White.
Science: Gold.
Engineering: Orange.
Business: Drab.
Technology: Silver grey.
Philosophy: Maroon.
Medicine: Red-White.

Masters

Gowns

As for the Cambridge M.A. gown.

Hoods

A black cloth of the full shape, lined with white and edged with 3" of the faculty colour, and the cowl bound with corporate gold braid. Except the M.A which is edged blue.
M.B.S: Edged 1½" drab, 1½" white, 1½" drab.

Doctors

Full Dress Robes

Ph.D.: As for the masters' gown in scarlet cloth.
Higher Doctors: A scarlet cloth robe of the Oxford doctors' shape with facings and sleeve cuffs of the faculty colour.

Hoods

Ph.D.: A black cloth hood of the full shape, lined with maroon and with the cowl bound with corporate gold braid.

Higher Doctors: A scarlet cloth hood lined with white, and bound with corporate gold braid.

Academical Caps

Bachelors, Masters, Doctors: In undress, wear a black mortar board.
Ph.D.: In full dress, wear a black velvet bonnet with maroon cord and tassels.
Higher Doctors: Wear the same bonnet with corporate gold cord and tassels.

St Patrick's College, Maynooth

(1795)

This college is made up of two distinct parts. One section is a constituent college of the National University of Ireland and awards degrees of that body. The second part is a component college in the Pontifical University of Rome. The latter section awards degrees only in Theology, and follows the continental system of academical dress, using an epitôge to signify the degree.

Gowns
A black gown with a closed cassock front.

Epitôges
B.D.: An epitôge in purple and green (Faculty of Theology colours). There is one 3" wide band of ermine, and the epitôge is not pleated.
S.T.L.: An epitôge in purple and green with two 3" bands of ermine and no pleats.
D.D.: An epitôge in purple and green with three 3" bands of ermine. The epitôge is pleated.
B.A.Theol.: An epitôge of purple and red with one 3" band of ermine (a combination of Philosophy and Theology Faculty colours).
M.Th.: An epitôge of purple and red with two 3" bands of ermine and no pleats.
D.C.L.: (Doctor of Canon Law, not yet awarded) An epitôge in red and green pleated velvet with three 3" bands of ermine.

Note: The bands of ermine on the epitôge for a Diploma are 1" wide, whereas those for a degree are 3" wide.

Luton University

(1955)

All hoods are of the full shape.

Certificates

Gowns
The basic bachelors' gown.

Hoods
1st year: A black hood lined with blue and bound with 1½" white.
2nd year: A black hood lined green and bound with 1½" white.

Bachelors

Gowns
The basic bachelors' gown.

Hoods
A blue hood lined green.

Postgraduate Diplomas & Certificates

Gowns
The basic masters' gown.

Hoods
A green hood lined with blue and bound with 1½" white.

Masters

Gowns
The basic masters' gown.

Hoods
A green hood lined with white and bound 1½" blue.
M.Phil.: A blue hood lined with white and bound green.

Doctors

Ph.D.: Wears the masters' gown and hood with a blue felt bonnet with silver tassel.